Prevention and Treatment of Severe Behavior Problems: Models and Methods in Developmental Disabilities

edited by

NIRBHAY N. SINGH
Medical College of Virginia
Virginia Commonwealth University

Brooks/Cole Publishing Company

ITP® An International Thomson Publishing Company

Pacific Grove • Albany • Belmont • Bonn • Boston • Cincinnati • Detroit • Johannesburg • London • Madrid
Melbourne • Mexico City • New York • Paris • Singapore • Tokyo • Toronto • Washington

Sponsoring Editor: *Vicki Knight*
Marketing Team: *Jean Thompson, Margaret Parks*
Editorial Associate: *Jana Garnett*
Production Editor: *Kirk Bomont*
Manuscript Editor: *Margaret Ritchie*
Cover and Interior Design: *Terri Wright*
Design Editor: *Roy R. Neuhaus*

Interior Illustration: *Accurate Art, Inc.*
Art Coordinator: *Lisa Torri*
Typesetting: *Bookends Typesetting*
Cover Printing: *Color Dot Graphics, Inc.*
Printing and Binding: *R. R. Donnelley/*
  Crawfordsville

For more information, contact:
BROOKS/COLE PUBLISHING COMPANY
511 Forest Lodge Road
Pacific Grove, CA 93950
USA

International Thomson Editores
Seneca 53
Col. Polanco 11560
México D.F. México

International Thomson Publishing Europe
Berkshire House 168-173
High Holborn
London WC1V 7AA
England

International Thomson Publishing GmbH
Königswinterer Strasse 418
53227 Bonn
Germany

Thomas Nelson Australia
102 Dodds Street
South Melbourne, 3205
Victoria, Australia

International Thomson Publishing Asia
221 Henderson Road
#05-10 Henderson Building
Singapore 0315

Nelson Canada
1120 Birchmount Road
Scarborough, Ontario
Canada M1K 5G4

International Thomson Publishing Japan
Hirakawacho Kyowa Building, 3F
2-2-1 Hirakawacho
Chiyoda-ku, Tokyo 102
Japan

Printed in the United States of America

10 9 8 7 6 5 4 3 2 1

Library of Congress Cataloging-in-Publication Data

Prevention and treatment of severe behavior problems : models and
  methods in developmental disabilities / edited by Nirbhay N. Singh.
    p. cm.
  Includes bibliographical references and index.
  ISBN 0-534-34418-6
  1. Developmentally disabled—Rehabilitation. 2. Mentally
handicapped—Behavior modification.   I. Singh, Nirbhay N.
HV1570.P74 1997
362.1'968—dc20
                                               96-9280
                                               CIP

THIS BOOK IS PRINTED ON ACID-FREE RECYCLED PAPER

The royalties from the sale of this book will be used to support the work of the Ekoji Buddhist Sangha in Richmond, Virginia.

This book is dedicated to Albert
for teaching me about self-injury.

Brief Contents

PART 2: METHODS

Contents

PART I: MODELS

2 *Comprehensive Assessment of Severe Behavior Problems*   *23*
MAURICE A. FELDMAN AND DOROTHY GRIFFITHS

3 *Procedures for Assessing and Increasing Social Interaction*   *49*
FRANK W. KOHLER AND PHILLIP S. STRAIN

4 *Intensive Behavioral Intervention with Young Children with Autism*   *61*
O. IVAR LOVAAS AND GREGORY BUCH

5   *Curricular Approaches to Controlling Severe Behavior Problems*   87

MARK WOLERY AND VINCENT WINTERLING

PART II: METHODS

About the Authors

Sharon H. Bonaventura (M.A., University of Richmond) is a senior-in-discipline for psychology at Central Virginia Training Center, Lynchburg, Virginia. Her research interests are in developmental disabilities and mental illness. She has co-authored papers on such topics as self-injurious behavior, Tourette's disorder, and the prevalence of mental illness in individuals with developmental disabilities. Her current research interests are in assessment of Alzheimer's in persons with Down's syndrome.

Gregory Buch (Ph.D., University of California, Los Angeles) has served as the assistant director of the UCLA Clinic for the Behavioral Treatment of Children. He is currently interested in disseminating intensive early intervention services and paraprofessional training outside university settings.

W. David Crews, Jr. (Ph.D., Virginia Polytechnic Institute and State University, 1995) is a clinical neuropsychology fellow in the Division of Neuropsychology at the University of Virginia Health Sciences Center, Charlottesville, Virginia. He also provides neuropsychological services at the Central Virginia Training Center in Lynchburg, Virginia. His current research interests and publications are in neuropsychology, mental retardation, and behavioral medicine.

Dee Duncan (M.S., North Dakota State University, 1988) is a doctoral candidate in clinical psychology at the Louisiana State University. His research in terests are in pediatric feeding disorders, developmental disabilities, and severe behavior problems. His publications are in the area of mental illness in individuals with mental retardation.

Kathleen Dyer (Ph.D., University of California, 1985) is the director of evaluation, research, and staff development at Bancroft, Inc. She has authored numerous articles and chapters in areas including providing positive behavioral support for individuals with challenging behaviors, enhancing communication, and organizational and developmental disabilities. She has been on the faculty at Temple University and the University of Massachusetts and has served on the editorial boards of several professional journals. She is currently the director of the Delaware Valley Association for Behavior Analysis.

Cynthia R. Ellis (M.D., University of Nebraska Medical Center, 1985) is an assistant professor of pediatrics and psychiatry and director of the Child Development Center at the Medical College of Virginia/Virginia Commonwealth University. She has published in the areas of behavior problems, psychopathology, and psychopharmacology in children and individuals with developmental disabilities. Her clinical and research interests are in developmental and behavioral pediatrics, mental retardation, ADHD, and psychopharmacology.

Maurice Feldman (Ph.D., McMaster University, 1977) is associate professor of psychology and psychiatry at Queen's University and chief psychologist of Ongwanada Centre in Kingston, Ontario, Canada. He holds several research grants, has published extensively in scientific and professional journals and books, and has given numerous addresses and workshops in Canada, the United States, and Europe. He currently is editor-in-chief of the *Journal of Developmental Disabilities,* on the board of editors of three journals, and president of the Ontario Association on Behaviour Analysis. His clinical and research interests include etiology, prevalence, assessment, prevention, and treatment of psychopathology in persons with developmental disabilities.

Jessica M. Gehin (M.S., East Central University of Oklahoma, 1989) is a psychologist at the Central Virginia Training Center in Lynchburg, Virginia. Her interests include psychological treatment and psychiatric disorders in individuals with developmental disabilities.

Dorothy Griffiths (Ph.D., University of Toronto, 1991) is an assistant professor in the Department of Child Studies at Brock University and vice-president of the National Association for Dual Diagnosis. She has authored and co-authored articles, chapters, and a book on such topics as community-based behavior intervention, quality assurance of behavior intervention, and social skills training. She also has co-authored a number of publications in the area of sexually inappropriate behavior. Her current research interests are in sexual abuse prevention.

David Hammer (Ph.D., University of Georgia, 1981) is the director of psychological services at the Nisonger Center and an adjunct associate professor of psychology at the Ohio State University. He is a licensed clinical psychologist, specializing in the assessment and intervention of challenging behaviors of individuals with mental retardation and autism. He has published numerous research articles in the areas of behavioral interventions, developmental disabilities, and psychopathology.

Frank W. Kohler (Ph.D., University of Kansas, 1987) is a research scientist with Allegheny-Singer Research Institute. His research interests include preschoolers with autism, children's social interactions and relations, and the implementation of effective instructional practices in primary grade classrooms. He has been associate editor and literature review editor for *Education and Treatment of Children* and has written several articles on school reform.

Tracy L. Kroeger (M.A., Ohio State University, 1993) is a doctoral student in psychology at the Ohio State University. She has published in the area of emotion recognition by individuals with mental retardation. Her research and clinical interests are in emotion recognition and mental illness in individuals with mental retardation.

Laura K. Lambert (M.A., University of Iowa, 1995) is a special education teacher in a small school district in eastern Iowa. She has taught a wide variety of special education students, including those with developmental disabilities, behavioral disorders, autism, and learning disabilities. Her research interests include self-injurious behavior and social interaction skills of students with disabilities.

Eric V. Larsson (Ph.D., University of Kansas, 1986) is the director of clinical services for REM Consulting & Services in Minneapolis, Minnesota. He has co-authored several chapters and research articles on autism, intensively early childhood intervention, self-injurious behavior, applied behavior analysis, legal issues, community development, and child abuse. He also serves on several editorial review boards. He maintains a full clinical and consulting practice and serves as a director for several regional and state service agencies and professional associations.

O. Ivar Lovaas (Ph.D., University of Washington, 1958) is a professor and director of the Clinic for the Behavioral Treatment of Children in the Department of Psychology at the University of California, Los Angeles. His treatment research has been supported by grants from the National Institute of Mental Health and Office of Education almost continuously since 1962. Among his many awards, he has received a Guggenheim Fellowship, Honorary Doctor of Letters, Edgar Doll Award from the American Psychological Association, and the Research Award from the American Association on Mental Retardation. His current research centers on intensive and early behavioral intervention for children with autism and pervasive developmental disabilities.

Johnny L. Matson (Ph.D., Indiana State University, 1976) is a professor and director of clinical training at Louisiana State University. He has also held positions at Northern Illinois University and the University of Pittsburgh School of Medicine. He is the author of 29 books and 280 journal articles and book chapters and is editor of *Research in Developmental Disabilities.* The bulk of his work has been on the mental health needs of persons with mental retardation. He is past president of the Mental Retardation and Developmental Disabilities Division of the American Psychological Association.

John A. Northup (Ph.D., University of Iowa, 1991) is an assistant professor of school psychology at Louisiana State University. He completed a post-doctoral fellowship at Kennedy-Krieger Institute, where he worked in the Neurobehavioral Unit. His current interests involve children with ADHD as well as children with developmental disabilities. He is a member of the editorial board of the *Journal of Applied Behavior Analysis.*

Teresa L. S. Parr (M.S., Virginia Commonwealth University, 1995) is a doctoral student in the Department of Psychology at Virginia Commonwealth University, Richmond, Virginia. Her research interests are in child psychopathology.

Robert W. Ricketts (M.S., Abilene Christian University, 1980) is a private practitioner providing behavior management consultation to service providers for individuals with developmental disabilities. He has authored and co-authored a variety of research articles and book chapters in the areas of severe problem behavior and mental retardation. His research interests are in ecobehavioral assessment and treatment, and behavioral pharmacology.

Johannes Rojahn (Ph.D., University of Vienna, Austria, 1976) is a professor of psychology and psychiatry at the Ohio State University. He also serves as the coordinator of the doctoral program in psychology of mental retardation and developmental disabilities and as the director of training and evaluation at the Nisonger Center for Developmental Disabilities. Much of his research has focused on behavior problems and other forms of psychopathology in mental retardation. More recently he has conducted studies exploring the role of emotion in the development of psychopathology in people with mental retardation. He has served as an associate editor for the *American Journal on Mental Retardation* and *Research in Developmental Disabilities* for several years.

Nirbhay N. Singh (Ph.D., University of Auckland, New Zealand, 1976) is a professor of psychiatry and pediatrics at the Medical College of Virginia, clinical professor of psychology at the Virginia Commonwealth University, and director of the Commonwealth Institute for Child and Family Studies in Richmond, Virginia. He has published widely in the areas of mental retardation, autism, psychopharmacology, and psychiatric disorders of children and adolescents. His current interests are in cultural competency in mental health service delivery, quality of life issues, social construction of knowledge, and the general area of consciousness in eastern psychology. He currently edits the *Journal of Behavioral Education* and the *Journal of Child and Family Studies.*

Yadhu N. Singh (Ph.D., University of Strathclyde, Glasgow, 1979) is an associate professor of pharmacology at South Dakota State University. His research interests include bioactive agents that affect neuromuscular transmission and muscle contractility, as well as drugs used in the treatment of neuropsychiatric disorders.

Phillip S. Strain (Ph.D., Peabody College, 1974) is professor of educational psychology at the University of Colorado at Denver. His major research interests are in the assessment and purposeful development of children's social skills, and he has published numerous articles, chapters, and books on this topic. His current research focuses on the longitudinal outcomes of early intervention for children with autism and the generalization of children's social skills from school to home and community settings.

David P. Wacker (Ph.D., Arizona State University, 1979) is a professor of pediatrics (pediatric psychology and developmental disabilities) and special education at the University of Iowa. His research interests are related to the assessment and treatment of severe behavior problems. He is the current editor of the *Journal of Applied Behavior Analysis.*

Hollis A. Wechsler (B.A., Wake Forest University, 1992) is a doctoral student in counseling psychology at the Virginia Commonwealth University. She was previously a researcher at the Commonwealth Institute for Child and Family Studies at the Medical College of Virginia. Her publications are in the area of serious emotional disturbance in children and adolescents and their families. Her current research interest is in adolescent psychopathology.

Vincent Winterling (Ed.D., University of Kentucky, 1990) is the director of Devereux New Jersey Center for Autism. He has authored and co-authored a number of research papers on such topics as problem behavior, response prompting procedures, and safety instruction for persons with severe disabilities. His current interests include effective management practices for human services organizations and strategies to promote learning in persons with severe disabilities.

Mark Wolery (Ph.D., University of Washington, 1980) is a senior research scientist at Allegheny-Singer Research Institute and a professor in the Department of Psychiatry at the Medical College of Pennsylvania and Hahnemann University. His research interests are in establishing and transferring stimulus control, identifying the variables that influence observational learning, and evaluating instructional practices for children with disabilities in inclusive preschool programs and early elementary grades. His books and articles focus on these topics. He was the editor of *Topics in Early Childhood Special Education* from 1992 through 1996.

Preface

This book presents, in relatively nontechnical language, a number of models and methods that can be used to prevent and treat behavior problems in individuals with developmental disabilities. It was prepared with a wide audience in mind. First, the book will be of interest to students in special education, applied behavior analysis, and clinical psychology. These would be students who are seeking to have firsthand experience in developmental disabilities.

Second, the book will be of interest to teachers whose students include children with developmental disabilities. Given the current zeitgeist for inclusion, increasing numbers of teachers in regular education, as well as in special education, will need in-service training in the management of the behavior problems of their students. This book will serve as the basis for such a course.

Third, the book will be very useful to clinicians, therapists, and other direct-care staff in facilities, community-based residences, and group homes for individuals with developmental disabilities. Finally, family members will also find much of interest in the book that will assist them in enhancing the quality of life of their child or sibling with developmental disabilities.

Following an introductory chapter, the book is divided into two major parts, the first on models, the second on methods. The introductory chapter provides the conceptual framework for the care of individuals with developmental disabilities and briefly summarizes the rest of the chapters in the book. Part I presents a number of general methods for teaching and habilitating individuals with developmental disabilities. Chapter 2 presents an ecobehavioral framework for assessing behavior problems. Chapter 3 presents specific procedures for assessing and increasing social interaction in young children. Chapter 4 explains how to conduct intensive behavioral interventions with young children with autism. Chapter 5 describes how curricular approaches can be used to control severe behavior problems in the classroom. Chapter 6 discusses how functional communication training can be used to replace severe behavior problems. Chapter 7 provides basic information on behavior-modifying drugs that are used with children, adolescents, and adults with developmental disabilities.

Part II presents treatment strategies for controlling self-injury (Chapter 8), stereotypy (Chapter 9), aggression (Chapter 10), rumination (Chapter 11), and pica (Chapter 12). Although individuals with developmental disabilities exhibit many different types of behavior problems, these five are perhaps the most difficult to treat and also hinder the individual from learning adaptive behaviors. Taken together, the two parts of the book provide the reader not only with a conceptual framework for behavioral intervention but also with a basis for implementing a wide range of assessment and treatment procedures with some degree of confidence.

Many people assisted me in preparing this book, and I am grateful to each of them. Ennio Cipani had the original idea for this book, and we were going to edit it jointly. However, it did not work out that way, but I am grateful to him for his support and advice during the early stages of the preparation of the book. I am most grateful to my eminent contributors, who provided me with high-quality manuscripts to work with and showed much patience during the extended editorial process. I would like to express my sincere appreciation to the staff at Brooks/Cole who were instrumental in the production of this book. Vicki Knight, a wonderful friend and kindred spirit, has provided me with much support, understanding, and encouragement. Kirk Bomont not only did a magnificent job as the production editor but also was a delight to work with. Others of the Brooks/Cole family who enabled this book to look as good as it does include Jana Garnett, Roy Neuhaus, and Lisa Torri. The book also benefited from the reviewers who read the manuscript: Paul Bates, Southern Illinois University; Peter Leone, University of Maryland; Nancy Meadows, Texas Christian University; John Schuster, University of Kentucky; and Carl Smith, Drake University. I also thank Ettora Burrell, Cynthia R. Ilis, and Hollis Wechsler, who assisted me so ably in the preparation of the manuscript for this book. Finally, my gratitude to Judy Singh and Subhashni Singh, who assisted me with the indexes.

I undertook the final editing of this book while I was a visiting scholar at the Chinese University of Hong Kong in Sha Tin, N.T., Hong Kong. I am grateful to Dr. Jin Pang Leung for providing me peace and comfort, as well as academic stimulation, during my visit. Finally, a special acknowledgment is due to my family for enduring the preparation of yet another book.

Nirbhay N. Singh

Chapter 1

Enhancing Quality of Life through Teaching and Habilitation

NIRBHAY N. SINGH

INTRODUCTION

Almost all of our work with individuals with developmental disabilities is based on the belief that we can make a difference, that we can help them to enhance the quality of their lives. Perhaps the most humane reason why we built institutions for them is that we thought we could marshal our best resources in one place and provide a better quality of life than was available in the community. While our aims may have been praiseworthy, the actual standard of care that was provided in these institutions rarely met the needs of the individuals. Indeed, the individuals were often simply incarcerated in institutions that were large, staffed by poorly trained professionals, and offered very little therapy of any kind. When these individuals demanded attention, by means of self-injury and aggression, they were sedated with psychotropic medication.

Ever since the first institution was established, people have questioned the appropriateness of institutions as places for teaching and habilitating individuals with developmental disabilities (e.g., Bernstein, 1916; Fernald, 1919; Seguin, 1846). With the current zeitgeist for full inclusion in the community, we are much more vocal in asking the same question today. Perhaps we have been asking the wrong question. In fact, what we are concerned about is not whether we should have institutions, but whether we are providing individuals with developmental disabilities the *quality of life* that they deserve—a quality of life that is within the mainstream of society.

In an earlier paper (Singh, 1995b), I discussed a number of indicators within service delivery systems that we can use to determine if individuals with developmental disabilities who are in an institution have an acceptable quality of life. I noted that these indicators are necessary rather than sufficient conditions for providing an acceptable quality of life. In this chapter, I present the same indicators within a more general framework for assessing the nature and quality of the services provided to individuals with developmental disabilities, regardless of their residential status.

PSYCHOLOGICAL SERVICES

Behavior Reduction Programs

It is generally accepted that behavior problems that arise because of faulty or incomplete learning are best treated with behavioral methods. The assessment, analysis, and treatment of behavior problems is a multistage process that includes a structural and functional (experimental) analysis of the problem behavior. A structural analysis includes an assessment of the impact of the environment, both physical and medical, on the target behavior. If the behavior is controlled by environmental variables, programmatic intervention is focused on the manipulation of the environment, and if the behavior is a consequence of some medical problem (e.g., otitis media), the treatment is medically driven. A functional analysis includes an assessment of the functional relationships between various purported motivational variables and the rate of occurrence of the target behavior. An appropriate behavioral intervention is formulated once the motivation of the target behavior is identified.

Structural Analysis

In dealing with a person's behavior problems, it is generally accepted that a behavioral psychologist will perform a standard structural analysis of at least two components: the impact of the person's physical environment and the impact of the biological environment (Axelrod, 1987; Pyles & Bailey, 1992). Often psychologists undertake informal observations of the individual in different settings, read his or her records to ascertain previous treatments, and informally interview family members, teachers, and direct-care staff about the individual's behavior under different conditions. This practice is limited and does not meet generally accepted standards because there is no thorough and systematic investigation of the environmental and medical variables that may set the occasion for the emergence or maintenance of maladaptive or problem behaviors. In many cases, the critical motivational variables for the maintenance of problem behaviors are found in the individual's environment; unless there is a systematic method for gathering such data, they are likely to be overlooked, and ineffective treatments are likely to be prescribed. While it is the responsibility of psychologists to undertake the behavioral component of a structural analysis, physicians must be involved in the medical component. At the very least, a team effort of the psychological and medical staff is necessary for a thorough structural analysis.

Functional Analysis

Regardless of whether the target behavior problem is new or an escalation of a previously identified problem, a series of steps are typically followed before the treatment plan is written and implemented, and its progress reviewed: (1) a descriptive analysis of the target and collateral behaviors; (2) hypothesis formation; (3) experimental analysis under analog conditions; (4) development, implementation, and evaluation of the treatment; and (5) maintenance and generalization of treatment effects (Axelrod, 1987; Mace, Lalli, & Shea, 1992). A descriptive analysis requires (1) structured or unstructured observations in the natural setting; (2) interviews with family members, teachers, and staff who know the individual and the conditions under which the target behavior occurs; and (3) data collection on antecedents, target behavior, and consequences using a partial interval recording procedure. Analysis of the data thus obtained provides the basis for deriving tentative hypotheses about the functional relationships between various motivational variables and the occurrence of the target behavior. These hypotheses are tested under analog conditions that simulate the individual's natural environment and control as many extraneous variables as possible. Thus, only the function being tested could be responsible for any change in the rate of the individual's target behavior. Once the function of the target behavior is identified, this information is used to design an appropriate intervention that not only will reduce the problem behavior but will also make positive changes to the lifestyle of the individual.

Trial-and-Error Approaches

In the absence of a thorough assessment of the functions of the behavior problem, interventions are typically based on trial and error. A problem with the trial-and-error approach is that it entails an excessive reliance on a variety of restrictive procedures to gain control over problem behaviors. While the use of functional analysis does not by itself preclude the need for any aversive procedures, it does lead to hypothesis-driven interventions that are more comprehensive, generally more effective, and typically less intrusive than interventions developed on the basis of trial and error (Carr, Robinson, & Palumbo, 1990; Repp & Singh, 1990). An outcome of not basing an intervention on a thorough functional analysis is that generic positive reinforcement programs are often used to decrease problem behaviors. While it is praiseworthy that some form of intervention is provided, the treatment programs are typically of the boilerplate variety and not designed to make a *lifestyle* change for the individuals, who continue to engage in severe behavior problems, often for years. In this regard, one indicator of the quality of care is the number of years an individual has had a behavior reduction program for the *same* behavior. In my experience, some individuals have been on behavior reduction programs of one sort or another, often for years, before the target behavior is brought under control. Indeed, the successful interventions have often taken so long that it is questionable whether the behavior change can be attributed to the programmed behavioral treatment or merely to the passage of time.

Maintenance and Generalization

Another indicator is whether there is an adequate program for maintaining and generalizing the programmed behavior change. The lack of an explicit maintenance and generalization program may not be a critical omission if the behavior change is programmed to occur in situ—in the environment in which the individual is supposed to maintain the behavior, which is invariably the community. However, treatment programs in most institutions are designed to reduce behavior problems within the institutional environment without ever focusing on the most critical element of behavior change: Does it make a difference in the lifestyle or the quality of life of the individual? We must question the significance of such treatment programs when the individual continues to be incarcerated in a facility away from the natural rhythm of life in the community.

Unplanned Physical and Mechanical Restraints

A further indicator of the quality of care is the use of unplanned physical and mechanical restraints to control the problem behaviors of individuals. In the absence of effective treatment programs, restraints may be used to provide short-term control of some aggressive, explosive, violent, and self-injurious individuals. The repeated use of unplanned restrictive and invasive procedures should alert the family, teachers, and staff that the individual's behavioral treatment program is ineffective and needs revision. Allowing individuals to engage in high rates of severe problem behaviors that require repeated applications of physical restraints, whether for emergency protective purposes or as a part of a behavior treatment protocol, cannot be justified under any conditions. Unplanned restrictive procedures, as well as planned but ineffective restrictive procedures, cause physical, emotional, and psychological harm to the individuals and certainly depart substantially from generally accepted standards of care.

Timely Evaluation and Program Revision

Behavioral intervention programs are designed to produce changes in the individual's behavior in the context of daily life. Thus, if the program is effective, behavior changes should be evident within a few days. Indeed, we need a minimum of only three data points to see whether a trend is emerging. In many institutions, the effects of behavioral and psychopharmacological treatment programs are formally checked monthly and are then reviewed at the interdisciplinary team meeting. Also, it is often difficult to obtain the services of knowledgeable professionals in the community who are able to respond in a timely manner when treatment programs are not effective. Thus, when the program is not effective, it means that the individual is subjected to an inappropriate program as well as to the psychological and emotional effects of engaging in the challenging behavior for several weeks before the need for programmatic change is recognized and appropriate modifications are made. In a responsive system of care, data are checked daily for treatment trends, and modifications are made as soon as the pattern of responding is clear. Waiting a month or longer, while the challenging behaviors are likely to continue, is not a positive indicator of a good quality of care.

Reliability of the Data

The cornerstone of behavioral intervention is the reliable and systematic collection of data. In most institutions and family homes, no mechanism exists for the reliable and systematic collection of behavioral data. There are two major problems with unreliable data. First, the utility of a behavioral treatment based on unreliable data is inherently suspect and may harm the individuals through its inappropriate use. Second, programmatic and policy decisions are often based on these data. For example, the behavior management committee (BMC) in all institutions passes judgments on the worthiness of behavioral intervention programs based on the data provided to it. In these cases, the judgment of the BMC is questionable because it is based on data that are not trustworthy. A similar argument can be made about the decisions made by the institution's human rights committee. In short, individuals who need effective behavioral programming for their challenging behaviors are virtually assured of not receiving it if the first step in treatment planning (i.e., data collection) is unreliable.

Skills Training Programs

Historically, training programs for individuals with developmental disabilities emphasized skills acquisition, often in isolated behavioral domains rather than as part of a cluster of skills that resulted in comprehensive lifestyle changes. The overall impact of these programs was that, if they were successful, the individuals were able to perform a number of isolated skills at given mastery levels (e.g., 80% on three consecutive occasions), but often, the skills were not functional. For example, an individual was taught to discriminate between colors but not in the context of daily living (e.g., to cross the street when the light is green). Thus, the outcome of training programs was judged within the context of frequency counts of task performance within a narrowly defined context (e.g., Cindy will complete two matching-to-sample tasks per session when given five or fewer verbal prompts per task for 60% of the sessions for two consecutive months). Such programs are no longer acceptable, and currently accepted professional standards of care require that training programs produce more comprehensive lifestyle changes than the mere acquisition of isolated skills (Evans & Meyer, 1987; Horner, Sprague, & Flannery, 1993). While training programs may use discrete behaviors or skills as the unit of instruction, functional activities or skill clusters, and not mastery of isolated skills per se, are the appropriate units of outcome (Guess & Helmstetter, 1986). We must remember that the aim of training is not to enable individuals to achieve an arbitrary level of proficiency in isolated skills but to assist them to reach the "criterion of ultimate functioning" (Brown, Neitupski, & Hamre-Neitupski, 1976)—that is, to be able to engage in a behavior at the level accepted by the community. Thus, an indicator of quality of care is whether the outcomes of training programs show socially valid changes in the individual across a range of settings, people, and target behaviors.

Another critical issue is the integration of training and treatment programs so that the services are not fragmented. For example, it is standard practice in the behavioral field to integrate behavior-reduction and skills-training programs because we do not reduce a behavior in a vacuum; it has to be replaced by socially acceptable behaviors that will enhance the quality of life of the individual. Thus, another indicator of quality of care is the degree to which treatment and training programs are integrated.

MEDICAL SERVICES

The rights of individuals with developmental disabilities in institutions to adequate medical care is guaranteed under the Fourteenth Amendment of the U.S. Constitution and several federal statutes. However, there do not appear to be firm guidelines as to what constitutes "adequate" care in this context, and it is left to the best judgment of the professionals involved in providing such services to determine what is acceptable. Nonetheless, medical services provided to individuals with developmental disabilities must be substantially in compliance with currently accepted professional standards of care. The quality of the care provided in several areas of medical services, including basic medical care, emergency care, seizure monitoring and management, and the administration and monitoring of psychotropic drugs as well as their side effects, provides the basis for determining whether these individuals are receiving the medical services that they are entitled to. Another consideration is whether the medical services provided to residents in institutions are inextricably linked to institutional care or whether the medical needs of these individuals can be met in the community. Given that most medical professionals in institutions are not specifically trained in the medical care of individuals with developmental disabilities, there is little reason to believe that they provide any services above and beyond those provided by other medical professionals in the community. However, this does not imply that the level of medical care will invariably be superior in the community, only that it is unlikely to be worse.

PSYCHIATRIC SERVICES

Individuals with mental retardation have up to five times the prevalence of mental illness of their peers in the general population (Singh, Sood, Sonenklar, & Ellis, 1991). Thus, the services of a psychiatrist trained in the psychiatry of mental retardation is critical because this is a very difficult population to assess and diagnose, especially if the individuals are nonverbal and have severe behavior problems. General psychiatrists and family physicians do not have the specialized training that is required to provide adequate psychiatric services to this population. It is the responsibility of the psychiatrist to provide timely psychiatric services, including the assessment, diagnosis, and treatment of mental illness. Further, psychiatrists need to be available for consultation on medication management. The quality of psychiatric services can be judged on several indicators, including the psychiatrist's knowledge and training in mental retardation, the provision of psychiatric services to all individuals diagnosed as having or suspected of having a mental illness, and appropriate and reliable assessment, diagnosis, and treatment. Psychiatric services provided by general physicians without any training in mental health, in lieu of experienced psychiatrists, is a good indicator of the lack of appropriate services.

Integration of Behavioral and Psychopharmacological Treatments

It is often the case that individuals with developmental disabilities who are diagnosed with a psychiatric disorder are on medication. Further, while many behavioral problems can be treated with behavioral methods, some maladaptive behaviors are the result of biological dysfunctions (e.g., serotonergic dysfunction) for which medication may be the treatment of choice (Aman & Singh, 1988). Thus, it is likely that many individuals with developmental disabilities will be on both behavioral programs and medication. In such cases, it is of utmost importance that the two treatments be integrated not only at the functional level but also at the interaction level. For example, it is well known that the impact of behavioral procedures employing conditioned aversive stimuli or punishment procedures may be lessened if the individual is also on neuroleptic medication. Thus, the degree to which the behavioral and psychopharmacological treatments are integrated at both the functional and the interactional levels provides an indicator of the quality of the care provided in the community and in an institution.

Medication Management

Given that individuals with mental retardation are prescribed medication for behavioral as well as psychiatric problems, psychotropic medication management is a very important aspect of the care of individuals with mental retardation and/or mental illness. Thus, adherence to currently accepted standards of care is essential because medications used to control behavior problems have some potentially serious side effects, including undesired effects that may hinder learning in this population. Several excellent sources of information (e.g., Aman & Singh, 1988; Ellis, Singh, & Jackson, 1996; Gadow & Poling, 1988) can be used to provide guidelines for currently acceptable practice as well as indicators of the quality of medication management. In addition, two other indicators should be assessed. First, there is a tendency to use polypharmacy for behavior and psychiatric problems. Such a practice may indicate that the psychiatric and/or behavior problems have not been controlled well enough with either behavioral programming or single-drug management and that the psychiatrists and psychologists do not see an alternative to drug management for intractable problems. The use of polypharmacy deviates from generally accepted standards of care. Second, the long history of neuroleptic use in this population means that a minority of the individuals on these drugs have developed or are at risk for developing tardive dyskinesia (TD). These individuals need to be seen by a neurologist for further examination, confirmation of the diagnosis, and suggestions for the management of TD. The lack of referral for neurological services is also an indicator of the quality of care provided in the community or an institution.

Emergency Chemical Restraints

In addition to prescribed medication for behavior and psychiatric problems, emergency chemical restraints are often used to subdue an individual who is aggressive or violent. This practice grossly deviates from generally accepted standards of care. The repeated use of chemical restraints indicates that the behavioral and psychopharmacological treatments are not very effective and that staff have to resort to the emergency use of psychotropics to keep the individual's behavior under control. Repeated chemical restraints indicate poor treatment practices that adversely affect the quality of life of the individual.

LIVING ENVIRONMENTS

Current professional standards of care and federal law require that individuals with developmental disabilities be provided with an effective treatment environment to ensure an acceptable quality of life. It has always been somewhat difficult to determine what the parameters of an effective treatment environment ought to be, given the diversity of "local" environments in the community. Fortunately, behavioral psychologists have been evaluating the effects of different treatment environments on the behavior of individuals, and the data from their studies provide us with guidelines as to what such environments ought to be like. For example, Favell and McGimsey (1993) have suggested that the inherent quality of an effective treatment environment is that it is functional, by which they mean that such an environment must (1) be an engaging environment (i.e., How well do the individuals actively participate in the activities provided in the environment?); (2) teach and maintain functional skills (i.e., Does the environment provide the context for individuals to learn skills and functionally improve their independence and general quality of life?); (3) reduce or preempt the occurrence of behavior problems (i.e., How effective is the environment in actively and successfully treating behavior problems, as well as in providing an environment that preempts the occurrence of such problems?); (4) be the least restrictive alternative (i.e., How normalized is the living environment?); (5) be a stable environment (i.e., How consistent are the personnel, interactions, and activities in the lives of the individuals?); (6) be a safe environment (i.e., Are the individuals safe from physical and psychological harm as a consequence of their own behavior or the behavior of others in their living environment?); and (7) be the one in which the individuals *choose* to live (i.e., Would the individuals choose to live in this environment?). These dimensions of the environment are quantifiable and can be used as the basis for evaluating the quality of care provided by facility- or community-based service providers.

An Engaging Environment

Typically, the environment in the community, as well as in institutions, is not fully functional for individuals with mental retardation. Some aspects of an engaging environment can be observed with some individuals, some of the time. For example, some individuals do not find anything in the environment that is reinforcing enough to attract their attention. In some living areas, age-appropriate leisure activities are available that provide the individuals an opportunity to engage in activities that promote the development of their social skills. However, in the same living area, there may be other individuals who do not interact with the materials, a fact suggesting that the environment is not functional for them. Given that there is a negative correlation between engagement and problem behavior, some of the problem behaviors exhibited by these individuals may be related to the fact that the environment is not responsive to their needs. Whether or not the environment is functional for specific individuals is an indicator of the quality of the services provided.

Teaching and Maintaining Functional Skills

In many institutions and community-based facilities, each individual has a list of several skills that are priority goals on their individual program plan. These goals pertain to the achievement of specific skills in various areas of functioning, such as social-emotional, sensorimotor, communication, and vocational. These skills are taught in isolation in discrete training sessions in the hope that these individuals will be able to use them appropriately in their daily activities. Unfortunately, isolated skills taught in sequestered conditions are typically *not* observed in the daily activities of these individuals because they are unable to *apply* them unless generalization is specifically programmed. To maximize their application, these skills must be taught in situ, thereby obviating the need for programming generalization and maintenance. In acceptable treatment environments, training is conducted not in discrete, artificial training sessions, but in settings, times, and activities that are functional for the individual.

Reducing or Preempting the Occurrence of Behavior Problems

Behavior problems not only pose physical and emotional risks to the individual and to those around them (staff, family, and peers) but also interfere with the individual's learning and habilitation. One question that can be posed for this criterion is whether an institution or a community program effectively treats each individual's behavior problems. The proper implementation and timely revision of a behavior program based on appropriate and comprehensive structural and functional analyses of the individual's behavior will eliminate the challenging behavior or, at least, will reduce it to manageable levels. One indicator of this criterion is how successfully the individual's behavior problems are treated. The longer a problem behavior remains in an individual's repertoire, the less acceptable is the treatment environment. Other indicators include the timeliness of revisions made in the treatment program based on accurate outcome data and the fidelity with which the treatment program is implemented.

Least Restrictive Living Environment

The continuum of living environments for individuals with developmental disabilities ranges from large segregated institutions to community living, with fully integrated work, education, and leisure opportunities (Favell & McGimsey, 1993). The placement of individuals with developmental disabilities in an institution and some community-based facilities does not provide the least restrictive living environment. For example, living in an institution does not lead to fewer restrictions than the individuals would experience in the community or to increased participation in the work, education, and leisure opportunities experienced by their peers living in the community. Thus, the basic question is: How normalized is the living environment? Unfortunately, the living environments in institutions and some community-based facilities are very restrictive and not normalized. Most do not offer much privacy because many individuals have to share bedrooms with others, do not have any personal belongings on the walls or at their bedside, and do not have a homelike environment. Further, some individuals may have their rights to liberty, as guaranteed by the Fourteenth Amendment, denied for a number of reasons. One of the most common reasons for the denial of their rights is the use of restrictive procedures as a part of their treatment plans. When individuals engage in aggressive or destructive behaviors, physical or mechanical restraints or emergency chemical restraints are often used in lieu of effective behavioral and psychopharmacological management.

Stable Environment

The basic question is whether there is order in the individual's life: Is there predictability and continuity in terms of services and personnel? Because staff in an institution and in some community-based facilities and workshops are rotated through several programs, individuals often encounter new staff in their daily activities, and the implementation of behavioral programs is often inconsistent because the new staff do not know how to implement them. This situation often leads to an unstable environment for the individuals.

Safe Environment

Individuals with developmental disabilities must be protected from physical and psychological harm, as well as injury from behavior problems. Given the large number of individuals in an institution who engage in self-injurious behavior or physical aggression toward others, the residents are not protected from injury. Another indication of a safe environment is whether there are "incidents" above and beyond the number expected to be found in a "regular" family home in the community. A further indicator of a safe environment is the number of abuse, neglect, or mistreatment investigations undertaken at an institution. Although community environments may be safer in a physical sense because fewer individuals with severe behavior problems reside together, there is always the danger that others in the community may cause psychological harm through insensitivity toward individuals with developmental disabilities. Until a society accepts all individuals as equal members of the community, there will always be the potential of harm to some of its members, either psychological or physical. Unfortunately, those with developmental disabilities are particularly vulnerable to such harm because they are unable to defend themselves.

Choice of Residential Placement

A final indicator of the quality of life of individuals with developmental disabilities is the choice they make regarding their residential status. The critical indicator is whether these individuals choose to live in the environment where they currently reside. Are the residents of institutions or their guardians given an opportunity to choose community placement? In some institutions, one of the reasons why individuals are not transitioned to the community is that they do not have the consent of their parents. Many families initially oppose the transfer of their children from a residential facility to the community because they have strong feelings of uncertainty, fear, betrayal, and guilt. However, after the transfer occurs, the great majority become strong supporters of community placement (Larson & Lakin, 1991). Further, institutions have been found to be "consistently less effective than community-based settings in promoting growth, particularly among individuals diagnosed as severely or profoundly mentally retarded" (Larson & Lakin, 1989, p. 330). These are very strong reasons for devising individualized community placement programs that include parent education on placement outcomes and an assurance that their child's quality of life is what will drive the placement. Further, in the few cases in which the initial placement fails to be of advantage to the individual, additional training and other placement options must be provided by the facility until a suitable community placement is found. The effort an institution makes in community placement is one indicator of the quality of the services it provides. Further, keeping individuals in residential institutions because of a lack of local and state funding is untenable and cannot be condoned on any grounds.

When asked for their opinion, most staff in institutions will indicate that, with appropriate supports, most, if not all, residents under their care can be successfully placed in the community. I totally agree that, with adequate supports, all residents in institutions can be successfully placed in the community.

Indeed, there are a small number of states in this country that do not have any facilities at all and have successfully accommodated their citizens with mental retardation in the community. A question often posed by skeptics is: What about the medically fragile residents? Well, what about them? Where would they be if they did not have an underlying mental retardation? The mere fact that they have mental retardation should not condemn them to be segregated from their peers and placed in institutions. In any case, most institutions provide little meaningful programming for the medically fragile and often contract with a local hospital for medical services for these residents. The old medical chestnut that institutions provide total care for individuals with mental retardation is a myth that can no longer be sustained.

According to the National Association of Superintendents of Public Residential Facilities for the Mentally Retarded (1974), deinstitutionalization encompasses three interrelated processes: (1) prevention of admission by finding and developing alternative methods of care and training; (2) return to the community of all residents who have been prepared through programs of habilitation and training to function adequately in appropriate local settings; and (3) establishment and maintenance of a responsive residential environment that protects human and civil rights (pp. 4–5). While I wholeheartedly agree with the first two options, let us take another look at the third. The issue here is whether institutions provide "a responsive residential environment that protects the human and civil rights" of individuals with mental retardation. If we take into account even the limited number of indicators we have discussed (i.e., psychological services, medical services, psychiatric services, and living environments), it is hard to imagine an institution fulfilling all of these requirements and still remaining an institution. For example, if an institution were to meet all the indicators of an acceptable living environment, then, by default, it would not be an institution because it would be providing its services in family homes in the community, where the individual has access to everything that the community has to offer all its citizens.

Thus, the issue is not whether we should have institutions but what the quality of life is that we offer to our brothers and sisters who are mentally retarded. Further, we must never forget that living in the community is not inherently better if the services we provide to individuals in the community are not of the same quality as those we provide for ourselves. Indeed, one can well argue that the measure of a community is how well it takes care of those who cannot fully take care of themselves. We have the choice of providing a quality lifestyle in the community to individuals with mental retardation or making the community a larger institution for them.

The authors who have contributed to this book have devoted their clinical, teaching, and research careers to providing models and methods by which we can enhance the quality of life of individuals with developmental disabilities. I will briefly summarize each of the chapters in terms of the central theme of this book.

PART 1: MODELS

In Chapter 2, Feldman and Griffiths describe ecobehavioral strategies for assessing behavior problems that can be used with individuals with developmental disabilities, both in the community and in institutions. This model is derived from the view that all phenomena in the environment are interrelated and, therefore, that assessment and treatment should be undertaken in the context in which the behavior occurs (Singh, 1995a). Feldman and Griffiths note that an ecobehavioral approach to the assessment and treatment of behavior problems can be encapsulated by asking the individual's family members, teachers, and caretakers four critical questions: (1) Why is he or she doing that? (2) What is the payoff for the behavior? (3) What is he or she trying to tell us? and (4) Could he or she be doing something more meaningful and appropriate to obtain the same (or an even better) payoff?

The authors provide a general methodology that parents, teachers, and caretakers can use to answer these four questions. They advocate using three sources of information to answer these questions: (1) informant interviews, (2) naturalistic observations, and (3) controlled analog assessments, if necessary. Further, they suggest that only essential data that is needed to generate testable hypotheses of the motivation for the behavior problem be collected. If a hypothesis is proved correct, it will lead directly to the design of interventions that not only reduce the behavior problem but also teach the individual alternative, functional skills. When taken together, the reduction of the behavior problem and the learning of new functional skills will contribute to an enhanced quality of life for the individual.

The quality of life of individuals with developmental disabilities can be greatly enhanced if they are taught appropriate social interaction skills. In Chapter 3, Kohler and Strain note that few people have demonstrated the long-term effects of social skills training in this population. They suggest that the reason may be that most social skills studies have (1) focused on global behaviors, (2) targeted the behavior of an individual instead of the interactions between individuals, and (3) failed to investigate the functions of specific social behaviors in an individual's subsequent social acts. In response, Kohler and Strain present an assessment tool that provides a fine-grained analysis of social behavior in terms of its magnitude, function, reciprocity, and duration. Interventions derived from this type of analysis have the potential to prevent the development and maintenance of behavior problems, as well as to enhance a broad range of social behaviors in individuals with developmental disabilities.

Lovaas (1987) has developed and evaluated an intensive behavioral treatment program for young children with autism. His results show that about half the children with autism who participate in the intensive treatment program achieve normal intellectual and educational functioning as measured on standardized intelligence tests and the successful completion of first grade in regular education classrooms. The children in this program gained an average of 30 IQ points above similar children who did not receive the intensive treatment. Follow-up data collected after a mean of five years showed that more of the children who had participated in the treatment program remained in regular education classrooms than those who did not (McEachin, Smith, & Lovaas, 1993).

In Chapter 4, Lovaas and Buch describe their model of intensive behavioral intervention with young children. The Young Autism Project at the University of California at Los Angeles is a 40-hour-per-week, 2- to 3-year treatment program for 2- to 3-year-old children with autism. They describe in some detail the procedures involved in implementing this program, as well as the critical components of the model. Finally, they discuss the knowledge and skills that therapists and teachers will need for successfully implementing this program.

Curricular modifications can be used to deal with behavior problems. In Chapter 5, Wolery and Winterling discuss the roles that curriculum can play in the design of intervention plans for controlling behavior problems. They suggest that curriculum can be used as (1) prevention, (2) the context for other interventions, (3) an adjunctive intervention, and (4) the primary intervention. They also describe specific curricular modifications that teachers can use to deal with behavior problems: teaching replacement behaviors, promoting adaptive responding that is incompatible with the behavior problem, teaching self-management behaviors, and manipulating contextual variables, such as teacher interaction. The authors conclude the chapter by describing how major teaching functions, such as managing instructional time, presenting instructional strategies, and providing feedback to children, can be skillfully used by the teacher to preempt and control behavior problems. This chapter suggests that the manipulation of the teaching environment and the curriculum can provide the setting events for learning without the occurrence of behavior problems.

There is abundant data to show that some individuals, typically those with limited forms of communication, engage in behavior problems as a form of communication. This finding suggests that some forms of behavior problems in some individuals may be purposeful. Carr, McConnachie, Levin, and Kemp (1993) have noted that behavior problems may serve as a primitive form of communication and will drop out of the individual's repertoire when replaced by more sophisticated forms of communication. This finding suggests that, if behavior problems in individuals with developmental disabilities have a communicative intent, then teaching them alternative, socially acceptable forms of communication will eliminate these problems. This issue is at the heart of Chapter 6, in which Dyer and Larsson describe functional communication training methods for individuals with limited forms of communication. They discuss the general principles of functional communication training and the research that demonstrates the effectiveness of this method of controlling behavior problems. Further, they provide clear guidelines for assessing the communicative functions of behavior problems and specific strategies that can be used to provide alternative methods of communicating. This chapter provides simple methods for enhancing the quality of life of individuals with developmental disabilities by teaching them communication skills that are socially acceptable and easily understood by those who interact with them.

A large number of prevalence studies have shown that between 30% and 50% of institutionalized individuals with developmental disabilities are on psychotropic medication for their behavior problems (Singh, Ellis, & Wechsler, in press). The prevalence is a little lower in the community, with 12% to 31% of children and 18% to 24% of adults being on psychotropic medication. Given the high prevalence of psychotropic drug use, Ellis, Singh, and Singh suggest in Chapter 7 that anyone who works with individuals with developmental disabilities should have some basic knowledge of behavior-modifying drugs as used in this population. In this chapter, they briefly present the basic principles of psychopharmacology, as well as the indications, effects on behavior, and side effects of the most frequently used psychotropic medications. Further, they discuss the role of interdisciplinary professionals in delivering and monitoring the effects of these drugs. Clearly, if we are going to use behavior-modifying drugs to enhance the quality of life of individuals with developmental disabilities, we must be sure that there is a good rationale for their use with specific individuals. As the authors correctly point out, like any other treatment, behavior-modifying drugs should be used to enhance the individual's general functioning and quality of life as opposed to merely controlling an undesirable behavior.

PART 2: METHODS

Chapters 8 through 12 present simple and clear guidelines for using various proven behavioral strategies for managing the five most common behavior problems in individuals with developmental disabilities: self-injury (Wacker,

Northup, and Lambert), stereotypy (Rojahn, Hammer, and Kroeger), aggression (Matson and Duncan), rumination (Ellis, Parr, Singh, and Wechsler), and pica (Ellis, Singh, Crews, Bonaventura, Gehin, and Ricketts). Management of each of the target behaviors is based on the model of behavioral assessment and treatment described above. Further, each chapter includes a brief outline of standard behavioral treatments that have been empirically evaluated and found to be effective with some individuals. Both aversive and nonaversive treatments are included, and it is up to the clinician to determine through thorough structural and functional analyses which treatment option would be least intrusive and most effective for a given individual. As I have noted elsewhere (Singh, 1995b), the effectiveness dimension must include an enhancement of the individual's quality of life and not just a reduction in the rate of the behavior problem. We must remember that, when we teach and habilitate individuals with developmental disabilities, our goal is to make positive changes in the entire fabric of their lives.

REFERENCES

Aman, M. G., & Singh, N. N. (1988). *Psychopharmacology of the developmental disabilities.* New York: Springer-Verlag.

Axelrod, S. (1987). Functional and structural analyses of behavior: Approaches leading to reduced use of punishment procedures? *Research in Developmental Disabilities, 8,* 165–178.

Bernstein, C. (1916). Minutes. *Journal of Psycho-Asthenics, 21,* 94–112.

Brown, L., Neitupski, J., & Hamre-Neitupski, S. (1976). The criterion of ultimate functioning. In M. A. Thomas (Ed.), *Hey, don't forget about me.* Reston, VA: Council for Exceptional Children.

Carr, E. G., McConnachie, G., Levin, L., & Kemp, D. C. (1993). Communication-based treatment of severe behavior problems. In R. Van Houten & S. Axelrod (Eds.), *Behavior analysis and treatment* (pp. 231–267). New York: Plenum Press.

Carr, E. G., Robinson, S., & Palumbo, L. W. (1990). The wrong issue: Aversive versus nonaversive treatment. The right issue: Functional versus nonfunctional treatment. In A. C. Repp & N. N. Singh (Eds.), *Perspectives on the use of nonaversive interventions for persons with developmental disabilities* (pp. 361–379). Sycamore, IL: Sycamore Press.

Ellis, C. R., Singh, N. N., & Jackson, N. (1996). Problem behaviors in children with developmental disabilities. In D. X. Parmelee (Ed.), *Child and adolescent psychiatry* (pp. 263–275). St. Louis, MO: Mosby.

Evans, I. M., & Meyer, L. H. (1987). Moving to educational validity: A reply to Test, Spooner, and Cooke. *Journal of the Association for Persons with Severe Handicaps, 12,* 103–106.

Favell, J. E., & McGimsey, J. F. (1993). Defining an acceptable treatment environment. In R. Van Houten & S. Axelrod (Eds.), *Behavior analysis and treatment* (pp. 25–45). New York: Plenum Press.

Fernald, W. (1919). State programs for the care of the mentally defective. *Journal of Psycho-Asthenics, 24,* 114–122.

Gadow, K. D., & Poling, A. (1988). *Pharmacotherapy and mental retardation.* Boston: Little, Brown.

Guess, D., & Helmstetter, E. (1986). Skill cluster instruction and the individualized curriculum sequencing model. In R. H. Horner, L. H. Meyer, & H. D. Fredericks (Eds.), *Education of learners with severe handicaps* (pp. 221–248). Baltimore: Paul H. Brooks.

Horner, R. H., Sprague, J. R., & Flannery, K. B. (1993). Building functional curricula for students with severe intellectual disabilities and severe problem behaviors. In R. Van Houten & S. Axelrod (Eds.), *Behavior analysis and treatment* (pp. 47–71). New York: Plenum Press.

Larson, S. A., & Lakin, K. C. (1989). Deinstitutionalization of persons with mental retardation: Behavioral outcomes. *Journal of the Association for Persons with Severe Handicaps, 14,* 324–332.

Larson, S. A., & Lakin, K. C. (1991). Parent attitudes about residential placement before and after deinstitutionalization: A research synthesis. *Journal of the Association for Persons with Severe Handicaps, 16,* 25–38.

Lovaas, O. I. (1987). Behavioral treatment and normal educational/intellectual functioning in young autistic children. *Journal of Consulting and Clinical Psychology, 55,* 3–9.

Mace, F. C., Lalli, J. S., & Shea, M. C. (1992). Functional analysis and treatment of self-injury. In J. K. Luiselli, J. L. Matson, & N. N. Singh (Eds.), *Self-injurious behavior: Analysis, assessment, and treatment* (pp. 122–152). New York: Springer-Verlag.

McEachin, J. J., Smith, T., & Lovaas, O. I. (1993). Long-term outcome for children with autism who received early intensive behavioral treatment. *American Journal on Mental Retardation, 97,* 359–372.

National Association of Superintendents of Public Residential Facilities for the Mentally Retarded. (1974). *Contemporary issues in residential programming.* Washington, DC: President's Committee on Mental Retardation.

Pyles, D. A. M., & Bailey, J. S. (1992). Behavioral diagnostic systems. In J. K. Luiselli, J. L. Matson, & N. N. Singh (Eds.), *Self-injurious behavior: Analysis, assessment, and treatment* (pp. 155–180). New York: Springer-Verlag.

Repp, A. C., & Singh, N. N. (1990) *Perspectives on the use of nonaversive interventions for persons with developmental disabilities.* Sycamore, IL: Sycamore.

Seguin, E. (1846). *Traitement moral, hygiene et l'éducation des idiots et descuetres enfants arreere's.* Paris: J. B. Bailliere.

Singh, N. N. (1995a). In search of unity: Some thoughts on family-professional relationships in service delivery systems. *Journal of Child and Family Studies, 4,* 3–18.

Singh, N. N. (1995b). Moving beyond institutional care for individuals with developmental disabilities. *Journal of Child and Family Studies, 4,* 129–145.

Singh, N. N., Ellis, C. R., & Wechsler, H. A. (in press). Psychopharmacoepidemiology in mental retardation. *Journal of Child and Adolescent Psychopharmacology.*

Singh, N. N., Sood, A., Sonenklar, N., & Ellis, C. R. (1991). Assessment and diagnosis of mental illness in persons with mental retardation: Methods and measures. *Behavior Modification, 15,* 418–422.

PART
1

M O D E L S

Chapter
2

Comprehensive Assessment
of Severe Behavior Problems

MAURICE A. FELDMAN AND DOROTHY GRIFFITHS

INTRODUCTION

About 30% to 50% of individuals with developmental disabilities (DD) have behavioral or psychiatric disorders, such as aggression, self-injury, stereotypy, property destruction, and depression (Bouras & Drummond, 1992). Individuals with DD may be predisposed to behavior disorders because of limited appropriate cognitive, communicative, social, and problem-solving skills. Also, life experiences involving stigmatization, rejection, abuse, restrictions on personal freedom, dependency on others, difficulty in learning, or lack of opportunities to learn socially appropriate behaviors through typical interactions with nonhandicapped individuals may also make individuals with DD more prone to behavioral and emotional problems.

Numerous treatments have been investigated, the behavioral and the pharmacological being the two most popular forms. Often, these treatments are employed in a "cookbook" fashion (e.g., "if aggression, then use time-out") without thorough analyses of the underlying causes and maintaining conditions of the aberrant behavior. Recently, there has been renewed interest in the assessment of behavior problems. For example, the National Institutes of Health consensus report of practitioners and researchers (National Institutes of Health, 1991) concluded that, to promote more effective nonintrusive interventions for individuals with DD and destructive behaviors, more emphasis should be placed on the initial identification of the variables influencing the individual's maladaptive behavior.

Various assessment strategies have been developed that increase the likelihood of isolating functional variables. Usually, when these agents are uncovered, effective and (preferably) nonintrusive treatments can be directly derived from the assessment findings. We describe the assessment strategies that can be used in community and institutional settings. This model incorporates quality assurance recommendations (Griffiths, 1989) and government-sanctioned standards of practice (Blake, Feldman, Keller, Moore, & Munn, 1987) for treating individuals with DD and behavior disorders. We have adopted an ecobehavioral approach to the assessment and treatment of aberrant behavior in individuals with DD. The assumption underlying this approach is that most forms of aberrant behavior are learned and are potentially influenced by a wide array of contextual factors (Schroeder, 1990; Singh & Aman, 1990).

Sources of Motivation for Learned Maladaptive Behavior

Positive and negative reinforcement are the two primary sources of motivation for learned maladaptive behavior. Automatic reinforcement, wherein the behavior directly generates positive or negative reinforcing physiological, nonsocial consequences, has also been considered a source of motivation by some investigators (e.g., Iwata, Vollmer, & Zarcone, 1990). However, as all automatic reinforcement effects can be explained within the context of positive and negative reinforcement, for the sake of parsimony and clinical utility we have subsumed automatic reinforcement phenomena under positive (e.g., sensory reinforcement) or negative (e.g., pain reduction) reinforcement. We do recognize the value, however, of identifying possible physiological consequences when trying to identify sources of motivation for aberrant behavior.

Positive Reinforcement

Positive reinforcement involves the contingent presentation of events that increase the probability of occurrence of the behaviors they follow. Three general types of positive reinforcers have been implicated in the maladaptive behavior of individuals with DD: (1) attention from others; (2) tangibles such as food and toys; and (3) sensory stimulation. From a communication perspective, the individual engaging in the aberrant behavior is assumed to be saying, "I want you" for attention, "I want this" for tangibles, and "This feels good" for sensory stimulation.

In identifying reinforcement contingencies, one must also examine not only the consequences of the behavior in question, but also the setting events and immediate antecedents. Setting events, which may occur before or concurrently with the target behavior, establish the condition (i.e., motivation) for reinforcement of the behavior. Box 2-1 presents setting events and antecedents typically associated with positively reinforced maladaptive behavior in individuals with DD. Aberrant behaviors such as aggression, self-injury, and stereotypy may be the most successful responses in consistently obtaining high rates of social, tangible, and sensory positive reinforcement in environments lacking in social interactions, stimulating activities, and opportunities to engage in meaningful, socially appropriate behaviors. Likewise, such behaviors may be highly effective in preventing the removal of, or in restoring, positive reinforcers.

Negative Reinforcement

Negative reinforcement involves the increased probability of the occurrence of a behavior that is successful in avoiding ("I don't want to do that"), escaping from ("Get me out of here"), delaying ("Let's see how long I can put this off"), or attenuating ("I won't do all of it") aversive events. Box 2-2 presents various setting events and antecedents, usually considered aversive or unpleasant by

<table>
<tr><td>

**Box
2-1**

</td><td>

EXAMPLES OF POSITIVE-REINFORCEMENT-BASED BEHAVIOR: SETTING EVENTS, ANTECEDENTS, AND CONSEQUENCES

</td></tr>
</table>

Setting Events
1. Lack of social interactions
2. Lack of stimulating activities
3. Lack of opportunities to respond in socially appropriate ways

Antecedents
1. Ending social interaction
2. Turning attention to someone else
3. Ignoring person
4. Terminating preferred activity
5. Taking away preferred objects

Consequences
1. Attention or reactions from other individuals
2. Tangibles and activities
3. Sensory stimulation and environmental change

the person, that are associated with negatively reinforced maladaptive behavior in individuals with DD. Aberrant behaviors (e.g., aggression against the instructor, destroying instructional or work materials, and engaging in high-rate stereotypy) may be effective in allowing the person to escape these aversive stimuli, particularly in settings where there are limited choices and more appropriate escape behaviors (e.g., asking to leave) are not reinforced.

Multiple Factors Influencing Current Behavior

An ecobehavioral perspective maintains that, in addition to contemporaneous reinforcement contingencies, there are many contextual factors that influence the development and maintenance of aberrant behavior in individuals with DD. Figure 2-1 illustrates some of the more obvious historical and contemporary variables that intermingle to yield the person's current behavioral repertoire. The recognition that current behavior is very likely a result of complex biobehavioral interactions discourages dichotomous explanations (e.g., genetic vs. environmental, or psychiatric vs. behavioral) and fosters an interdisciplinary approach to the assessment and treatment of aberrant behavior.

The view that aberrant behavior is a product of complex biobehavioral relationships is illustrated in the following example. A child who engaged in self-injurious behavior consisting of hitting his ear was referred for assessment

> ### Box 2-2
>
> **EXAMPLES OF NEGATIVE-REINFORCEMENT-BASED BEHAVIOR: SETTING EVENTS, ANTECEDENTS, AND CONSEQUENCES**
>
> *Setting Events (Aversive)*
> 1. Pain, illness, discomfort
> 2. Crowding, presence of nonpreferred individuals
> 3. Bright lights, noise
> 4. High demands, rapid pacing of instructions
> 5. Monotonous, boring situations
> 6. Staff changes
> 7. Regimented environments with no choices or control over one's own life
> 8. Unpredictable chaotic environments
>
> *Antecedents*
> 1. Demands to engage in nonpreferred activities
> 2. Physical guidance
> 3. Materials associated with boring or difficult tasks
> 4. Frightening stimuli
> 5. Criticism, correction
>
> *Consequences*
> 1. Avoidance (prevention of aversive event)
> 2. Escape (termination of aversive event)
> 3. Delay in start of aversive event
> 4. Attenuation of aversive event

and treatment. A medical examination revealed that he had otitis media, an ear infection that results in a fluid buildup that increases pressure in the ear, thereby causing pain and discomfort. The child may have accidentally discovered that hitting the ear temporarily reduces the pressure and hence the pain. This was a learning experience based on negative reinforcement, which increased the probability that hitting the ear would occur again if it continued to successfully reduce pain. Thus, although self-injury appeared to have been "caused" by a biological condition (the ear infection), in fact the infection was a setting event (i.e., it established the conditions) whereby hitting the ear was reinforced by pain reduction and thus occurred more frequently under similar circumstances. While treating the infection eliminated the pain-reduction function of self-injury, it did not result in a reduction of the behavior to zero. It appeared that other consequences for ear hitting had now assumed a maintaining role (e.g., positive reinforcement of the parents' attention to the behavior). This example shows how biological, learning, and environment factors interact to produce and maintain aberrant behavior.

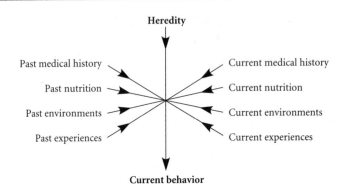

Figure 2-1

A variety of historical and current biological and environmental events interact to produce current behaviors

ECOBEHAVIORAL ASSESSMENT

A fundamental goal of an ecobehavioral assessment is to gather sufficient information to make a hypothesis of the likely reinforcement contingencies (i.e., the sources of motivation) that are maintaining the aberrant behavior. Basically, we ask the question: "Why is the person doing that?" We have found it useful in communicating with nonbehavioral professionals and care providers to ask this question metaphorically: "What is the payoff for that behavior?" or "What is the person trying to tell us?" Then, we derive treatments directly from the hypothesis by asking, "Could the person be doing something more meaningful and appropriate to obtain the same (or an even better) payoff?"

General Methodology

An assessment should investigate the current sources of motivation for the aberrant behavior and the conditions under which it occurs. The basic components of a comprehensive ecobehavioral assessment include the identification of:

1. Specific behavioral excesses and deficits and their impact on the person's life.
2. Biological and medical factors that may be associated with the aberrant behavior.
3. Circumstances (i.e., physical and social environments, activities, physiological conditions, and specific antecedents) in which the aberrant behavior

tends to occur (and not occur) using life-space (Brown, Shiraga, York, Zanella, & Rogan, 1984) and structural analyses (Axelrod, 1987).

4. Possible reinforcers of the aberrant behavior by examining its typical consequences via a functional analysis. As the term will be used here, a *functional analysis* could involve, but does not necessarily require, an experimental validation of a causal relationship between the behavior and specific consequences.

5. Other potentially reinforcing consequences that could be used to teach new skills and override the existing reinforcement for aberrant behavior.

6. The person's current abilities to perform adaptive behaviors (e.g., communication, leisure, and self-care) that could be used as replacements for the aberrant behavior.

Hierarchy of Ecobehavioral Assessment

In conducting ecobehavioral assessments, we have extended the concept of the least intrusive treatment to that of the least intrusive assessment. That is, we endeavor to use the most efficient, least intrusive way of obtaining sufficiently accurate information to generate hypotheses from which effective non-intrusive interventions can be derived. We use the least-intrusive-assessment approach across three levels of fact finding: informant interviews, natural observations, and controlled analog assessments. Each subsequent level represents an increasing (1) likelihood of accurately determining the relevant variables affecting behavior; (2) level of required practitioner knowledge and sophistication in conducting ecobehavioral assessments; (3) amount of assessor time and effort; and (4) level of intrusiveness from the client's and the caregivers' perspectives.

Level 1: Informant Interviews

The first step in gathering information pertinent to an ecobehavioral assessment is to interview individuals familiar with the client (of course, if the client is capable, he or she should also be interviewed). Knowledgeable informants for individuals with DD usually include family members, teachers, and residential and work/day programming staff. The following information is obtained.

Nature and definition of the behavior problem.   Various checklists, such as the Aberrant Behavior Checklist (Aman & Singh, 1986, 1994), the Child Behavior Checklist (Achenbach & Edelbrook, 1981), and the Parent Attitude Test (Cowen, Huser, Beach, & Rappaport, 1970), are available to help infor-

---

Box 2-3

QUESTIONS TO ASK REGARDING THE TARGET BEHAVIOR(S)

1. Describe the problem behavior in detail. What does the person do?
2. How often does the behavior occur each day or week?
3. How long does the behavior or episodic outburst (rapid repetitions) usually last?
4. How intense is the behavior? Does it cause injury or destruction?
5. Is there a group of different behaviors that tend to occur together (e.g., biting own arm, screaming, and crying)?
6. Are there early warning signs that the aberrant behavior is about to happen? What are they?
7. Does the problem behavior occur regularly, or is it cyclic (e.g., seasonal or premenstrual)?
8. Why is this behavior a problem to the individual? Does it threaten self or others' health and safety? Does it interfere with (a) learning, (b) social acceptance, and (c) opportunities for less restrictive, more independent and integrative placements and outings?

---

mants identify general problem areas. Two scales can also be used that are designed to identify possible psychiatric aspects of behavior disorders in individuals with DD: the Reiss Screen (Reiss, 1988) and PIMRA (Psychopathology Instrument for Mentally Retarded Adults) (Matson, Kazdin, & Senatore, 1984). The informants usually require guidance in pinpointing the specific behaviors that are likely to become the targets for treatment. Box 2-3 presents a list of questions we can ask informants about the problem behaviors of the client.

Client and family history and current caregiver status. In addition to basic demographic information, we are interested in when and where the problem started, how it may have changed over the years, previous medical conditions, treatment efforts (including medications), and their effects. We can use this information so as not to reinvent the wheel or make the same mistakes others may have made before.

For clients living at home, we use the Parenting Stress Index (Abidin, 1983) and other questions to ascertain the parents' current levels of stress, attitudes toward their child, and social and professional supports. From an ecobehavioral perspective, we use this information to understand how life events may affect the parents' receptivity to intervention (and their role as mediators), and to determine whether the members of the family would benefit from other services (e.g., family therapy, stress management, or sibling counseling). We also ask potential implementers of the treatment (usually the natural care providers) about their knowledge of, experience with, and acceptance of behavioral procedures to determine the structure and extent of

> ## Box 2-4
>
> ### QUESTIONS TO ASK REGARDING POSSIBLE BIOLOGICAL AND MEDICAL CONDITIONS ASSOCIATED WITH ABERRANT BEHAVIOR
>
> 1. Does the individual have a diagnosed syndrome (e.g., Down, Prader-Willi, fragile X, Rett, or premenstrual)? If yes, are the behaviors typical of the syndrome?
> 2. Are there any medical conditions that may contribute to the problem (e.g., allergies, epilepsy, otitis media, or diabetes)?
> 3. Has the individual's health changed recently? If so, how, and was this change related to a change in behavior?
> 4. What medications is the individual receiving? Could the behavior problem be related to side effects or drug interactions? Has there been a recent change in medication associated with a change in behavior? List all medications, dosages, purposes, and length of time used.
> 5. Have there been recent mood changes or fluctuations?
> 6. Have there been recent changes in activity and energy levels?
> 7. Have there been recent changes in the individual's skill levels or social behavior?
> 8. Have there been eating, sleeping, or toileting problems?

mediator training they are likely to require to willingly and effectively implement the recommended interventions.

Biological and medical assessments of behavior disorders. Often, challenging behavior has a biomedical basis. Thus, one of the first steps in the assessment of behavior disorders in individuals with DD should be to investigate possible biological and medical influences. Pinpointing specific target behaviors may aid the physician in recognizing possible underlying biological conditions. Box 2-4 lists the questions we can ask informants (or clients) about current biological and medical conditions and treatments. Conditions often associated with an increased risk of behavior problems include genetic disorders (e.g., the Lesch-Nyhan, Rett, fragile X, and Prader-Willi syndromes), other biological insults (e.g., traumatic brain injury and fetal alcohol syndrome), food and sleep deprivation, adverse medication effects (e.g., side effects, long-term effects, polypharmocological interactions, and withdrawal reactions), and conditions that result in pain and discomfort (e.g., premenstrual syndrome, headaches, infections, dental problems, seizures, constipation, hemorrhoids, and allergies).

Given the high prevalence of psychiatric disorders in individuals with DD who have behavior problems, ideally a psychiatrist should be part of the assessment team. The client should also receive a thorough examination by other relevant medical specialists (e.g., a neurologist, a geneticist, and an aller-

---

Box 2-5

QUESTIONS TO ASK REGARDING THE CLIENT'S QUALITY OF LIFE

Answer yes or no as to whether the client is involved in making personal decisions about the following aspects of his or her life:

1. When to get up and go to bed
2. Meal planning and grocery shopping
3. Furniture and decorations for bedroom
4. Access to the entire house (except others' private areas)
5. How to spend his or her money
6. Choice of room- or housemates, friends, and visitors
7. Access to peers without disabilities
8. Communicating with others via telephone and letter writing
9. Pets
10. Availability of a personal space and privacy
11. Personal belongings
12. Choice of work activities
13. Choice of recreational and leisure activities
14. Choices of what to do with his or her time; scheduling own time
15. Access to transportation
16. Access to a variety of community environments
17. Freedom to refuse requests made by others

---

gist) to determine if a current biomedical condition may be related to the occurrence of the aberrant behavior. If so, then these underlying conditions should obviously receive appropriate medical treatment. In addition, the side effects and long-term effects of medications should be closely monitored, as these, too, may directly or indirectly cause behavior problems. Even when there is an underlying medical condition, nonmedical treatments may help to reduce the associated maladaptive behavior.

Structural analysis of current environments. We can conduct an informant-based ecological and quality-of-life assessment using a life-space analysis (Brown et al., 1984). Over a typical week, the informant indicates in what settings and activities and with whom the individual is involved and the extent of his or her participation in the domains of domestic, school/work, leisure/recreational, community integration, and interactions with peers who have no disabilities. We can supplement this information with questions (Box 2-5) about the client's opportunities to make personal decisions about daily activities. We then conduct a discrepancy analysis in which we compare the client's lifestyle across situational domains with that of peers who have no disabilities; discrepancies that may be attributed to behavioral excesses and deficits are particularly noted. We relate the life-space information to the occurrence of the target behaviors to identify possible behavioral deficits and setting events (e.g., an uncomfortable setting, periods of time without meaningful social interactions or activities, high-demand situations, and lack of choices).

Motivational analysis.   We use the Motivational Assessment Scale (MAS; Durand & Crimmins, 1988) to obtain the care providers' perceptions of the possible reinforcers of the client's target behavior(s). The MAS consists of 16 items and yields rank scores for four common reinforcement categories: (1) attention, (2) tangibles, (3) sensory, and (4) escape. Although the MAS is an appealing and efficient functional analysis device, we interpret the results of the MAS cautiously because of its weak psychometric properties (Singh et al., 1993). Further, we have found low interrater reliability of MAS scores among different care providers, as well as a poor correspondence between MAS ratings of possible reinforcers and ratings found through natural observations or analogs (Feldman, Griffiths, Condillac, & Tough, 1992). However, we have found that the MAS is apparently more accurate and consistent when filled out by an informant who has had training in behavior analysis.

Client reinforcers.   The care providers and, if possible, the client complete a client reinforcer checklist to help identify possible reinforcers that can be used during interventions (e.g., differential reinforcement and skill training). The reinforcers include social (e.g., praise, affection, and favorite individuals), tangibles (e.g., food, toys, and possessions), sensory (e.g., music, TV, and video games), activities (e.g., games, sports, outings, and free time), environments (e.g., calm setting, own room, and shopping mall), and money. This information is used cautiously, as we recognize that there may be a discrepancy between the care providers' perceptions and the client's actual reinforcers (Green et al., 1988). Whenever possible, we augment this information by using a reinforcer sampling procedure in which we observe what the client typically chooses when given an array of potentially reinforcing items or activities (Green et al., 1988).

Current skill level.   We ask knowledgeable care providers to fill out the Vineland Adaptive Behavior Scale to determine skill strengths and training needs. The caregivers also fill out the Communicative Functions of Problem Behavior checklist (LaVigna & Donnellan, 1986), which examines the various aberrant and appropriate behaviors the client may be using to communicate her or his feelings, opinions, needs, and desires. Skill information is utilized in the identification of target adaptive responses, which can be taught to replace maladaptive behavior and to increase independence.

Level 2: Observations in the Natural Environment

Informant interviews represent a relatively easy, nonintrusive, and socially valid way of obtaining relevant information for designing interventions. However, rarely is this level of assessment sufficient, as the clinical validity of some of this information is questionable. Other people, even when they know the client well, may have difficulty accurately identifying specific target behaviors, their functions, and other reinforcers. Hypotheses concerning the function of aberrant behavior are not likely to be correct or to lead to effective treatments if they are based on faulty information. The next level of eco-behavioral assessment, naturalistic observations, is usually needed.

Baseline.   After the target behaviors have been pinpointed and defined in measurable terms, it is necessary to determine the current extent of the problem by actually measuring the frequency of occurrence of the target behaviors. Baseline data can also be used to evaluate the effectiveness of the intervention by comparing the treatment results to the baseline. Usually, a daily data sheet is designed, and mediators are given instructions on how to monitor and record the frequency of the target behaviors.

We have found that mediators (e.g., parents and care providers) sometimes do not fill out the data sheets accurately or at all. Most mediators do not place as much emphasis or value on objective observational data as do behavior analysts, and we have to search for alternative ways to obtain observational data. Thus, the behavioral consultants themselves may often conduct videotaped or live probes in the natural environment. Even when the mediators do collect data, we still conduct probes to ensure that their observations are reliable.

Probes can be conducted at various times and can be of varying duration, depending on the frequency of the target behaviors, the urgency of collecting data, the availability of observers or video equipment, and the mediators' tolerance of the presence of observers in their home or workplace. At the very least, we try to conduct probes during the times when the informants say the client's aberrant behaviors are most likely to occur. Not only does this approach give us more opportunities to see the behaviors in order to conduct a functional analysis, but it also allows a rigorous test of the efficacy of the subsequent treatment. When we have the opportunity, we also try to conduct probes when the maladaptive behavior is least likely to occur, in order to identify (1) variables that may be inhibiting the aberrant behavior and (2) behaviors that the client is already performing in the absence of aberrant behavior, which may serve as replacement skills.

Scatter plot.   As part of an ecobehavioral approach, we conduct an observational structural analysis of the possible controlling stimuli in order to isolate patterns of responding in different environments and contexts throughout the day. The scatter plot is helpful in depicting these patterns, and we have found that many mediators are more willing to fill it out than to collect detailed frequency data (Touchette, MacDonald, & Langer, 1985). The scatter plot form allows us to determine the pattern of occurrence of the target behavior for a fixed duration (e.g., every half hour) on each day of a particular week.

Scatter plots often reveal time- or environment-dependent patterns of behavior that are not obvious to the care providers until they see them emerge on the scatter plot form. For example, Figure 2-2 shows the representative results of a scatter plot for a young woman, Mary, living in a group home. She was regarded by the staff as noncompliant. The scatter plot revealed that her temper tantrums tended to occur at night. Further probing of staff revealed that there was a house rule that all clients must be in bed by 9 P.M. Mary's tantrums appeared to be effective in delaying the bedtime and in making her the center of attention. In other words, Mary may have engaged in tantrums to communicate that she did not want to go to bed at 9. Discussions with staff focused on arbitrary non-age-appropriate rules that restrict the right of adults with developmental disabilities to have control over their lives. Staff agreed to remove this house rule and let Mary stay up until she responded affirmatively when asked if she wanted to go to bed or until she started to doze on the living room couch. She usually stayed up no later than 11 P.M., and more important, the nighttime tantrums stopped.

Figure 2-3 illustrates a scatter plot form representative of a young boy, Jerry, with whom we worked at home. The scatter plot clearly shows that Jerry exhibited aggression (i.e., hitting and kicking others) most frequently during the morning routine, and again when asked to brush his teeth before bed. Despite some concerns at school, his aggression was not as frequent there as it was at home. The scatter plot information collected by his parents (and confirmed by videotaped probes) quickly identified those situations and times that required intervention. However, it did not provide us with enough information to formulate a hypothesis about the function of the behavior and to propose a treatment. For this, we needed to conduct the more detailed observations described below.

Antecedent-Behavior-Consequence (ABC) Observations

In order to identify possible reinforcement contingencies, it is often necessary at least to conduct naturalistic observations of the pattern of antecedents that may control the behavior, as well as the consequences that may serve as reinforcers for the target behaviors (O'Neill, Horner, Albin, Storey, & Sprague,

Figure 2-2

Representative results of a scatter plot of a young woman, Mary, living in a group home

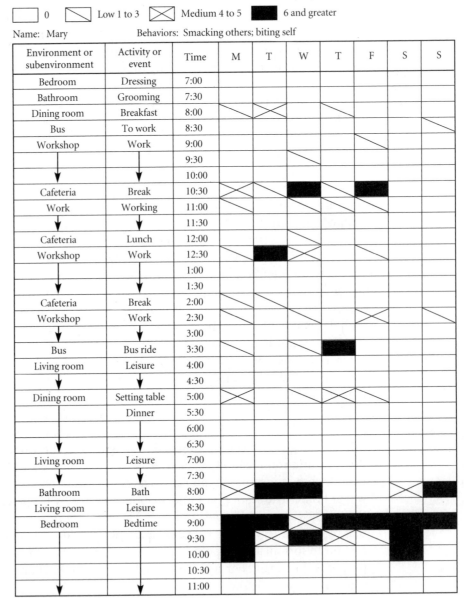

Name: Mary   Behaviors: Smacking others; biting self

Legend: □ 0   ◺ Low 1 to 3   ⊠ Medium 4 to 5   ■ 6 and greater

Environment or subenvironment	Activity or event	Time	M	T	W	T	F	S	S
Bedroom	Dressing	7:00							
Bathroom	Grooming	7:30							
Dining room	Breakfast	8:00	◺	⊠		◺			◺
Bus	To work	8:30							
Workshop	Work	9:00				◺			
		9:30			◺		◺		
		10:00							
Cafeteria	Break	10:30	◺		■	◺	■		
Work	Working	11:00	◺			◺			
		11:30							
Cafeteria	Lunch	12:00				◺			
Workshop	Work	12:30		■	⊠				
		1:00							
		1:30							
Cafeteria	Break	2:00	◺		◺				
Workshop	Work	2:30					⊠		
		3:00							
Bus	Bus ride	3:30	◺		◺	■			
Living room	Leisure	4:00							
		4:30							
Dining room	Setting table	5:00	⊠		⊠		⊠		
	Dinner	5:30							
		6:00							
		6:30							
Living room	Leisure	7:00							
		7:30							
Bathroom	Bath	8:00	⊠	■	■			⊠	■
Living room	Leisure	8:30							
Bedroom	Bedtime	9:00	■		⊠	■	■		■
		9:30	■	⊠	■	⊠		■	
		10:00	■					■	
		10:30							
		11:00							

Figure 2-3

Representative results of a scatter plot of a young boy, Jerry, living at home

Legend: ☐ 0   ◨ Low 1 to 3   ⊠ Medium 4 to 5   ■ 6 and greater

Name: Jerry   Behaviors: Hitting, punching, biting, kicking others

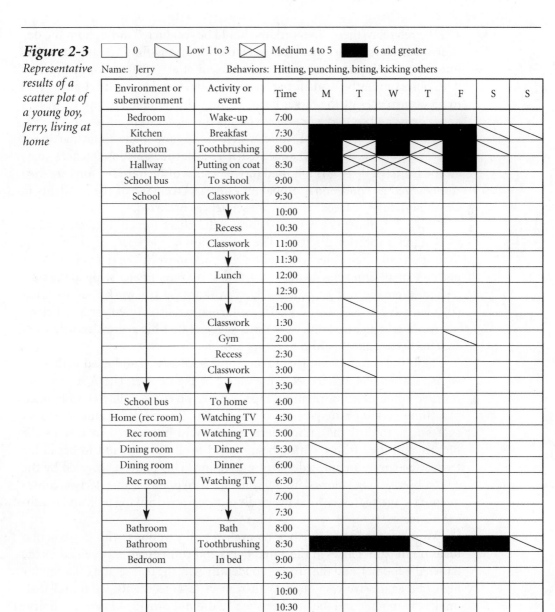

Environment or subenvironment	Activity or event	Time	M	T	W	T	F	S	S
Bedroom	Wake-up	7:00							
Kitchen	Breakfast	7:30	■	■	■	■	■	◨	◨
Bathroom	Toothbrushing	8:00	■	⊠		⊠	■	◨	
Hallway	Putting on coat	8:30	■	⊠	⊠	⊠	■		
School bus	To school	9:00							
School	Classwork	9:30							
	↓	10:00							
	Recess	10:30							
	Classwork	11:00							
	↓	11:30							
	Lunch	12:00							
		12:30							
	↓	1:00		◨					
	Classwork	1:30							
	Gym	2:00					◨		
	Recess	2:30							
	Classwork	3:00		◨					
		3:30							
School bus	To home	4:00							
Home (rec room)	Watching TV	4:30							
Rec room	Watching TV	5:00							
Dining room	Dinner	5:30	◨			⊠			
Dining room	Dinner	6:00	◨			⊠			
Rec room	Watching TV	6:30							
	↓	7:00							
		7:30							
Bathroom	Bath	8:00							
Bathroom	Toothbrushing	8:30	■	■	◨	■	■	◨	
Bedroom	In bed	9:00							
		9:30							
		10:00							
		10:30							
↓	↓	11:00							

1990). Preferably, these observations should be conducted throughout the day over many days to decrease the chance of spurious findings and to reveal intermittent reinforcement schedules. O'Neill et al. (1990) recommend that ABC observations be made for at least 2 to 5 days, and that a minimum of 10 to 15 occurrences of the target behavior must be observed before consistent antecedents and consequences are typically revealed. Over a series of observations of the target behavior, we can determine how many times particular antecedents (e.g., demands) preceded it and particular consequences (e.g., escape from the demand) followed it. The results of the observations are then summarized as conditional probabilities or a percentage of the incidents in which particular antecedents and consequences occurred.

Table 2-1 illustrates a hypothetical ABC chart for an aggressive client working in a vocational setting. The calculation of the series of 10 incidents indicates that, when Peter was told to "get back to work," he slapped the staff person 6 of 10 times (Incidents 1, 2, 4, 5, 6, and 8); after Peter slapped the staff person, Peter did not go right back to work, or he left work 7 of 10 times (Incidents 1, 2, 3, 5, 7, 8, and 9). This information, if representative of Peter's interactions at the worksite over time, suggests that his aggressive behaviors are effective in allowing him to escape work.

Table 2-2 is representative of some of the ABCs we conducted with Jerry, whose scatter plot results were presented in Figure 2-3. The ABC analysis revealed some new information. First, a more precise baseline was obtained indicating very high frequencies of aggression. Second, it became clear that aggressions toward the father were much more frequent than toward the mother and the brother. Third, being asked to drink milk and to brush his teeth were common antecedents of aggression. This pattern, revealed by the ABC observations, allowed us to generate a hypothesis that Jerry's consequence for the aggression was primarily escape from drinking milk and brushing his teeth.

We also conducted further naturalistic observations with a particular focus on the differences in the antecedents and consequences provided by the father, the mother, and the brother to identify why the dad set the occasion for high-rate aggressive responses. With respect to antecedents, we found that, unlike the mother and the brother, the dad did not provide Jerry with choices (e.g., orange juice, or partial participation in toothbrushing), positioned himself within reach of Jerry's blows, and gave instructions at a rapid pace. With respect to consequences, Jerry was able to land his hits on his dad's body, and his dad failed to acknowledge Jerry's appropriate attempts to communicate that he did not want milk or that he wanted to brush his teeth himself. Teaching the father to interact with Jerry more in the manner used by other family members significantly reduced Jerry's aggression and increased his cooperation during the morning routine.

TABLE 2-1

Hypothetical Antecedent–Behavior–Consequence Chart

ABC LOG

Client Name: Peter (31 years old)
Target Behavior: Slapping others

No.	Date	Time	Setting	Person Recording	Antecedent	Behavior	Consequences
1	July 7	9:46 A.M.	Front of workshop	Fred	Fred instructed Peter to go back to workstation.	Slapped Fred (staff) on back	Fred said nothing; Peter hung around front door; did not go to workstation.
2	July 7	10:45 A.M.	Coffee room	Sue	Sue told Peter that break was over and that it was time to go back to work on sorting bolts.	Slapped Sue (staff) across face	Peter continued to sit in chair; Sue asked him if he would like to go outside, he agreed and went outside with Sue.
3	July 7	1:47 P.M.	Workstation	Sue	Fred went over to ask Peter if he needed any help.	Slapped Fred on chest	Fred didn't say anything and walked away; Peter stopped working for 10 minutes.
4	July 7	2:41 P.M.	Bathroom	Fred	Fred asked Peter to leave the bathroom and go back to work.	Slapped Fred on chest	Fred repeated request, and this time Peter went back to workstation.
5	July 8	10:02 A.M.	Workstation	Fred	Peter was getting up from his chair; Fred instructed Peter to stay in his seat and continue working.	Slapped Fred across chest	Peter got up and walked around the workshop for 15 minutes before returning to workstation.

(continued)

TABLE 2-1

Hypothetical Antecedent–Behavoir–Consequence Chart (*continued*)

Client Name: Peter (31 years old)
Target Behavior: Slapping others

ABC LOG

No.	Date	Time	Setting	Person Recording	Antecedent	Behavior	Consequences
6	July 8	10:50 A.M.	Coffee room	Fred	Fred told Peter that break was over and to go back to work.	Slapped Sue, who was walking by	Fred repeated request, and Peter went back to work.
7	July 8	11:56 A.M.	Workstation	Sue	Sue told another client that it was almost time for lunch.	Slapped Sue on back	Sue ignored Peter; Peter stopped sorting bolts until lunch break.
8	July 8	1:30 P.M.	Lunchroom	Sue	Group told that lunch was over and to go back to work.	Slapped Fred on chest	Fred repeated request directly to Peter, but Peter remained in his seat for 15 minutes and then got up and wandered around.
9	July 8	3:20 P.M.	Outside bathroom	Sue	Sue walked by Peter.	Slapped Sue across arm	Sue ignored Peter and walked away; Peter got up and went to the bathroom for 10 minutes.
10	July 8	3:45 P.M.	Outside	Sue	Sue said, "Goodbye, see you tomorrow" to Peter.	Slapped Sue across chest	Sue ignored Peter; Peter got on the van.

TABLE 2-2

Antecedent–Behavior–Consequence Chart

ABC LOG

Client Name: Jerry (9 years old)
Target Behavior: Hitting, punching, biting, kicking

Date	Time	Setting	Person Recording	Antecedent	Behavior	Consequence
Oct. 2	7:45 A.M.	Kitchen	Dad	Dad asked him to drink milk.	Hit dad (×36)	Ignored; drank some milk.
Oct. 2	8:00 A.M.	Bathroom	Dad	Dad helped him brush teeth.	Hit, kicked, punched dad (×28)	Ignored; dad brushed Jerry's teeth for him.
Oct. 3	7:50 A.M.	Kitchen	Mom	Mom asked him to drink milk.	Attempted to hit mom (×2)	Ignored; drank some milk.
Oct. 3	8:05 A.M.	Bathroom	Dad	Dad helped him brush teeth.	Hit, kicked dad (×58)	Told to stop after 30th hit; restrained; dad brushed Jerry's teeth for him.
Oct. 4	7:39 A.M.	Kitchen	Brother	Brother asked him to drink milk.	Attempted to bite brother (×3)	Ignored; drank some milk.
Oct. 4	8:00 A.M.	Bathroom	Brother	Brother helped him brush teeth.	Kicked brother (×1)	Ignored; let brother help him brush his teeth.
Oct. 5	7:45 A.M.	Kitchen	Dad	Dad asked him to drink orange juice.	Hit dad (×4)	Ignored; drank all of the orange juice.
Oct. 5	8:09 A.M.	Bathroom	Dad	Dad helped him brush teeth.	Hit, kicked, bit dad (×36)	Told to stop; restrained; dad brushed teeth for him.

Level 3: Experimental Analog Assessments

It is important to remember that ABC observations are descriptive analyses in that they only reveal correlations between the aberrant behavior and its surrounding events; they do not by themselves confirm cause-and-effect relationships between behavior and environmental events. Moreover, the ABC observations sometimes fail to reveal the likely reinforcers, especially when the behavior is maintained on thin schedules of reinforcement. Thus, it may be necessary to resort to experimental analyses, which allow us to systematically examine the impact of different conditions on the target behavior (e.g., giving attention contingent on self-injurious behavior, or allowing escape from demands contingent on aggression). Experimental analog assessments involve the planned manipulation of specific variables under tightly controlled, somewhat artificial conditions to isolate cause-and-effect relationships between the behavior and the environmental variables.

Structural analog assessments.   In structural analog assessments, setting events or antecedents are manipulated, while consequences (and other variables) are held constant. A variety of setting events can be manipulated, such as the physical environment (e.g., a small vs. a large room), schedules (few vs. many breaks), demands (e.g., difficult vs. easy tasks), people (e.g., friends vs. staff), and activities (e.g., exercising vs. watching TV). For example, we worked with a woman with severe disabilities who would, on occasion, get into a frenzy of biting herself on the arm. Informal observations suggested that loud noises were related to these outbursts. After padding her arm to prevent injury, we conducted a structural analog assessment in which we played segments of tape-recorded loud noises that she experienced regularly (e.g., a telephone ringing, the dropping of a metal pot on the floor, and a lawn mower), alternated with segments of ambient background noise. All other aspects of the sessions were consistent (same staff, same rooms, same times of day, no interactions, and no response to biting). Until we had conducted this systematic assessment, we did not realize that virtually all of her self-injurious outbursts occurred in response to these sudden loud noises. Our treatment consisted of gradually increasing the volume of the tape-recorded segments from barely audible to very loud (over sessions) while reinforcing her with praise and preferred activities for not biting. Over time, she was able to tolerate louder and louder taped and live noises without biting herself.

Analysis of consequences.   Currently, the most accurate way to identify the likely reinforcers maintaining an individual's aberrant behavior is to conduct an experimental manipulation of consequences in tightly controlled settings. The analog analysis was developed by Iwata, Dorsey, Slifer, Bauman, and

Richman (1982) with subsequent refinements by others (e.g., Derby et al., 1992; Sturmey, Carlsen, Crisp, & Newton, 1988). In the Iwata et al. (1982) version, four different types of sessions were presented repeatedly in mixed order: (1) attention contingent on self-injury; (2) escape from demands contingent on self-injury; (3) the client was left alone with no stimulation (to test whether the behavior was self-stimulatory); and (4) attention for the absence of self-injury (a control condition). Many variations of the analog assessment procedure can be used to analyze the consequences of a target behavior. Notice, for example, that the Iwata et al. (1982) procedure does not include an evaluation of possible tangible reinforcement. If informant and observational information suggests that the individual exhibits aberrant behavior to obtain and keep a desired object, then a condition should be included in which the person is allowed to have the item contingent on the occurrence of the aberrant behavior.

Figure 2-4 illustrates the results of an analog functional analysis of the behavior of Robert, a preschooler who engaged in headbanging. Over 5 days, we conducted 10-minute sessions in which different consequences were provided for his headbanging. The context (play activities) was the same across sessions. In the attention condition, each time Robert hit his head, the teacher said in a conversational tone, "Don't hit your head." In the tangible condition, he was given his favorite toys when he hit his head. In the escape condition, he was allowed to leave the play situation for 1 minute. In the sensory condition, he was simply left alone to do as he pleased. The order of the sessions was mixed over days, and there were free-play breaks between the sessions. We recorded the occurrence or nonoccurrence of headbanging every 10 seconds from videotapes made of the sessions. As can be seen in Figure 2-4, the brief functional analysis showed that Robert's headbanging was primarily a function of escape, although attention and tangibles also accounted for numerous occurrences. These functional analysis results are typical. While one consequence sometimes emerges as the most likely reinforcer, all too often the behavior is multiply determined.

Necessary and Sufficient Components of an Ecobehavioral Assessment

The need for the various levels of assessment (i.e., informant interviews, naturalistic observations, and experimental analogs) ultimately depends on the information required to formulate a reasonable and testable hypothesis concerning the operating variables controlling and maintaining the aberrant behavior. Although it is recommended that experimental analogs be con-

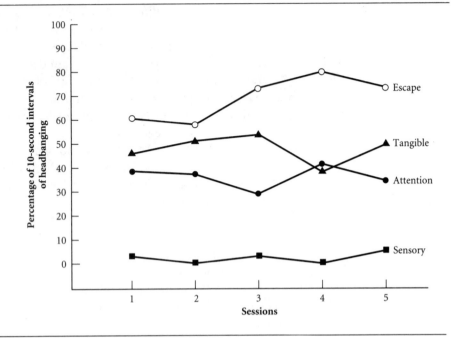

Figure 2-4

Results of an analog functional analysis conducted in a day care center with a preschooler who engaged in head-banging

ducted to ascertain functional relationships, in practice this may not always be accepted, practical, or necessary. We have found that the data gathered through scatter plot and ABC naturalistic observations are often sufficient for experienced behavioral clinicians, who are familiar with the functional analysis literature, to formulate correct hypotheses regarding cause-and-effect relationships between stimuli and responses and to create effective interventions. For example, in the case of Jerry, whose assessment results were described above, the observations made on the different styles of interaction between family members were sufficient to decrease Jerry's aggression significantly. The father, who was the primary target of Jerry's aggression, was taught to interact with Jerry in a manner that promoted nonaggressive, prosocial, and communicative behaviors.

In keeping with the least intrusive assessment model, we typically use experimental analog assessments only as a last resort when the combination of interviews and naturalistic observations fails to yield sufficient information concerning the variables controlling and maintaining the target behaviors. Even then, the nonanalog assessment information is often valuable in narrowing the range of variables to be manipulated in the experimental analog assessment.

The primary reason we are reluctant to use analog assessments is that their intent is to identify conditions that (temporally) increase the aberrant behaviors. Although we carefully explain the rationale to parents and care providers and take measures to reduce the risk of injury (e.g., using protective measures such as padding and stopping the session if the client becomes too agitated), we often find that care providers are not keen to engage in this type of assessment. This lack of enthusiasm is especially troublesome when we must rely on them to conduct the analysis because we ourselves are unable to elicit the behavior in the client. Care providers have also reported carryover effects from the assessment sessions to other times. Whether these effects are real or not, the tendency for mediators to blame a "bad day" on analog assessment sessions may affect their acceptance of and cooperation with the ongoing assessment and treatment package. The use of brief (5-minute) sessions sometimes alleviates some of the concerns expressed by mediators (Derby et al., 1992).

Putting It All Together

The purpose of the medical and ecobehavioral assessments is to gather sufficient information to be able to formulate a hypothesis identifying the biological and environmental variables that influence the aberrant behavior. To the extent that these variables can be manipulated, the hypothesis should lead directly to the design of interventions that not only reduce the maladaptive behavior but also teach more adaptive replacement skills and improve the person's quality of life.

Hypothesis statements should be in nontechnical language and should "make sense" to care providers. If we continue with some of the examples described above, the hypothesis formulated for Peter would be "When asked to go back to work, Peter is likely to hit the staff person because Peter's aggression consistently results in his avoiding or escaping the task." For Mary, the hypothesis would be "When Mary is asked to go to bed at 9 P.M., she is likely to engage in a temper tantrum that delays her bedtime." The validity of these hypotheses is strengthened by the success of the treatments derived from them. After completing the structural analysis, we use this information to generate answers to two related questions: What are the high-risk conditions, and can they be eliminated or altered? and What are the low-risk conditions, and can they be increased? The answers to these questions sometimes yield nontechnical solutions to the problem (e.g., allowing Mary to go to bed later). Functional analysis, communication, and adaptive-skill-assessment information is combined to answer three questions: What is the reinforcer maintaining the aberrant behavior? What simple, appropriate replacement behavior can the person be taught that will (at the very least) obtain the same reinforcer? and Is it possible to totally eliminate the reinforcement for the aberrant behavior?

CONCLUSIONS

We have presented an overview of an ecobehavioral model for assessing the behavior problems of individuals with DD. The model balances the least intrusive model with the right to effective treatment. We have been guided throughout by research findings, clinical experience, and program evaluation as well as consumer input and feedback. The ecobehavioral model examines a wide range of biomedical and environmental variables to identify the factors that control and maintain an individual's aberrant behavior. Often, structural analyses of setting events and antecedents lead to reductions in aberrant behavior through simple environmental manipulations, such as giving individuals more choices and control in their lives or building tolerance to the eliciting stimuli. The identification of the reinforcers maintaining aberrant behavior through functional analyses can also lead to effective interventions, in which mediators are able to teach clients to replace aberrant behavior with more adaptive and socially appropriate ways of obtaining the same reinforcers.

REFERENCES

Abidin, R. R. (1983). *Parenting Stress Index: Manual.* Charlottesville, VA: Pediatric Psychology Press.

Achenbach, T. M., & Edelbrook, C. S. (1981). *Behavioral problems and competences reported by parents of normal and disturbed children aged four through sixteen.* Monograph on Social Research in Child Development, 46 (1, Serial No. 188).

Aman, M. G., & Singh, N. N. (1986). *The Aberrant Behavior Checklist and Manual.* East Aurora, NY: Slosson.

Aman, M. G., & Singh, N. N. (1994). *The Aberrant Behavior Checklist: Community.* East Aurora, NY: Slosson.

Axelrod, S. (1987). Functional and structural analyses of behavior: Approaches leading to reduced use of punishment procedures? *Research in Developmental Disabilities, 8,* 165–178.

Blake, M., Feldman, M., Keller, M., Moore, C., & Munn, F. (1987). *Standards for the use of behavioral training and treatment procedures in settings for developmentally handicapped individuals.* Toronto, Canada: Ontario Ministry of Community and Social Services.

Bouras, N., & Drummond, C. (1992). Behavior and psychiatric disorders of people with mental handicaps living in the community. *Journal of Intellectual Disability Research, 36,* 349–357.

Brown, L., Shiraga, B., York, J., Zanella, K., & Rogan, P. (1984). *A life-space analysis strategy for students with severe handicaps.* Madison: University of Wisconsin and Madison Metropolitan School District.

Cowen, E. L., Huser, J., Beach, D. R., & Rappaport, J. (1970). Parent perceptions of young children and their relation to indexes of development. *Journal of Consulting and Clinical Psychology, 34,* 97–103.

Derby, K. M., Wacker, D. P., Sasso, G., Steege, M., Northup, J., Cigrand, K., & Asmus, J. (1992). Brief functional assessment techniques to evaluate aberrant behavior in an outpatient setting: A summary of 79 cases. *Journal of Applied Behavior Analysis, 25,* 713–721.

Durand, V. M., & Crimmins, D. B. (1988). Identifying the variables maintaining self-injurious behavior. *Journal of Autism and Developmental Disorders, 18,* 99–117.

Feldman, M. A., Griffiths, D., Condillac, R., & Tough, S. (1992, May). *Determining the function of maladaptive behavior: Agreements between a careprovider informant scale and antecedent-behavior-consequence time sampling event recording in the natural environment.* Paper presented at the 18th Annual Convention of the Association for Behavior Analysis, San Francisco.

Green, C. W., Reid, D. H., White, L. K., Halford, R. C., Brittain, D. P., & Gardner, S. M. (1988). Identifying reinforcers for individuals with profound handicaps: Staff opinion vs. systematic assessment of preferences. *Journal of Applied Behavior Analysis, 21,* 31–43.

Griffiths, D. (1989). Quality assurance for behavior interventions. *Psychiatric Aspects of Mental Retardation Reviews, 8,* 73–80.

Iwata, B. A., Dorsey, M. F., Slifer, K. J., Bauman, K. E., & Richman, G. S. (1982). Toward a functional analysis of self-injury. *Analysis and Intervention in Developmental Disabilities, 2,* 1–20.

Iwata, B. A., Vollmer, T. R., & Zarcone, J. H. (1990). The experimental (functional) analysis of behavior disorders: Methodology, applications, and limitations. In A. C. Repp & N. N. Singh (Eds.), *Perspectives on the use of nonaversive and aversive interventions for individuals with developmental disabilities* (pp. 301–330). Sycamore, IL: Sycamore Press.

LaVigna, G. W., & Donnellan, A. M. (1986). *Alternatives to punishment: Solving behavior problems with non-aversive strategies.* New York: Irvington.

Matson, J. L., Kazdin, A. E., & Senatore, V. (1984). Psychometric properties of the Psychopathology Instrument for Mentally Retarded Adults. *Applied Research in Mental Retardation, 5,* 81–89.

National Institutes of Health. (1991). *Treatment of destructive behaviors in individuals with developmental disabilities.* Bethesda, MD: Author.

O'Neill, R. E., Horner, R. H., Albin, R. W., Storey, K., & Sprague, J. (1990). *Functional analysis of problem behavior: A practical assessment guide.* Sycamore, IL: Sycamore Press.

Reiss, S. (1988). *Test manual for the Reiss Screen for Maladaptive Behavior.* Orland Park, IL: International Diagnostic Systems.

Schroeder, S. R. (1990). *Ecobehavioral analysis and developmental disabilities.* New York: Springer-Verlag.

Singh, N. N., & Aman, M. G. (1990). Ecobehavioral analysis of pharmacotherapy. In S. R. Schroeder (Ed.), *Ecobehavioral analysis and developmental disabilities* (pp. 182–200). New York: Springer-Verlag.

Singh, N. N., Donatelli, L. S., Best, A. M., Williams, D. E., Barrera, F. J., Lenz, M. W., Landrum, T. J., Ellis, C. R., & Moe, T. L. (1993). Factor structure of the Motivation Assessment Scale. *Journal of Intellectual Disability Research, 37,* 65–74.

Sturmey, P., Carlsen, A., Crisp, A. G., & Newton, J. T. (1988). A functional analysis of multiple aberrant responses: A refinement and extension of Iwata et al.'s methodology. *Journal of Mental Deficiency Research, 32,* 31–46.

Touchette, P. E., MacDonald, R. F., & Langer, S. N. (1985). A scatter plot for identifying stimulus control of problem behavior. *Journal of Applied Behavior Analysis, 18,* 343–351.

**Chapter
3**

*Procedures for Assessing and Increasing
Social Interaction*

Frank W. Kohler and Phillip S. Strain

INTRODUCTION

There has been much progress over the last 20 years in the development and refinement of assessment procedures and intervention protocols for understanding and improving the social interactions of young children. We know something about how global attributes of the social environment, such as the available play areas, materials, and group size, affect children's interactions. A wealth of research has also examined how adult direction and feedback influence the quality and amount of children's interactions. Finally, the most recent wave of studies has addressed the role of peer modeling and peers' initiations as critical components of social skills interventions.

In spite of this emerging knowledge base, there are few demonstrations in the literature of social skills interventions that have produced truly powerful, long-term, and socially validated outcomes. It is our view that too narrow a focus on outcomes or target behaviors is largely responsible for our limited success. With few exceptions, the social skills literature is characterized by a focus on global behavioral categories, the behavior of individuals rather than mutual interactors, and a general failure to examine the functions of specific social behaviors in participants' subsequent social acts. Partially in response to these concerns, our research group has developed an observational protocol that allows for a fine-grained analysis of social behavior, including measures of magnitude, function, reciprocity, and duration. We describe the development of this assessment tool with children who are developmentally disabled and discuss procedures for increasing social interaction. We believe that successful interventions derived from a thorough analysis of social interaction deficits have wide-ranging implications in preempting the development and maintenance of problem behaviors in children with developmental disabilities. Increasing appropriate social skills allows children to access reinforcers directly in their natural environments without having to resort to problem behaviors to obtain the same reinforcers.

DEVELOPMENT OF THE EARLY CHILDHOOD SOCIAL INTERACTION CODE

The Early Childhood Social Interaction Code was developed as part of an effort to improve the social interactions between preschoolers with disabilities

This chapter was supported by Grant Number G008730076-88 from the U.S. Department of Education and Grant Number MH37110-07 from the National Institute of Mental Health to the Allegheny-Singer Research Institute. The authors are indebted to numerous individuals who have contributed to this effort. Special thanks are expressed to Denise Shearer, Marilyn Hoyson, Bonnie Jamieson, and the remainder of the LEAP teachers for their assistance and cooperation.

and their typical peers. An initial concern was that the primary behavioral units of the code be consistent with empirically derived conceptualizations of preschool children's social interactions. Our examination of the existing research literature led to the development of five primary units for coding and analysis. Both initiations and immediate responses have been identified as critical components of preschool children's social exchanges. Initiations begin an interaction and are not closely preceded by codable social exchanges. Responses immediately follow and occur in direct reply to a preceding initiation. Two additional coding units pertain to children's ongoing interaction. *Continued play* refers to all associative play or cooperative activity that follows children's initiations and responses. For example, all mutual block construction that follows an initiation "Let's build a schoolhouse" and a response "OK" is coded as continued play. Similarly, concurrent behaviors are topographically identical to initiations but occur within the context of continued play. Unlike initiations, these behaviors occur concurrently with ongoing continued play. Finally, our code examines the teacher behaviors that facilitate children's social exchanges.

A second task was to establish a range of subcodes for each primary interaction unit. Our primary concern was that these subcategories represent functional dimensions of children's social interaction. The existing research literature was very informative in this regard. For example, studies examining the different impacts of preschool children's social initiations have found that play organizer suggestions, share offers and requests, assistance offers and requests, and compliments and affection lead to a higher proportion of immediate positive responses than do questions, general statements, or imitative behaviors (Hendrickson, Strain, Tremblay, & Shores, 1982; Tremblay, Strain, Hendrickson, & Shores, 1981). Furthermore, play organizer suggestions, share offers and requests, and assistance initiations also lead to exchanges that are highly reciprocal and enduring (Kohler & Fowler, 1985).

On the basis of the existing literature, we developed 21 different categories for our five primary units of the code. The initiation and concurrent units comprise the same seven subcodes: play organizers, shares, assistance, affection, compliments, negative behaviors, and general statements. Five different types of responses are coded, including yes, no, ignores, general comments, and negatives. *Continued play* refers to the single category of associative play, while both prompts and approval are coded within the teacher behavior unit. The five primary code units and their range of subcategories are listed and described in Table 3-1. Copies of our coding manual, complete with definitions and scoring procedures, are available from either of the authors.

Several additional considerations went into the development of the code. A wealth of evidence has emphasized the importance of reciprocity as a critical dimension of children's social development. Therefore, our code examines

TABLE 3-1

Primary Units and Subcategories of the Social Interaction Code

Behavioral Unit	Number of Codes	Specific Codes	Examples
Social initiations	7	Play organizer	A suggestion for play
		Share	Offer of or request for a play item
		Assistance	Verbal request for help
		Compliment	A statement of praise
		Affection	Hugging another child
		Negative	Hitting or name-calling
		General comment	Statements not coded above
Immediate responses	5	Yes	Accepting a help offer
		No	Refusing a play idea
		Ignores	Turning away from a share offer
		General	Answering a general question
		Negative	Yelling no to a suggestion
Social concurrents	7	Same as initiations	Same as initiations
Continued play`	1	Associative play	All intervals of mutual block building that follow a play organizer initiation and a yes response
Teacher behavior		Prompts	A direction to share
		Praise	A compliment for accepting help

the mutual exchange of discrete initiations, responses, and concurrents between an observed child and peers. Another consideration was the reliability of the instrument. Many existing codes for preschool children's interactions have utilized time-sampling systems with intervals ranging from 3 to 10 seconds in duration. The recording system selected for our code was based on two criteria: (1) It enabled the reliable recording of behaviors that were often fleeting, diverse in form, and exhibited by two different children within a brief time period, and (2) it minimized the likelihood that an observed child or peer would exhibit more than one initiation, response, or concurrent behavior within a single observational interval. Based on these two considerations and approximately three months of pilot research, we selected a 6-second partial-interval time-sampling procedure.

A sample block for one interval of the observer scoring sheet is illustrated below. All discrete social initiations, concurrents, or responses are recorded by slashing the appropriate code across from the *O* (observed child) or *P* (peer) letters at the beginning of the block. Responses are coded to initiations only and are never coded to children's concurrent behaviors. Following positive initiations and responses, the occurrence of associative or cooperative play between an observed child and peers is indicated by the *C* code under "Continued Play." Finally, any prompts and/or praise that the teacher uses to facilitate observed child-peer interaction are marked with the *Prp* (prompt) and *Pra* (praise) codes.

Child	Initiations and Concurrents							Responses					Continued Play	Teacher	
O	Po	Sh	As	Cp	Af	Gn	Ng	Ys	No	Gn	Ig	Ng	C	Prp	Pra
P	Po	Sh	As	Cp	Af	Gn	Ng	Ys	No	Gn	Ig	Ng		Prp	Pra

An observer might mark codes for any combination of behaviors occurring during a 6-second interval. The three blocks of codes that follow illustrate a possible sequence of scoring combinations. If an observed child offered a toy to a playmate during Interval 1, then the observer would slash an *Sh* initiation across from the *O*. A peer might accept that item during the next interval, and the teacher might say, "Nice sharing, you two." In this case, the observer would mark the *Ys* code across from the *P* and mark the *Pra* for both the observed child and the peer. Finally, the two children might exchange trucks during the third interval. This would be noted by marking the *Sh* for both children. The *C* code of continued play is also slashed during Interval 3 to indicate that the shares are concurrents rather than initiations (i.e., the behaviors occurred concurrently with associative play rather than beginning a new interaction).

Interval 1

Child	Initiations and Concurrents							Responses					Continued Play	Teacher	
O	Po	S̸h	As	Cp	Af	Gn	Ng	Ys	No	Gn	Ig	Ng	C	Prp	Pra
P	Po	Sh	As	Cp	Af	Gn	Ng	Ys	No	Gn	Ig	Ng		Prp	Pra

Interval 2

Child	Initiations and Concurrents							Responses					Continued Play	Teacher	
O	Po	Sh	As	Cp	Af	Gn	Ng	Ys	No	Gn	Ig	Ng	C	Prp	P̸ra
P	Po	Sh	As	Cp	Af	Gn	Ng	Y̸s	No	Gn	Ig	Ng		Prp	P̸ra

Interval 3

Child	Initiations and Concurrents							Responses					Continued Play	Teacher	
O	Po	S̶H̶	As	Cp	Af	Gn	Ng	Ys	No	Gn	Ig	Ng	C̶	Prp	Pra
P	Po	S̶H̶	As	Cp	Af	Gn	Ng	Ys	No	Gn	Ig	Ng		Prp	Pra

Several rules exist for scoring intervals during which an observed child or peer exhibits more than one type of initiation, response, or concurrent. First, negatives take precedence over all other behaviors. For example, if an observed child exhibits both a share and a negative initiation, then only the negative is recorded. Second, all alternative forms of initiations, responses, and concurrents take precedence over generals. If a peer makes both a yes and a general response to an observed child's play suggestion, then only the yes is coded. Finally, if two or more forms of prosocial initiations or concurrents (excluding generals) occur in the same interval, then only the first overture is coded. More specifically, if a peer hands a block to an observed child (share) and says, "You can put this on top of your tower" (play organizer), then only the share is coded.

Code Training and Interrater Agreement Procedures

Observer training activities are generally conducted for three to four hours a day over the course of three to four weeks. Phase 1 of training lasts one week and entails memorization of the various code definitions and scoring procedures. Trainees finish this phase by completing a quiz that ascertains their mastery of the following: (1) definitions of the five primary code units; (2) the range and definitions of subcodes within each primary unit; and (3) the procedures for recording child and teacher codes, including rules for coding intervals during which children exhibit more than one initiation, response, or concurrent behavior. Trainees must pass this 35-item multiple-choice test with 80% accuracy before beginning the second phase of training.

Observer trainees begin coding children's interactions during Phase 2. Many individuals joining our projects have minimal observation experience. Therefore, they receive one or two hours of practice per day in classroom play situations to obtain the following skills: (1) maintaining the position and proximity necessary to monitor children's overtures; (2) structuring obser-vations around a 6-second partial interval system; (3) identifying and discriminating between fleeting episodes of children's various behaviors; and (4) recording children's overtures on the designated coding sheet within the correct interval block. Trainees practice observations with an experienced partner, who provides continual monitoring and coaching. This phase of training is generally completed within four to six days, totaling 6 to 12 hours of actual practice.

TABLE 3-2

Average Percentage of Agreement Coefficients on the Occurrence of Individual Subcodes within Each Primary Coding Unit

Study	Initiation	Response	Concurrent	Continue	Teacher	Total
1	95	93	88	96	80	93
2	90	81	85	89	83	86
3	91	87	91	92	76	87
4	89	77	94	71	82	81
5	91	87	83	91	81	88
Overall means	91	85	88	88	80	87

The final phase of observer training entails the establishment of interrater agreement. The trainee continues to conduct daily observations with an experienced partner. Initially, the pair may code independently for only 1-minute time periods (ten intervals) before comparing records and discussing discrepancies. When their observations maintain high agreement, however, the team gradually increases the duration of their independent coding until the trainee is scoring children's interactions without coaching for an entire 6- to 12-minute period. At this point, the pair begins the formal calculation of interobserver agreement.

Occurrence reliability is calculated by dividing the total number of agreements regarding a specific behavior by the total number of agreements plus disagreements and multiplying by 100. Agreement about occurrence is calculated for each primary social interaction unit as well as all individual subcodes within these five categories. Table 3-2 shows the interrater agreement coefficients from five of our studies. Collectively, these studies have included 14 preschoolers with disabilities and their typical classmates. Interrater agreement checks were conducted during at least 20% of each child's play sessions across all experimental conditions in each study. With only a few exceptions, occurrence reliability scores consistently met or exceeded 80%.

PROCEDURES FOR INCREASING SOCIAL INTERACTION

The Early Childhood Social Interaction Code was developed to evaluate the impact of efforts to improve the interactions between preschoolers with disabilities and their peers. We have developed a protocol comprising social skills training and peer-mediated intervention to improve children's social inter-action skills (Kohler, Shearer, & Strain, 1990; Kohler, Strain, Maretsky, & DeCesare, 1990; Kohler, Strain, & Shearer, 1992; Kohler et al., 1995).

Classwide Social Skills Training

We have developed a training package that can be used with an entire class of preschoolers, including children with disabilities and their peers without dis-abilities (Kohler, Shearer, & Strain, 1990). The training procedures are de-signed to be used during structured classroom-play activities. Children participate in daily sessions of 15 minutes in groups of three (consisting of one child with disabilities and two peers) to learn the following skills: (1) play organizer suggestions; (2) share offers and requests; (3) assistance offers and requests; and (4) compliments and affection (when developmentally appro-priate). These specific skills are learned in the sequence indicated above, and three different strategies are taught for using each skill. First, each skill is used to initiate and extend or continue play interactions with another child. For example, peers might direct a share offer to a target child who is playing alone. Second, children learn to respond positively to such overtures. For example, a youngster might either accept the item being offered or request an alternative play material. Finally, children learn to be persistent in their use of initiations and responses. Overtures that are ignored or refused are followed by different or more elaborate offers or requests.

Social skills training is typically planned for 15 days and entails three steps in the teaching of each skill. Teachers introduce and model a particular skill during Stage 1, which lasts one or two sessions. During Stage 2 (two to three days), children rehearse that skill with the teacher and with one another. The teacher provides ongoing instructions, models, and feedback (correction and praise) to individual children at this time. During Stage 3, the children practice the skill with one another independent of close teacher direction. Two criteria are set for terminating the final stage of training in each skill: (1) The target child and each peer can exchange at least four newly taught skills during a 6-minute period; and (2) the majority of peers can exhibit at least 50% of their skills independent of adult prompts. After the children meet these criteria, the teacher begins Stage 1 with a new social skill (i.e., training in share begins after the children have completed all three stages of training in play organizers).

The training protocol can be tailored to fit a diverse range of play activi-ties, which can be rotated on a daily basis. For example, play organizer, share, and assistance overtures are suited to dramatic, manipulative, and gross motor activities. Conversely, compliments are most appropriate for manipulative tasks (e.g., blocks or Legos), while affection (e.g., holding hands) is generally limited to gross motor activities. The sequence and scope of training can also be tailored to meet children's individual needs and abilities. Target children who can exhibit spontaneous language learn to direct social initiations to their peers. Youngsters lacking language skills might initially learn only to respond positively to other children's overtures. Some youngsters can learn to respond positively to a wide range of different initiations, while others initially learn to respond positively to share offers only. In any case, training is completed when all participants can exhibit their targeted skills with a high degree of consistency and independence.

Peer-Mediated Intervention Procedures

Following social skills training, the teacher can implement a peer-mediated intervention consisting of either an individual or group-oriented reinforcement contingency to maintain children's frequent exchange of newly taught overtures. An example of an intervention is described below.

The teacher begins each session by reviewing the activity with a group of one target child and two typical peers. After describing various play materials and roles, the teacher introduces the targeted skills and reinforcement contingency to the children. The teacher might also encourage the children to help one another exhibit the desired interaction skills. Several of our studies have included formal supportive skills training to teach children how to help one another meet the reinforcement contingency (Kohler, Strain, Maretsky, & DeCesare, 1990; Kohler et al., 1995). More specifically, children spend two or three days learning to monitor a happy face chart and to remind their friends to earn happy faces by exchanging the targeted social skills.

Following the introduction, the target child and the peers receive happy faces for exchanging the targeted prosocial skills. The specific reinforcement contingency is always tailored to the children's individual needs and abilities. Target children capable of initiating are expected to direct specific overtures to their peers, whereas less capable youngsters are expected to respond positively to initiations received from peers. The actual number of happy faces that each child must earn for individual or group reinforcement also varies with their abilities. Teachers generally provide only two to four prompts per session in order to promote children's spontaneous and independent exchanges.

CONCLUSIONS

We have described a social interaction code that was developed to examine the reciprocal exchanges and associative play between children with disabilities and their typical peers. The instrument contains five primary units for coding and analysis, including various forms of child initiations, responses, and concurrent behaviors, as well as children's continued or associative play and two types of teacher behavior. This code was developed to evaluate the effectiveness of social skills training and intervention and has been used with a wide range of different children and types of activities.

A package consisting of social skills training and intervention was also described. We have developed a standardized procedure that entails teaching children specific skills that have been identified as critical dimensions of social interactions. Both children with disabilities and their typical peers learn a variety of strategies for incorporating these skills into their interactions. Following training, teachers implement a peer-mediated intervention that encompasses either an individual or group-oriented reinforcement contingency to maintain the children's newly taught social exchanges. This intervention can be implemented on a daily basis across diverse play activities.

Our social skills protocol also pertains to the prevention and remediation of children's problem behaviors. Teachers are encouraged to be intimately involved in the intervention process by providing specific prompts to promote children's positive social exchanges. A high proportion of prompts should be directed to target children who exhibit limited initiation and/or language skills. In addition, teachers should also provide immediate praise and happy faces as well as delayed backup rewards to reinforce children's social interaction exchanges. This form of teacher involvement is similar to the compliance training generally conducted with children who exhibit oppositional behaviors. Finally, teachers' and peers' frequent overtures to children with disabilities appear to interrupt and even prevent a range of problem behaviors such as self-stimulation, echolalic speech, and the inappropriate use of materials.

REFERENCES

Hendrickson, J. M., Strain, P. S., Tremblay, A., & Shores, R. E. (1982). Interactions of behaviorally handicapped children: Functional effects of peer social initiations. *Journal of Applied Behavior Analysis, 6*, 323–353.

Kohler, F. W., & Fowler, S. A. (1985). Training prosocial behaviors to young children: An analysis of reciprocity with untrained peers. *Journal of Applied Behavior Analysis, 18*, 187–200.

Kohler, F. W., Shearer, D. L., & Strain, P. S. (1990). *The preschool social skills procedure: A teacher's manual for teaching social interaction skills to young children.* The Early Childhood Intervention Program, Allegheny-Singer Research Institute.

Kohler, F. W., Strain, P. S., Hoyson, M., DeCesare, L., Donina, W. M., & Rapp, N. (1995). Using a group-oriented contingency to increase social interactions between children with autism and their peers: A preliminary analysis of corollary supportive behaviors. *Behavior Modification, 19,* 10–32.

Kohler, F. W., Strain, P. S., Maretsky, S., & DeCesare, L. (1990). Promoting positive and supportive interactions between preschoolers: An analysis of group-oriented contingencies. *Journal of Early Intervention, 14,* 327–341.

Kohler, F. W., Strain, P. S., & Shearer, D. D. (1992). The overtures of preschool social skill intervention agents: Differential rates, forms, and functions. *Behavior Modification, 16,* 525–542.

Tremblay, A., Strain, P. S., Hendrickson, J. M., & Shores, R. E. (1981). Social interactions of normally developing preschool children: Using normative data for subject and target behavior selection. *Behavior Modification, 5,* 237–253.

Chapter 4

Intensive Behavioral Intervention with Young Children with Autism

O. IVAR LOVAAS AND GREGORY BUCH

INTRODUCTION

We provide an introduction, in nontechnical terms, to how and why to conduct intensive behavioral interventions with young children with autism. The UCLA Young Autism Project's 40-hour-per-week, two- to three-year treatment program for 2- to 3-year-old children is described and procedures are discussed, ranging from how to conduct the first hour of treatment to how to teach children with autism to play with their average peers. Next, a description of the critical components of effective behavioral treatment is presented as a rationale for the intensive procedures described and to provide guidelines for persons who wish to develop their own treatment programs. Finally, we offer a description of the knowledge and skills that should be required of a competent behavioral therapist or teacher. This is not a "how-to" manual of behavioral treatment. Such a manual would require one or two substantial texts by itself, examples of which are offered by Lovaas et al. (1980) and Koegel, Rincover, and Egel (1982). Rather, our intent is to interest the reader in seeking further information about this approach to treatment.

A brief word about terminology. Because there are few clear distinctions between the roles of therapists and teachers in the intensive early-intervention programs we describe here, the words *therapist* and *teacher* are used interchangeably throughout the chapter.

THE FIRST HOUR OF TREATMENT

When working in the field of autism, one soon learns that tremendous individual differences exist among children diagnosed as autistic. These differences are particularly evident when children are placed in educational or treatment programs. Some children respond with immediate tantrums or aggression, while others remain placid and unresponsive. Some children acquire new skills rapidly, while others appear to learn very little at all. Those who work with children with autism should be prepared for significant variability in how the children respond to behavioral treatment, in terms of both outcome after years of intervention and responsiveness during the first hour of treatment.

Work on this chapter was supported by Grant H133G80103 from the U.S. Office of Education. We would like to acknowledge Tristram Smith's advice and assistance in the preparation of this chapter. Persons interested in learning more about intensive early intervention or in receiving reprints are encouraged to contact the authors.

Despite their diversity, a constructive way to approach most children with autism is to think of them as people who have hardly ever succeeded in doing what their parents wanted them to do. Day after day, year after year, their parents and teachers have talked to them, tried to comfort them when they were upset, tried to cheer them to get a smile, and tried to inform them about the world in general, to no avail. These are children who have largely met with failure in life. Not surprisingly, many tend to be very frustrated, whiny, and subject to tantrums whenever anyone tries to teach them. These children probably anticipate failure and typically respond with objections to their first hour of treatment.

To counteract this negative emotional state, the therapists' job is to (1) guarantee that the children will succeed at what they are asked to do, (2) reward the children as effectively as possible when they do succeed, and (3) minimize the opportunities for the children to make mistakes. To do these things, therapists must first select a task that is so simple that failure is impossible. Therapists must then identify the specific rewards that particular children want the most and must provide them contingent on the children's success. Let us first concentrate on the task or behavior to be taught.

We usually begin by teaching a child to "sit down" when asked. Parents and all teachers or therapists who are going to work with the child are present for the first session. An experienced therapist places a chair directly behind the child and stands the child between his or her legs. The therapist then says, "Sit down," and gently but firmly guides the child to a sitting position in the chair. Teaching this simple task first has four distinct benefits:

1. The response can be easily guided or prompted. The child has, in effect, no choice but to succeed and be rewarded.
2. The children's opportunities to make mistakes or run away are reduced by the physical restrictions of the teaching situation.
3. The task is very discriminable. The gross motor action of sitting down provides the child with substantial sensory feedback that a response has been performed and maximizes the chances that the child will discriminate (be "aware" of) the relationship between the response and the reinforcing consequences that follow.
4. It provides a useful skill. Most of the children that we see have failed to learn to sit down when asked, and it is very difficult to teach a child who is running around the room.

As soon as the child has been seated for 3 to 5 seconds, everything that the child wants is provided in the form of two basic kinds of rewards: First, the child is immediately allowed to escape to Mom or Dad and seek comfort. This is an example of negative reinforcement or escape-avoidance learning.

Second, the child is given his or her favorite food or drink. Favorite objects (e.g., twigs, pieces of string, or other small objects) that the children may use in their ritualistic behaviors are also provided. In technical terms, the foods and objects are positive reinforcers. This rewarding condition may initially last for 20 to 30 seconds, after which the child is brought back to the chair. As soon as the child sits down, therapists and parents offer their approval in the form of enthusiastic clapping and cheering. In order to maximize the child's number of learning opportunities, the length of time that the child is required to sit is gradually lengthened while the duration of the rewarding condition is gradually reduced. The most important thing that the child can learn during this early interaction is not the act of sitting per se, but that there are predictable, rewarding consequences for his or her actions. The sitting task is repeated many times (trials are "massed") to ensure that the child will make this association.

Shortly, a new behavior is introduced. Once a child has succeeded in sitting in the chair, we may put a small wooden block on an adjacent table and then place the child's hand on top of the block. The teacher then moves the child's hand over a large bucket and prompts the child to release the block. The block falls into the bucket with a loud bang. Now, the child has to sit down and then drop a block in a bucket before being reinforced. In technical terminology, the teacher is shaping increasingly lengthy behaviors—from sitting in the chair for 5 seconds and dropping one block to sitting in the chair for 1 minute and dropping five blocks.

A third task often worked on in the first hour of treatment involves teaching children to come when their parents call them. A parent and a therapist sit face to face, in chairs about five feet apart. The child stands in the arms of the therapist, facing the parent. The parent briefly shows the child a small piece of a favorite food and says, "Come here." If the child does not respond, the therapist gently pushes the child into the arms of the parent, who immediately gives the child the food reinforcer, hugs and kisses, and lots of verbal praise. The process is then repeated. Every two to three trials, the adults scoot their chairs a few inches farther apart. As the distance between the chairs increases, the children eventually have to take several unguided steps between the adults. In addition to gradually increasing the distance between themselves, the adults gradually fade out their manual prompts. Eventually, the therapist is faded out altogether, and the children learn to come from any location within hearing range of their parents. In addition to the behaviors that are explicitly taught, appropriate spontaneous behaviors such as eye contact and random vocalizations are also reinforced. Eventually, teaching sessions are increased to 5 minutes, and the sessions are alternated with 2- to 3-minute breaks, in which children may spend time with their parents or at play.

Children demonstrate several different responses to the first hour of treatment. Some children change their fussing to more succinct and pointed anger. When returned to the teaching situation, they may kick or bite the attending adult or hurl the block into the bucket. Any appropriately directed aggression is appreciated and reinforced. Assaultive and self-injurious behavior is ignored by "working through" the tantrum. It has been our clinical experience that aggressive behavior during first hour of treatment is a positive predictor of future success in treatment. The reason may be in part that inappropriate behaviors can be relatively easily redirected into appropriate behaviors. Similarly, it has been our experience that indifferent or oblivious responses to the first hour of treatment are suggestive of less favorable prognoses. Late in the first hour or two of treatment, some children appear to experience a sense of achievement after completing successful trials. They may look to their parents for approval, give a fleeting smile of mastery, or return to the chair of their own accord. Some children cry for most of the first hour, while others stop crying in the first 5 minutes. However, it is the rare child who does not learn to sit or place the block in the bucket during these first 60 minutes. Success in the first hour is as important for parents and therapists as it is for children. The reason is that it gives the adults a sense of having identified a situation, however limited, that resulted in some learning. In technical terms, this is referred to as the achievement of reinforcement control. In everyday terms, one may say that there is evidence that the children are beginning to accept directions from adults.

As the first hour begins, the parents and the therapists may be more anxious than the children are. The parents are already anxious from living with children who constantly "shut them out," behave as if their family members do not exist, or have not learned to talk or play. The parents have tried very hard to teach their children, and though they may have succeeded with their average offspring, they have failed with their children with autism. The therapists are under pressure to produce some results, that is, to have some positive effect on the children. Even therapists who have previously succeeded with many other children may be anxious because they know that each child is different and that failure is always possible. It is difficult to hide one's lack of knowledge about how to proceed in such an open environment with parents and teachers together. Of course, therapists and teachers can lessen their apprehension by telling themselves (or the parents) that the children may have some form of irreparable brain damage and that they cannot be taught. At this stage of our knowledge, however, this strategy would be dishonest. It is better to use the anxiety that one feels in this first encounter in more constructive ways, such as developing or implementing procedures that will ensure the children's success. When the therapists and parents sense that the children are learning something, no matter how trivial it may be, they know that the children are teachable. Just being able to reduce the physical prompts of guiding the child to the chair or the child's hand to the bucket is evidence that the child is learning. If the first hour goes well, both therapists and parents should congratulate each other and feel great relief, which is a therapeutic side effect for all parties involved.

During the first hour at the clinic, each person in the three- to six-member treatment team, including the parents, takes turns working with the child. The most experienced therapists usually start the first half hour because they are the most likely to enable the children to be successful. However, it is critical that the experience of successful teaching be immediately generalized to everyone else on the treatment team, especially the child's parents. Just as the child is lavishly reinforced, members of the treatment team reinforce one another for successful teaching performances. The team faces a long and demanding task. Therefore, we try to arrange a collaboration between team members that will produce mutual reward and reinforcement, regardless of whether the child is progressing quickly or slowly. On the same day as the first hour at the clinic or school, treatment is transferred to the home. To maximize consistency and minimize the children's chances of failure, each team member uses exactly the same procedures in all situations. One or two new behaviors may be introduced into treatment during the first week, but only with the knowledge of all parties involved. For example, we may try to "get hold" of (bring under reinforcement control) some simple behavior that the parents tell us the child can already perform at home.

An enriched learning environment can be seen as one in which a child has many opportunities to be reinforced. When working one-to-one, we give anywhere from five to ten trials per minute so that the interaction between the adult and the child is almost continuous. In an optimal classroom situation, a child may be reinforced for appropriate behaviors once every five minutes. In a one-to-one teaching situation, a child may be reinforced 25 times in five minutes. This rapid pace also prevents the child from "spacing out" into self-stimulatory or inattentive behavior. Verbal interactions with the children are limited to succinct instructions or praise for correct behavior. Any other form of verbalization (e.g., "What's wrong?" "Is this fun?" or "Oh, please, just try!") may only complicate the task of children who are just learning the meanings of words.

This short description of the first hour of treatment could well be extended 10- or 100-fold, but in summary, the key is to protect children from failure and to help them build a sense of mastery over their social environment.

EARLY RECEPTIVE LANGUAGE

As a bridge between the first hour of treatment and later, more complex programs, we teach children to follow an increasing array of simple instructions. As before, to ensure the children's success, we choose nonverbal responses that can be easily prompted. For example, children are taught to give objects to people, give hugs, close doors, take their parents' hands, stand up, wave, and so on. Children frequently still have tantrums and are whiny at this stage in treatment. Therefore, these programs are intended to allow the therapists to prompt appropriate responses while ignoring tantruming behavior. As the children learn that they will get plenty of treats and attention for their new and appropriate behaviors and that their tantrums have no effect on their parents and teachers, their tantrums gradually decrease. Further progress in receptive language follows on the children's mastery of nonverbal imitation.

Nonverbal Imitation

The first hour of treatment and the teaching of early receptive language skills provide examples of the gradual shaping of behaviors through the reinforcement of successively more accurate approximations of target skills. This shaping procedure has the advantage of being relatively simple for both teachers and children. However, it is extremely time-consuming and is ultimately inadequate as a learning process when the children need to acquire many skills. In addition, some behaviors are simply too complex to be shaped in a stepwise, trial-and-error fashion. Average children learn by imitating or modeling others. Consequently, they can pick up behaviors in "bigger chunks." Many children with retardation and children with autism do not spontaneously learn this way. Therefore, we explicitly teach nonverbal imitation. Once children have acquired this skill, they no longer have to be manually prompted through new behaviors; instead, they can learn simply by having behaviors demonstrated for them. For example, in teaching receptive language, one can simply demonstrate a nonverbal behavior and pair it with the appropriate spoken word. In order to teach a child the meaning of *wave,* a therapist may give the instruction "Wave" while simultaneously waving. The child is then reinforced for imitating the therapist's wave. Over a series of trials, the teacher fades out the physical wave until the child can wave solely in response to the verbal instruction "Wave."

When teaching the imitation of physical actions, therapists first select one distinct, discriminable, and easily observable behavior. Arm raising is a good example. Therapists raise their arms over their heads and say, "Do this!" Simultaneously, a second therapist provides a physical prompt by lifting the children's arms over their heads. As soon as the children's arms are up, they are immediately reinforced. Over subsequent trials, the physical prompts are faded until the children can raise their arms without any help. Next, raising arms is temporarily set aside, and a second behavior (e.g., touching a table) is taught. As before, the adults model the behavior, physically prompt the children to respond, and fade the prompts until the children are able to imitate their therapists without any help.

Next comes the hard part, teaching a subtle discrimination. Therapists randomly (using no discernibly consistent pattern) either touch the table *or* raise their arms. The children are consequently faced with one of their first difficult discrimination tasks: They must raise their arms if their therapists raise their arms, but they must touch the table if their therapists touch the table. The therapists may again use physical prompting to help the children respond correctly, then slowly fade the prompts until the children are actually responding solely by imitating their therapists' actions. Depending on the children's rate of learning, new imitative tasks are introduced until the child is said to have achieved "generalized" nonverbal imitation. At this point, children are able to observe novel behaviors and accurately imitate them without any previous practice.

This procedure for teaching nonverbal imitation provides a highly simplified example of a basic discrimination-training task. Teaching children to discriminate in imitating two different actions may sound straightforward, but it can present a challenge for even the most skilled therapist. Children can learn a startling variety of strategies for responding that have nothing to do with imitation. For example, some therapists alternate raising their arms and touching the table in a consistent pattern (ABAB). Many children quickly learn to alternate their responses in a similar pattern rather than learning to imitate their teacher. Other therapists may frequently repeat blocks of the same behavior (AAAABBBBAAAA). Under these circumstances, the children learn simply to repeat one response until they are prompted to begin repeating the other response. Another potential problem is that, even if the children respond randomly, they will be right half the time. Many children are quite satisfied with being reinforced 50% of the time and will pay little attention to their therapists' actions.

Some children may learn their first discrimination between two imitative responses within five trials, while other children may take hundreds of trials. As we will note later, skill in discrimination training should be a fundamental tool in the repertoire of every behavioral treatment program designed for clients who are developmentally disabled. Virtually every skill we teach is introduced in the form of as simple and clear a discrimination task as therapists can present. In the example above, nonverbal imitation was introduced as a discrimination between just two responses, raising the arms and touching a table.

Skill in discrimination training is equally important in teaching abstract language skills. When learning prepositions, children are first taught to discriminate between only two concepts. For example, they may learn to discriminate placing a block "on top" from "under" a box. Once this discrimination is mastered, additional prepositions are systematically introduced, and the skills are generalized to objects other than blocks and boxes.

Nonverbal imitation serves as a foundation for teaching literally hundreds of language, academic, play, and self-help skills. For example, children may learn to comb their hair by imitating their therapists' use of a comb. Children may learn to play with blocks by building structures similar to those built by their teachers and peers. Rather than laboriously shaping each letter of the alphabet, children may learn how to write by imitating their therapists' writing.

Matching to Sample

Matching skills are closely related to nonverbal imitation skills. Both procedures require children to observe stimuli and then, in varying ways, to replicate what they have observed. In a typical matching task, two distinctly different objects (e.g., a book and a car) are placed on a table before a child. The child is then given a duplicate of one of the objects (e.g., a second car) and is instructed, "Put with same." The child is then prompted to place the second car with the car on the table. New materials to be matched are gradually introduced, just as new behaviors to be imitated were introduced within nonverbal imitation. Children may be taught to match colors, shapes, letters, numbers, faces, categories, two-dimensional pictures of objects to the actual three-dimensional objects, and so on. Matching is unique in that virtually all children, regardless of their level of functioning, learn the skill very quickly and seem to enjoy the task. Soon after the skill is acquired, we often do not need to extrinsically reward the children for responding. The visual match appears to become a reinforcing event for the children.

Verbal Imitation

Just as it is impossible to shape individually every physical action that we wish to teach our children, it is also impossible to shape individually every verbalization that we wish our children to use. Consequently, children need to learn how to imitate what other people say. Just learning to imitate words, regardless of learning any meaning associated with them, can be an extremely complex task for mute children. Likewise, *teaching* mute children just to imitate words, regardless of teaching any meaning associated with them, is one of the most difficult tasks faced by teachers, therapists, or speech pathologists.

Lovaas, Berberich, Perloff, and Schaeffer (1996) developed a four-step procedure for teaching mute children to imitate words. In the first step, children are reinforced for making any vocalizations, regardless of whether they resemble words. The goal of this step is to increase the children's rate of random vocalizations. In the second step, the children are reinforced for any vocalization that occurs immediately after a therapist's vocalization. The goal of this step is to teach the children to make vocalizations in response to their teachers' vocalizations. In the third step, the therapists select a single sound that each child commonly makes during random vocalizations. The therapists then repeat that sound and reinforce the children only if they respond with that distinct sound. The goal of this step is to teach the children to accurately imitate this one specific sound. In the fourth step, the children are taught to discriminate between and imitate different sounds made by their therapists.

While almost all children find matching physical objects intrinsically rewarding, only about half of the children who receive intensive treatment enjoy verbal imitation to the point where they begin spontaneously to echo the words of others. This behavior is known as *echolalia*. Average children typically go through an echolalic stage as they are learning to speak. Therefore, we view the development of echolalic behavior as a positive prognostic sign. As may be expected, children who do not develop echolaliclike behavior typically have great difficulty in further language programs.

Observational Learning

Observational learning is another example of a learning strategy. It involves learning new behaviors through the observation of other persons' learning experiences. Although nonverbal and verbal imitation skills are typically taught in the first months of treatment, observational learning skills are usually not emphasized until the second year. Observational learning is a particularly important ability for children as they enter normal preschools and begin to interact with average peers, because it allows them to acquire a variety of complex skills without having to directly experience reinforcement or punishment. For example, Child A may observe Child B tamper with Child C's sand castle. Child C may then smack Child B with a sand shovel. If Child A has observational learning skills, he or she can learn not to disturb other children's projects simply by observing what happened to Child B. In an academic setting, Child A may observe a classroom teacher asks Child B, "Do you know what doctors do?" After Child B responds "No," the teacher may explain,

"Doctors help us when we are sick. They give us medicine and fix people when they get hurt." If Child A has observational learning skills, he or she can learn about doctors without one-to-one instruction.

To build observational learning skills, children are initially taught to observe simple interactions between a teacher and one peer. The teacher asks the peer a series of questions, reinforces the peer for correct responses, and informs the peer if the responses are incorrect. After each question to the peer, the teacher asks the child with autism the same question. The child is reinforced for imitating the peer's correct responses and for ignoring the peer's incorrect responses. Subsequently, the children are taught to observe longer interactions between teachers and peers before questions are asked, more peers are introduced into the situation, more elaborate behaviors are modeled, and ultimately, the procedure is generalized to the children's preschool classes.

Sadly, our experience is that the great majority of professionals either overlook the fundamental skills involved in nonverbal imitation, verbal imitation, and observational learning or consider them unteachable. Some professionals may observe that children lack nonverbal and verbal imitation skills but will not try to teach these because they believe that such abilities "emerge" only as part of a developmental process. Other professionals may attempt to mainstream children with autism without first teaching them imitation and observational learning skills. In all probability, such children will learn little or nothing from being placed in group learning situations with their average peers.

Research has shown, however, that children can be taught these strategies for learning (Lovaas, Freitas, Nelson, & Whalen, 1967; Schroeder & Baer, 1972). Further, we have found that these skills are essential to the building of the vast number of more complex behaviors that people with developmental disabilities need to learn.

Teaching Language

The majority of our treatment programs for young children with autism involve teaching language skills, the beginnings of which were illustrated in our description of the first hour of treatment. Over the course of treatment, the children may experience well over 100 discrete language programs. More complete details of these programs than can be presented in this chapter are available in Lovaas (1987).

Initial language programs are broken down into receptive and expressive skills. *Receptive language* refers to the ability to understand the meaning of others' speech. *Expressive language* refers to the ability to produce vocalizations (words) that have meaning associated with them (that is, are not merely imitative). In technical terms, receptive and expressive language requires children to make two different kinds of discriminations. In receptive language, children must learn to listen to verbal stimuli and give nonverbal responses. The previous example of teaching a child to wave in response to the instruction "Wave" involved a receptive discrimination. Alternatively, teaching a child to say "Wave" when observing another person wave requires that the child make an expressive discrimination. While receptive and expressive skills may seem to be closely linked, we have found that it is not safe to assume that children who demonstrate one are capable of the other, or that both can be effectively taught simultaneously. Because receptive responses are relatively easy to prompt, receptive skills are typically taught before expressive skills. For example, it is easier to prompt a child to touch or point to a ball than it is to prompt a child to say "Ball." Surprisingly, however, a minority of the children in our program have acquired expressive labels before receptive labels.

Receptive Language

The beginnings of receptive language were introduced in our examples of teaching children to "sit down" and "come here." In order to perform these tasks, the children had to learn to associate adults' words with concrete actions. In addition to associating words with actions, the children also need to learn to associate words with objects. To make the learning situation as easy as possible, the children are initially taught to discriminate between only two objects, for example, a ball and a cup. The objects are placed on a table before the children. The therapists clearly say "Ball" or "Cup" and then use one of several different prompts to help the children select the correct object. The therapists may facilitate a correct response by positioning the correct object significantly closer to the children, repeating the same object for many trials, pointing to the correct object, or physically guiding the children's hands. As the children begin to respond correctly, the prompts are faded until the children can respond with no help. As the children succeed, new objects are added. Once again, this is a highly simplified example of teaching a basic discrimination task. Without supervised training, novice teachers may make many mistakes that will slow or stop learning. For example, when teaching the above discrimination between a ball and a cup, a novice therapist might say, "Please touch the ball," and "Please touch the cup." These two phrases may sound virtually identical to a child who is just beginning to associate words with objects. An experienced therapist knows that simply saying "Ball" or "Cup," without the extra words, makes the children's task much easier. It is also easy to provide inadvertent prompts. For example, therapists frequently glance at the object that they are going to request before they request it. Rather than listening to what their teachers are saying, the children often learn to touch the last object that their teachers looked at. Clearly, children with autism are able to learn, though they do not necessarily learn what adults are trying to teach them.

Expressive Language

In expressive language programs, children are taught to use their own words to label objects and actions. As usual, the children are initially taught to discriminate between two maximally distinctive stimuli. A ball and a cookie are a good example because their names sound distinctly different and they are quite different in appearance. The therapists present one of the objects (e.g., the ball), ask, "What is it?" and immediately prompt the children to respond by saying, "Ball." The children imitate the word *ball* and are reinforced. Over subsequent trials, the therapists' verbal prompt of "Ball" is faded out until the children can answer the question, "What is it?" unprompted.

The ball is then set aside, and the children are taught to label the cookies in the same way that they were taught to label the ball. Finally, the cookie and the ball are presented in randomly alternating trials. Once the children can expressively label two objects correctly, additional objects are added one at a time. After the children have learned to expressively label a variety of objects, they are taught to label actions. For example, children are taught to observe a therapist performing an action and to answer the question, "What is he (or she) doing?"

Advanced Language

Once children have learned to receptively and expressively label objects and actions, they are taught to label such relatively abstract concepts as colors, prepositions, sizes, pronouns, and emotions. Children are then taught to use all these skills to speak in complete sentences to describe their wants and desires, their own and other people's behaviors, and their immediate environment in general. Next, the children are taught time concepts and how to use the past and future tenses of verbs to give increasingly lengthy and detailed descriptions of their previous experiences and plans for future activities. Concurrently, the children are taught to *listen* to increasingly complex language. For example, the children initially listen to "stories" that are one to two sentences in length ("Dad went to the store. He bought juice.") and are asked questions ("Where did Dad go?" "What did he buy?"). The stories are gradually lengthened and made more detailed. At advanced stages, children are read age-appropriate books and are asked questions regarding cause-and-effect relationships, the emotions of the characters, and the probable outcomes of events. In the area of social language, children are taught how to initiate and maintain conversations as well as how to listen to other people's conversations and then join in.

Teaching Community and Self-Help Skills

As noted earlier, teaching language skills affects primarily only language skills. Despite significant gains in communicative skills, children's self-help and community skills typically show little change unless they are directly targeted. On the other hand, it is easier to teach self-help and community skills to a child who is starting to follow verbal direction and who can imitate models. The actual self-help and community skills that young children with autism need to learn are no different from those that average children are taught: how to dress and undress, how to use the toilet, how to feed oneself, how to behave appropriately in public places, how to avoid getting lost, how to cross the street safely, and how to behave with strangers. Although average children may acquire these skills through informal interactions with their parents, children with developmental disabilities typically need more explicit practice. For example, one of the most common problems reported by the parents of children with autism is difficulty in taking their children to restaurants, out shopping, or to friends' and relatives' homes. Often, after several traumatic experiences at the grocery store, these parents stop taking their children into the community at all.

Once children's tantrums have been reduced and the children are compliant with their parents' requests at home, the therapists work with the parents to transfer this control to community situations. Brief (5- to 10-minute) trips to grocery stores or to fast-food restaurants are planned. Before each trip, the parents and the therapists review all the problems that may occur (e.g., tantrums, running away, or annoying other customers) and exactly how they will be dealt with if they occur (e.g., ignoring, reprimanding, leaving, or time-out). The therapists accompany the parents and the children and coach the parents in following through with their pretrip contingency plans. As the parents feel more in control of the situation, the therapists fade out, and longer trips are taken to locations that demand more appropriate behaviors.

School Integration and Teaching Peer Play

As we noted earlier, children with autism demonstrate substantial individual differences in response to behavioral interventions. These differences are particularly important to remember as we discuss mainstreaming children with autism in regular classrooms and teaching them to interact socially with their average peers. In our research on the effects of intensive early intervention, we have seen at least two groups of children emerge. One group, roughly half of the children, appears to show substantial and long-term benefits from treatment. Children in this group progress rapidly through our language programs and make spontaneous use of the skills that they have learned. The second group, roughly the other half of the children, progresses relatively slowly in treatment. Some children in this group have tremendous difficulty in acquiring verbal imitation. Others may develop verbal imitation skills but move slowly in further language programs. The school and peer integration procedures that we will describe may be of some benefit to the children in the slower-moving group, but they are geared primarily to those children who are maximally responsive to intensive early intervention. Even with children in the maximally responsive group, successful integration requires the active intervention of the treatment team. Children are never placed in social or academic situations with the assumption that they will catch on by themselves.

Integration into regular preschools and building friendships with peers are critical to the long-term success of early intervention programs. Children will maintain the skills that they have learned in treatment only if they are able to use these skills under enjoyable circumstances in the real world. For example, a girl who has been taught how to talk will maintain her language skills if she enjoys (is reinforced by) conversing with her average peers. Integration into schools and establishing friendships with peers are equally important in teaching new behaviors. Once children are hooked on the reinforcers that their schools and peers provide, they begin to learn from regular classroom settings and to pick up the language from their friends, just as average kids do. For those children who have learned some basic sentence structure, are cooperative with instruction from adults, and are toilet-trained, preparations are made for placement in regular preschool classrooms. The parents and the therapists observe the school routines before the children are enrolled, and programs are implemented at home to prepare the children for the demands of the classroom. Initially, the children may spend only 30 to 40 minutes in class, two or three times a week. The parents and the therapists select the exact times by finding out when the class is doing activities that the children will be the most successful at and will enjoy the most. The therapists attend class with the children, prompt appropriate behavior, and note any behavioral deficits that may be worked on at home. For those children who are successful, time in class is gradually increased to full-time attendance. Meanwhile, the therapists' attendance is gradually faded out.

For those children who are maximally responsive to treatment, an emphasis is also placed on building friendships with peers. Peers are selected from preschools or from the children's neighborhoods and are invited to the children's homes for play sessions supervised by the therapists. For those children who show fewer gains in treatment, an emphasis is placed on helping the parents take full advantage of other services offered by the community, such as special-education classes, speech and language therapy, and alternate approaches to treatment.

An important first step to peer integration involves teaching children to attend to their peers' verbalizations. Despite learning to listen to their therapists and their parents, many children with autism still largely ignore their peers. During play sessions, the children are prompted to respond to their peers' questions and instructions. If necessary, the therapists may prompt the peers to repeat questions or to ask additional questions in order to give the clients practice in attending and responding.

Another important early step in peer integration involves giving children an age-appropriate level of "cultural literacy." Before children with autism can successfully play or converse with their average peers, they need to share a range of interests and experiences with them. They need to know how to play with the toys that their peers play with, they need to watch the television shows and movies that their peers watch, and they need to be able to engage in imaginative or pretend play based on the same topics that their peers' imaginative play is based on. Consequently, therapists must be knowledgeable about what's "hot" in the world of preschool children. Not only do they need to know how to teach children how to play with toys, but they also need to know which toys average children are playing with. In addition, they need to know which cartoons and movies average children are watching and the current topics of average children's imaginative play.

After children have acquired a degree of cultural literacy and have learned to respond to their peers' explicit questions and instructions, they are taught to imitate their peers' nonverbal play behavior. Initially, the children are taught to imitate their *therapists'* play activities with a wide selection of age-appropriate toys. Teaching takes place in the children's homes, where the therapists arrange a room with approximately ten toys or activities (e.g., cars, paper and crayons, Ninja Turtles, games, Legos, and dolls). The children are told that they need to "play" with their therapists. Therapists select a toy and begin to use it (for example, they may begin to color). The children are then prompted to color, too. After a moment, and without any announcement, the therapists switch to a new activity (e.g., setting up a race track). If the children also switch, they are immediately reinforced. If the children do not switch, they are briefly told, "No," and are prompted to move on to the new activity. Once the children can play along with their therapists, the therapists are replaced with peers. Peers are brought into the same play situation, and the clients are rewarded for imitating their peers' activities with toys. In later phases of the program, the children are taught to respond with their own comments to their therapists' comments during play. Subsequently, the therapists are again replaced with peers, and the children are rewarded for responding to their peers' comments during play.

MAJOR CHARACTERISTICS OF EFFECTIVE BEHAVIORAL TREATMENT

The following description of the critical components of effective behavioral treatment programs will provide a rationale for the intensive and time-consuming procedures we have described. This description will also offer guidelines for persons who wish to construct their own early-intervention programs for children with autism.

One-to-One Teaching

The great majority of children with autism learn very little in group settings. Most procedures that have been shown to improve these children's functioning are delivered in a one-to-one, adult-to-child format (Newsom & Rincover, 1989). Exposure to average peers and placement in classroom settings can be therapeutic for children with developmental disabilities, but only if they have the skills that will allow them to learn from these situations.

What to Treat

Examples of a large variety of teaching programs have been illustrated in this chapter. We developed these many programs out of necessity because we have found no critical or pivotal behaviors that, once acquired, produce concurrent spontaneous improvements in other areas of behavior. In technical terminology, this is known as response specificity or limited generalization across behaviors. So far as the practice of behavioral interventions is concerned, this means that one gets very few treatment gains "for free." All the behaviors that children with autism need to learn must be taught. If one teaches these children to sit in a chair or to place blocks in a bucket, the children have probably learned only those tasks. At best, it may be easier to teach the children additional skills. Similarly, if one teaches children to maintain eye contact, the children do not at the same time begin to "see" their teachers and parents or to become more "aware" of what is going on. They are simply able to attend visually to adults' faces. Later in treatment, one should not assume that, because children are successfully learning complex language skills, they will automatically decrease their assaultive or self-injurious behaviors or begin to interact appropriately with their peers. The world is full of people who have developed superior speaking skills yet have maintained vast repertoires of aggressive and destructive behaviors. Virtually all behaviors that children with autism need to function effectively and constructively in society have to be taught or modeled.

Where to Teach

Children with autism do not readily generalize the behaviors they have learned in one environment to other environments (Lovaas, Koegel, Simmons, & Long, 1973). From what we know now, there is no particular reason to believe that the skills the children learn in a clinic or a classroom will automatically transfer to home. Similarly, if home and classroom are covered, the skills may not transfer to community settings such as restaurants or supermarkets. In technical terminology, this is known as limited stimulus generalization or situation specificity in treatment effects. In practical terms, this means that the children have to be taught in all their environments. Therefore, we go home with the children after the first hour of treatment. If we give 40 hours of one-to-one treatment, 39 of those hours are delivered in the children's homes or immediate communities.

Who Should Teach

It follows from the three previous sections that all significant persons in the children's environment need to become behavioral teachers or therapists. This does not mean that each person needs to know enough to supervise treatment or construct new programs. Rather, each person should know enough about behavioral interventions to help the children maintain the skills that they have learned and to help them generalize these skills to new environments. Whether the children live at home or in the community, competent treatment requires that all significant persons in the children's environment receive some training. There is nothing more frustrating for a person who has achieved some degree of control over a child's tantrums than to observe another person actively reinforcing tantrums or other regressive behaviors. These are ideal circumstances for producing children with Jekyll-and-Hyde personalities. Contrary to what many people thought in the past, and to the position that many professionals still defend, children with autism are able to learn different sets of behaviors from different environments. This ability suggests that these children are very teachable, that many of their inappropriate behaviors are learned, and that one has to guard continually against counterproductive interventions, be they prescribed by a professional or informally provided by a relative. Parental participation in treatment is particularly important.

Without parental collaboration, the treatment will not work. The parents in our program attend all the weekly meetings of their treatment team, participate in all aspects of the treatment, and are always the final authority on what treatment their children receive. The parents also work as teachers for 10 of the 40 hours of treatment that we provide (so that they are free to engage in other activities for the remaining 30 hours). The parents may supplement or extend teaching in the evenings and on weekends in formal and informal teaching situations. Six months into the program, most parents know enough about behavioral treatment to help train new student therapists assigned to their families. The majority of our parents become very competent teachers and know more about behavioral treatment than most professionals.

How Long to Teach

The data on behavioral treatment show quite clearly that the longer treatment lasts, the more effective it is. This holds true across hours of the day, days of the week, weeks of the year, and years of a lifetime. Therefore, persons with developmental disabilities should ideally be in formal or informal learning situations all their waking hours, 7 days a week, 365 days a year, as long as they live. We know that the only way to prevent a relapse once treatment is terminated is not to terminate treatment. The only known exception to this rule about relapse is half of the young children who receive intensive behavioral intervention and who are successfully mainstreamed (Lovaas, 1987). Clearly, this treatment outcome is the exception rather than the rule because of the current lack of facilities that provide intensive intervention.

Based on the intensity and scope of the treatment procedures we have described, one may be led to conclude that children with developmental disabilities are really quite different from average children. Is this really so? Our answer is a definite no. All new parents learn that raising an average child involves much more work than they were led to believe. Children need to learn how to feed themselves, dress themselves, go to the bathroom, act nicely with their siblings, read and write, work, and engage in a whole host of other behaviors. Guiding them is a never-ending task. Furthermore, even average children need to learn to behave appropriately, not only at home but also in the community and at school. Wise parents communicate regularly with their children's teachers, keep their eye on what kinds of friends their children have, and reinforce their children for proper behavior. Average children have the advantage that they can be taught without their parents' needing a great deal of specialized knowledge of how to teach. Consequently, average children learn from the time they get up in the morning to the time they go to bed at night, 365 days a year. In order to grow as other children do, children with developmental disabilities need the same educational opportunities. They should be in environments in which they can learn 365 days a year, just as their average peers are.

Diagnosis and Assessment

Sadly, we commonly see parents who take their children to expert after expert, sometimes spending years and a considerable sum of money to acquire a stack of diagnostic reports. At present, accurate differential diagnoses are often difficult or impossible to make and appear to be of very little value to children with developmental disabilities and their families. Regardless of whether these children are diagnosed as retarded, autistic, pervasively developmentally disabled, or any combination of the above, the current treatment of choice is exactly the same: behavioral interventions focusing on teaching appropriate skills (Crnic & Reid, 1989).

Assessments in the form of standardized tests of intellectual and social functioning may be important for three reasons. First, they allow therapists and teachers to predict how the children would do if, at the time of testing, they were placed in regular classrooms or in ordinary social situations. Second, they allow researchers to compare subjects' level of functioning before and after treatment to gauge whether or not the children have improved with treatment. Third, they help researchers, clinicians, and teachers who work independently to ascertain whether they are working with similar clients or students.

Assessment is also critical in guiding behavioral treatment. However, the kind of assessment required differs from the standardized tests of intellectual and social functioning that most clinicians and educators are familiar with. The most important form of assessment in behavioral treatment is minute-by-minute, response-by-response measures of change in specific behaviors. During the first hour of treatment, and during all subsequent hours, one must continually and accurately observe whether the children are learning. A period of 10 to 20 minutes without progress should invite a discussion of what is wrong and what has to be changed. If no learning is occurring, then the treatment must be redesigned. Continuous assessment is also critical in directing what is being taught from moment to moment. For example, to teach a mute child to speak, a teacher needs to know exactly which sounds the child can currently produce and the exact status of each sound that is being shaped. The teacher may need to know if *soot* is currently being reinforced as an approximation of *foot*, or if the child is being required to pronounce the *f* correctly. Continuous assessment at this level of detail is essential to consistent progress.

It is important to note that the clinical problems (or dependent variables) that we choose to address with our treatment program are specific behaviors rather than global entities such as *autism* or *retardation*. Our focus on specific behaviors allows us to constantly assess whether we are helping the children we work with. The effectiveness of procedures for reducing tantrums or teaching children to imitate speech can usually be assessed within one hour of their implementation. If the procedures are ineffective, new procedures can be immediately attempted. On the other hand, the effectiveness of procedures for reducing autism or retardation may be assessed only after years of treatment. If the treatment is found to be ineffective, several more years must pass before the effectiveness of alternate procedures can be assessed.

The assessment of children's performance of specific skills may also allow us to predict who will benefit most from treatment. There appears to be a strong correlation between the acquisition of certain skills within the first three months of treatment (verbal imitation and expressive labeling of objects) and the most successful treatment outcomes.

EXPECTATIONS FOR OUTCOME

In one of our studies (Lovaas, 1987), 19 subjects were given two or more years of the 40-hour-per-week, one-to-one therapy described in this chapter. A group of 19 control children received fewer than 10 hours per week of therapy for a similar period of time. All the subjects were independently diagnosed as autistic and began treatment before the age of 46 months. The results of the study are briefly summarized below.

At the first follow-up, when the subjects were between 6 and 7 years old, the children in the experimental group had gained 20 IQ points, while the children in the control group had lost 5 IQ points. Of the 19 children in the intensive treatment group, 9 (47%) had successfully passed through regular first-grade classes in public schools and had scored in the normal or above-normal range on IQ tests ($M = 107$, range 94–120). No children in the control group had met these criteria of the achievement of normal functioning. In the intensive treatment group, 8 children had completed first grade in aphasia classes, while the remaining 2 children had been placed in classes for children with autism or retardation. In the control group, 8 subjects had been placed in aphasia classes, and 11 children had been placed in classes for children with autism or retardation. It is noteworthy that all children in the control group, in addition to receiving 10 hours per week of one-to-one behavioral treatment, had been enrolled in special-education classes and had full access to all services provided by the public school system. Apparently, this level of service was not sufficiently intense to allow these children with autism to catch up with their peers.

A more extensive follow-up of the normally functioning subjects in the experimental group was conducted when they were an average age of 13 (McEachin, Smith, & Lovaas, 1993). Blind examiners using IQ tests, scales of socioemotional functioning, and clinical interviews found that the gains of the experimental-group children had been maintained. Eight of the nine children described as functioning normally in the 1987 study were found to be indistinguishable from their average peers. For a more detailed discussion of these procedures and the results, the reader is encouraged to refer to the original citations to the last two studies.

Despite 40 hours per week of behavioral therapy over the course of several years, half of the 19 children in the intensive treatment group did not achieve normal functioning. One of these children was maintained in treatment until his early teens and received over 15,000 hours of therapy; yet he still learned very little functional speech and ultimately experienced a decrease in IQ. These results clearly demonstrate that time in treatment alone is not enough to ensure normal functioning for many children with autism and that the effectiveness of intensive early intervention varies significantly across individuals. These results also suggest the need for further research into how to help the many children who do not achieve normal functioning with the early behavioral intervention that we can currently offer.

For those children who do not achieve normal functioning, our treatment goals have shifted from an emphasis on developing vocal language to an emphasis on teaching alternate forms of communication and self-help, as well as vocational and recreational skills that may allow them to remain in and contribute to their natural communities. A similar treatment focus may be recommended for many children who are older and/or do not have access to intensive behavioral services.

Even though the results to date on the effectiveness of intensive early intervention are very encouraging, these results and procedures must be replicated by independent researchers before intensive early intervention can be given widespread endorsement. Currently, replication studies are beginning at independent research sites. At the UCLA project, Smith and Lovaas are currently investigating the effects of intensive early intervention with children who are diagnosed as mentally retarded but who do not have a primary diagnosis of autism.

REQUIREMENTS OF A COMPETENT BEHAVIORAL THERAPIST OR TEACHER

We have given some examples of the complex and intricate procedures that have been developed for the treatment of children with autism. In order to implement these programs successfully with persons with developmental disabilities, an extensive background in both the theoretical and the practical aspects of behavioral treatment is essential. This is particularly true when it comes to teaching language, the crux of our treatment program for clients with developmental disabilities.

The definitions of *behavior* and *behavioral treatment* vary considerably across professions. Within behavioral psychology, the term *behavior* refers to whatever one person can directly observe about another person. This observation ranges from observing another person smile, talk, eat, go to school, drive a car, or get married to the recording of physiological measures such as respiration and heart rate. In contrast, some treatment centers now employ "behavior specialists" who are assigned solely to reducing tantrums or aggressive behavior. Language instruction may be thought to belong to a group of professionals known as *language specialists*. And emotions may be thought of as something quite different from behavior altogether. This situation is clearly a gross distortion of what behavioral treatment is all about. In addition to being able to reduce inappropriate behaviors, a competent behavioral therapist must also be able to teach children how to imitate others, use language, sleep through the night, use the toilet, dress themselves, play with toys and with other children, understand cause-and-effect relationships, express affection, and anticipate or predict other people's feelings. In fact, the "behavior specialist" assigned solely to reducing aggressive behaviors will, in all probability, fail unless he or she is prepared to teach most or all the skills that will allow people to function adequately in the environments that are available to them. In the case of developmental disabilities, our task is to build "the whole person." Intervening on parts here and there will not do the job.

The reader should be wary of shortcuts to a competent education of children with autism. There are a host of programs on the market today that may be misunderstood as offering such shortcuts. These include "communication training," the "natural language paradigm," and "incidental teaching." These programs may supplement comprehensive behavioral treatment, but they are not replacements. A drift away from adequate treatment is regrettable, but predictable, considering the effort needed to obtain and carry out comprehensive behavioral interventions and the lack of adequate training facilities available to professionals. Because there are inadequate certification requirements at the state or federal level for "behavior therapists," this shameful situation is allowed to exist.

We can suggest several courses of action for a person who wishes to be a competent behavior therapist or teacher for persons with developmental disabilities. First, we advise that the prospective therapist become familiar with the basic research and theory within the psychological field of learning and behavior, by taking one or more courses at the upper division college level and/or studying several books in the area. Martin and Pear (1988) offer a good book for people new to the field, and Catania (1984) provides a more advanced text. Such study should emphasize operant principles and discrimination learning. Second, the person should have a detailed knowledge of the treatment programs that are currently available in professional journals and books. Third, the person must complete at least a three-month supervised practicum in one-to-one work with clients who are developmentally disabled. This practicum should emphasize procedures for building complex language. Fourth, given the complexity of the task at hand, persons should always consider themselves "in training." The teaching procedures are complicated, new procedures need to be constantly developed, old programs need continual refinements, and substantial individual differences exist between clients. No one person will be able to find answers to all the treatment problems that arise in any one client. In addition, it is easy for persons working in isolation to drift unwittingly from effective treatment procedures. Providing competent behavioral interventions requires that one work within a group of professionals who meet regularly to update their skills, evaluate treatment procedures, and jointly plan procedures for specific clients. At the UCLA Young Autism Project, each treatment team (parents, therapists, teachers, supervisory staff, and child) meets once a week. All adults work with the child in front of the group and receive feedback on their teaching skills. Improved procedures for old programs are discussed, and new programs are demonstrated.

Beyond knowledge and skills in behavioral theory and practice, many additional requirements should be imposed on those who have the major responsibility for the treatment or education of persons who are developmentally disabled. For example, "clinical sense," as acquired through supervised clinical training or other instructive interpersonal experiences, is important and often overlooked. Clinical sense is particularly important when working with the parents of children with disabilities. Being able to sense a person's stress and knowing how to alleviate it or how to work with it constructively are absolutely essential skills.

FUTURE NEEDS

It is clear that the technology that has been developed for the treatment of persons with autism and other developmental disabilities is not currently being implemented in the real world. Sadly, the result is that persons with developmental disabilities and their families continue to suffer from problems that we know how to treat. Intensive early intervention is labor-intensive and requires skilled personnel. Consequently, some have suggested that offering such treatment to all young children with autism is financially unrealistic. However, an analysis of the costs of lifetime custodial care for persons with autism suggests that intensive early intervention for all may actually produce a substantial savings over current spending levels. It would currently cost approximately $75,000 to provide a child with autism with three years of full-time, one-to-one services from a special-education teacher knowledgeable in behavioral treatment. For each child who is developmentally disabled and who reaches normal functioning with such treatment, the state would save the more than $2 million cost of lifelong institutionalization or group home care. Even for those children who do not achieve normal functioning, the savings resulting from reductions in the subsequent requirement of acute care would easily offset the initial expense of early intervention.

Cost-saving treatment procedures cannot be implemented until a competent group of professionals exists that knows how to use them. The university curricula for psychologists, speech therapists, occupational therapists, and special-education teachers should be enriched to include one-to-one behavioral instruction procedures for teaching language and other complex social behaviors to children who are developmentally disabled.

Approximately half of the children in the intensive treatment group in the studies described above did not appear to benefit significantly from intensive early intervention. Methods for helping those persons who do not respond to current treatment procedures need to be developed. In addition, we need to learn which factors predict who will benefit from intensive early intervention, so that our currently limited resources can be offered to those persons who will benefit most from them.

Helping those who are developmentally disabled represents one of the most significant challenges faced by educators and health care professionals. Many believe that the root of this challenge lies in the supposed intractability of developmental disorders. However, it has been our goal in this chapter to describe how, in trying to meet this challenge, we have found that behavioral treatment that addresses a large number of behaviors in a large number of situations can have a significant impact on the level of functioning of those who are developmentally disabled. In addition, it has been our goal to suggest that our most immediate challenge stem not from the inability of those who are developmentally disabled to learn, but from deficits in the training programs of the professionals who are supposed to help them. There is probably a 20-year gap between what is known about effective treatment and what is applied in the field.

REFERENCES

Catania, A. C. (1984). *Learning.* Englewood Cliffs, NJ: Prentice-Hall.

Crnic, K. A., & Reid, M. (1989). Mental retardation. In E. J. Mash & R. A. Barkley (Eds.), *Treatment of childhood disorders* (pp. 247–285). New York: Guilford Press.

Koegel, R. L., Rincover, A., & Egel, A. C. (1982). *Educating and understanding autistic children.* San Diego: College Hill Press.

Lovaas, O. I. (1987). Behavioral treatment and normal educational and intellectual functioning in young autistic children. *Journal of Consulting and Clinical Psychology, 55,* 3–9.

Lovaas, O. I., Ackerman, A. B., Alexander, D., Firestone, P., Perkins, J., & Young, D. (1980). *Teaching developmentally disabled children: The me book.* Austin, TX: Pro-Ed.

Lovaas, O. I., Berberich, J. P., Perloff, B. F., & Schaeffer, S. (1966). Acquisition of imitative speech by schizophrenic children. *Science, 151,* 705–707.

Lovaas, O. I., Freitas, L., Nelson, K., & Whalen, C. (1967). The establishment of imitation and its use for the development of complex behavior in schizophrenic children. *Behavior Research and Therapy, 5,* 171–181.

Lovaas, O. I., Koegel, R. L., Simmons, J. Q., & Long, J. (1973). Some generalization and follow-up measures on autistic children in behavior therapy. *Journal of Applied Behavior Analysis, 6,* 131–166.

Martin, G., & Pear, J. (1988). *Behavior modification: What it is and how to do it.* Englewood Cliffs, NJ: Prentice-Hall.

McEachin, J. J., Smith T. H., & Lovaas, O. I. (1993). Outcome in adolescence of autistic children receiving early intensive behavioral treatment. *American Journal of Mental Retardation, 97,* 359–372.

Newsom, C., & Rincover, A. (1989). Autism. In E. J. Mash & R. A. Barkley (Eds.), *Treatment of childhood disorders* (pp. 286–346). New York: Guilford Press.

Schroeder, G. L., & Baer, D. M. (1972). Effects of concurrent and serial training on generalized vocal imitation in retarded children. *Developmental Psychology, 6,* 293–301.

Chapter
5

Curricular Approaches to Controlling
Severe Behavior Problems

MARK WOLERY AND VINCENT WINTERLING

INTRODUCTION

In this chapter, we describe the role and modification of the curriculum in addressing problem behavior in individuals with developmental disabilities. There are many assumptions on which curricular modifications are based to treat problem behaviors, and we have summarized these in Box 5-1.

A curriculum includes an organized description of a body of content, assessment procedures for selecting goals for instruction, and methods for teaching selected skills. Also, each of these elements should be based on a conceptually consistent foundation (Dunst, 1981). A curriculum should contain a universe of potential content that is identified, defined operationally, and ordered by difficulty. The behaviors and skills that can be taught are identified and put in a logical and/or empirical order for instruction. This content may come from many sources: typical development (Bailey & Wolery, 1989), traditional academic domains (Mercer & Mercer, 1989), demands of the learner's ecology and the next most probable placement (Snell, 1987), and views of family members (Bailey & Wolery, 1989). Each is a legitimate source from which teachable skills can be identified.

The curriculum should include procedures for making a "match" between the potential content and the learner's needs and abilities. From the possible content, specific skills are selected that are valued (defined in various ways) for the learner. This match is usually established through an assessment of the learner's behavior in relation to the potential content (i.e., curriculum-based assessment) (Swanson & Watson, 1989). A number of assessment activities and strategies exist (Browder, 1987), such as interviews (Winton, 1988), direct observation (Cooper, 1981), direct testing (Bailey & Wolery, 1989), ecological inventories (Snell, 1987), and curriculum activity catalogs (Wilcox & Bellamy, 1987). The intent is to select a few behaviors that are important for the learner from a broad array of potential skills.

The curriculum should include instructional methods. The methods may include manipulations of the physical space, the social composition and structure of the environment, the schedule of activities, the materials, and interactions with others. Some of the manipulations are designed to increase the probability that the learner will engage in the targeted behaviors, and others are designed to structure the instructor's behaviors in promoting learning (Wolery, Ault, & Doyle, 1992). The purpose of instructional methods is to ensure that the learner will (1) acquire the important skills and (2) use them when and where they are appropriate.

These elements should be based on a conceptually consistent theoretical foundation (cf. Dunst, 1981). The theoretical model used to identify teachable skills should be the same as, or consistent with, the model used for

<table>
<tr><td>

Box 5-1

</td><td>

ASSUMPTIONS ON WHICH CIRCULAR MODIFICATIONS ARE DEVISED TO TREAT PROBLEM BEHAVIORS

</td></tr>
</table>

1. *Some problem behaviors are more serious than others.*
   Some require no intervention because they are transient and of little social consequence.
   Some are enduring, highly generalized with significant social impact, and worthy of careful intervention.

2. *Few reasons exist for allowing learners with disabilities to behave in ways that interfere with their learning and strengthen their antisocial behaviors.*
   Intervention is required from a competent and responsible team for selected problem behaviors.

3. *Changing the behavior of learners with disabilities should be done for their benefit rather than the expedience of others.*
   Intervention plans should contain a defensible rationale for changing the behavior that articulates the benefits of such change for the learner.

4. *Changing the behavior of learners with disabilities should be implemented with consultation from families and other professionals.*
   Society expects professionals to control problem behaviors in defensible ways. Therefore, decision models (Wolery, Bailey, & Sugai, 1988), assessment protocols (O'Neill, Horner, Albin, Storey, & Sprague, 1990), and intervention guidelines (Green, 1990; Wolery et al., 1988) have emerged. These models and guidelines urge continuing communication with family members and others to increase the likelihood that acceptable interventions will be used.

5. *Behavior, including problem behavior, is lawful but often controlled by multiple factors* (Iwata, Pace, Kalsher, Cowdery, & Cataldo, 1990).
   Assessment is necessary to identify how principles of learning are operating.
   This is a complex endeavor because:
   - The same behavior of two learners may occur for different reasons (Carr & Durand, 1985).
   - A learner may engage in multiple problem behaviors, each of which is controlled by different factors.
   - A problem behavior may be controlled by multiple factors.
   - The same problem behavior may be controlled by different factors in different contexts (Haring & Kennedy, 1990).
   - Two (or more) problem behaviors may be related or may covary; that is, changes in one are related to changes in the other.

6. *Interventions for problem behaviors should be based on the functions they serve* (O'Neill et al., 1990).
   Assessment is necessary to identify the functions. These functions can be divided into two broad categories: obtaining desirable events or avoiding and/or escaping from undesirable events. Each broad function can be divided into two sources: internal (e.g., automatic reinforcement) (Iwata et al., 1990) and external (e.g., to obtain attention or objects). Identifying the function(s) of problem behavior is useful knowledge in changing the existing conditions and in selecting replacement behaviors.

assessment and instruction. More than one model can be used, but the models must be conceptually compatible. For example, a merger of the operant and ecological models is appropriate because both have cultural transmission as their philosophical base. However, a merger of the operant and maturational models is inappropriate because they make incompatible assumptions about learning. A consistent conceptual base results in more coherent and defensible decisions about what is teachable, what to teach, and how to teach.

Operational Curriculum

We can agree on the elements that define *curriculum*, but what actually occurs constitutes the operational curriculum. Our intents about which goals to teach and how to teach them are, in practice, an abstract curriculum that may have little relationship to what actually occurs. The structure of the learner's environment, the responses of the environment to the learner's behavior, and the relationship of the learner to others constitute the actual curriculum.

The logic of the operational curriculum is that learning occurs as a result of interactions with and/or observations of the environment. Some of those interactions and observations are planned purposefully, and we call this *teaching*. Others happen incidentally or occur outside "instructional" times, and we call them *experience*. Both are potentially influential. They may result in learning; stimulus control may be established, transferred, broadened, or narrowed based on those interactions and observations. Some learning is desirable or valued by society, the team, the family, and the learner, and some learning is undesirable or problematic. Teaching and experience may produce desirable or undesirable learning. Thus, in problem situations, it is useful to ask, "What is actually being taught?" This question is different from "What do we want the learner to learn?" It focuses on the actual outcomes of interactions and observations. In this sense, the curriculum is the sum of the learner's exchanges with the environment.

Several implications follow from such a view of curriculum. First, the environment is continually instructing the learner. Existing events that teach the learner to behave in problematic ways must be addressed in intervention plans. If they are not, they may compete with the interventions designed to teach productive response patterns. Second, curricular modifications must extend beyond the times and situations that are usually viewed as instructional. They must focus on events and factors that are influential but are not part of the planned instructional exchanges. Third, our teaching may not have the desired results. An instructional strategy may be used to teach a given skill, but how it is used may actually teach problem responding (Billingsley, White, & Munson, 1980). For example, a team may identify reinforcers for a given learner, but unless those reinforcers are used contingently and appropriately, they are likely to have little influence on performance. The actual consequences will be those that are functional for behavior change. Thus, curricular modifications are manipulations designed to influence interactions and observations that result in learning.

The distinction between what is intended and what actually occurs is important from two perspectives. First, an analysis of what actually occurs will be more instructive in identifying the functions of problem behavior and the contribution of contextual factors to its occurrence. An analysis is needed of what is being learned, the learner's interactions with the environment, the environment's responses to the learner, and the context in which those interactions occur.

Second, an analysis of what is intended but not executed is useful in understanding the team's ability to carry out the intervention plans. Evidence indicating a failure to use the instructional plans or an inconsistent use of the plans is pivotal information in the planning of curricular modifications. If this evidence exists, the reasons staff fail to use plans should be identified because they may influence the implementation of subsequent plans. Staff may fail to use plans because of skill deficits, lack of resources, or lack of motivation. Each reason requires a different approach to eliminating the gap between the planned and the operational curriculum. If staff members do not have adequate skills or information, then training is needed or the plan must be designed within the limits of staff skills. If adequate resources are not available (e.g., staff or material shortages), an allocation of the needed resources may be necessary. If staff motivation is the primary reason the plans are not used, then incentives and/or sanctions may be needed. If the staff members do not have the skills needed for implementation, then provision of resources and incentives is not likely to correct the use problems. Similarly, if lack of resources or motivation is the reason for inadequate use, then providing additional training will probably not address the issue. Thus, the discrepancy, if one exists, between the intended and the operational curriculum and the reasons for that discrepancy deserve careful attention when one is planning curricular interventions for problem behaviors.

The curriculum for learners with disabilities should be viewed broadly. If the goal of education is to increase competence and quality of life, then any relevant skill that accomplishes these ends is appropriate content. Further, any reliable, legal, and ethically defensible means of securing information about what the learner knows or does and needs to know or do should be used to select goals. Finally, instruction should be viewed broadly, so that all relevant variables that influence performance and learning can be changed as needed. The term *curricular interventions* as used here refers to teaching specific types of behavior, efforts to modify the contextual variables related to problem behavior, and the instructional exchanges between teachers and learners.

ROLE OF CURRICULUM IN TREATING PROBLEM BEHAVIORS

The curriculum plays multiple roles in efforts to control problem behaviors. The curriculum can be used (1) as a means of preventing behavior problems, (2) as the context for other interventions, (3) as an adjunctive intervention, and (4) as a primary intervention.

Use of the Curriculum to Prevent Problem Behaviors

The primary purpose of this chapter is to discuss curricular modifications for treating existing problem behaviors, but it also can prevent the occurrence of problem behavior (Dunlap, Johnson, & Robbins, 1990). The experimental verification of preventive effects is a difficult proposition. However, numerous factors are thought to be related to prevention: maintaining a positive classroom climate, establishing a positive rapport with learners, and communicating respect to learners (DeLuke & Knoblock, 1987; Stainback, Stainback, & Froyen, 1987). Four guidelines are suggested for maximizing the curriculum's preventive effects.

First, useful skills should be taught. The usefulness of the skills is individually determined, but some skills may result in the prevention of problem behaviors. The logic is as follows: Given that many behavior problems occur because of deficient repertoires of appropriate responding, one can reasonably assume that increased competencies will provide an individual with opportunities and reinforcers that will reduce substantially the "need" for disruptive behavior patterns. If a person is provided with proficiencies in adaptive life skills and communication, and if these proficiencies are reinforced, problem behaviors used to obtain reinforcers would be redundant and unnecessary (Dunlap et al., 1990, p. 276).

Teaching communication skills appears to provide alternatives to problem behavior (Casey, 1978). It is clear that such skills are effective replacement behaviors for problem behaviors (Durand & Carr, 1987). If those skills had been well established in the learner's repertoire, then the functions they served would be redundant with those served by problem behaviors. If this occurred, then the problem behaviors may not have appeared or may have been less intense, frequent, or generalized. Similarly, many social skills (e.g., sharing, soliciting assistance and attention adaptively, and interacting appropriately) are topographically incompatible and/or functionally redundant with some problem behaviors. Thus, teaching such skills and ensuring that they are functional should be preventive. Teaching students classroom-demeanor skills (e.g., working independently, working in groups, waiting for a turn, and compliance) may also have a preventive function (Strain & Sainato, 1987). Also, problem solving, conflict resolution, and self-management skills may be legitimate targets of curricula designed to prevent problem behaviors (DeLuke & Knoblock, 1987). Teaching persistence in the face of failure may be useful (Fagen & Hill, 1987).

Second, the environment should be structured to promote adaptive rather than maladaptive responding. The physical space should be structured to reduce unnecessary movement, to promote easy traffic flow, and to allow easy visual monitoring by the teacher (Stainback et al., 1987). Further, the social environment should include models of appropriate behavior and may involve having misbehaving learners in close proximity to those who behave appropriately (Stainback et al., 1987). The groupings and activities within the class should focus on cooperative rather than competitive efforts (Stainback et al., 1987).

The schedule of activities should be predictable and contain variations within daily activities (Wolery & Fleming, 1992). Although predictability is important, greater learning appears to occur when tasks are varied rather than constant, and greater attention to tasks may be present in varied conditions (Dunlap & Koegel, 1980). Thus, variety in a predictable schedule seems important. Also, when possible, learners should have choices about how the time is spent, about how the activities are sequenced in the day (Wolery & Fleming, 1992), and about reinforcers (Mason, McGee, Farmer-Dougan, & Risley, 1989). Also, the expectations for learning and acceptable behavior should be stated and defined clearly. Classroom rules are a major means of communicating such expectations. The rules should be stated behaviorally, should be few in number, and should be accompanied by predictable consequences (Strain & Sainato, 1987).

Transitions between activities present multiple occasions for problem responding (DeLuke & Knoblock, 1987). The structure is often less controlled, more movement occurs, and opportunities for negative interactions are increased. Also, teachers are frequently attending to other issues (e.g., gathering materials or preparing for the next activity). Thus, smooth and rapid transitions between activities may prevent problem behaviors (Strain & Sainato, 1987).

Third, effective instructional strategies should be used. Instructional procedures that promote the acquisition of skills and are viewed as meaningful by the learners should be used. These may include strategies that reduce students' errors and increase opportunities for success. Several strategies, such as time delay, graduated guidance, decreasing assistance, and stimulus shaping, appear to meet these requirements (Wolery et al., 1992). The reduction or elimination of errors during instruction appears to result in three positive outcomes: (1) Stimulus control is transferred more quickly from prompts to target stimuli; (2) the student accesses reinforcement on a rich schedule; and (3) the frequent reinforcement leads to positive interactions between teachers and learners. Each of these outcomes may have preventive functions.

Effective strategies should result in increased engagement (McWilliam, 1991). Although engagement can be measured at many levels (McWilliam & Bailey, 1992), it includes active and appropriate interaction with materials, activities, and others in developmentally and contextually appropriate ways. Thus, it is often topographically incompatible with problem behavior and thus has preventive functions. Regular assessment of engagement, nonengagement, and waiting levels should occur. *Waiting* is defined as behaving appropriately but not having the opportunity for engagement (e.g., waiting in line, for a turn, or for materials, activities, or assistance). High levels of waiting (e.g., above 10% to 15% of the time) may indicate that the instructional environment should be adjusted to prevent the occurrence of nonengagement, which often takes the form of problem behavior (Wolery, Bailey, & Sugai, 1988). Many classroom variables, such as the activity schedule, the nature of the activities, staffing patterns, the novelty of the materials, and the timing of interactions, influence the levels of engagement (McWilliam & Bailey, 1992).

Fourth, the curriculum should result in a high ratio of positive to negative interactions. Evidence suggests that teachers generally provide relatively low levels of approval to learners (Heller & White, 1975; Thomas, Presland, Grant, & Glynn, 1978). However, other evidence suggests that the use of specifically identified reinforcers (Dyer, 1987) or the provision of choices about reinforcers before activities (Mason et al., 1989) results in decreases in problem behavior. Also, teachers should respond to the intent of students' interactions and behavior (DeLuke & Knoblock, 1987). The evidence suggests that adult responsiveness and positive development are correlated, at least for young children (Bailey & Wolery, 1992). Further, predictability in interactions is related to less troublesome child behaviors (Wahler & Dumas, 1986).

Problem behaviors appear to become functional as a result of exchanges between the learner and the environment, particularly the social environment (Kozloff, 1995). These exchanges may have a relatively brief history, may result in patterns of responding that lead to enduring problem behaviors, and may be unwittingly engaged in by adults. Some data indicate that the presence of problem behaviors may result in adults' avoiding teaching interactions with students (Carr, Taylor, & Robinson, 1991). Thus, the prevention of problem behavior requires reducing the occurrence of negative interactions, attending to the actual outcomes of each interaction, and monitoring interactions to note the occurrence of negative response patterns.

Thus, one role of the curriculum is to prevent problem behavior. This is accomplished by teaching useful skills, structuring the environment to promote adaptive response patterns, using effective strategies, and engaging in frequent, predictable, and positive interactions with the learner. Another role of the curriculum is to serve as the context for other interventions.

Use of the Curriculum as the Context for Other Interventions

In most instances, efforts to control problem behaviors often occur simultaneously with efforts to address instructional goals. Guidelines for the use of behavior control strategies often state that the procedures, when used, should be implemented concomitantly with attempts to promote adaptive responding (Green, 1990; Wolery et al., 1988). As a result, interventions for problem behaviors must take into consideration the nature of the existing curriculum (i.e., the operational curriculum). At the most basic level, the operational curriculum must be analyzed to ensure that it does not contain practices that will compete with the intervention (i.e., Does the curriculum contain variables that set the occasion for the problem behavior or support its occurrence?). If such variables exist, they should be corrected in the intervention plan.

Also, the team must determine which interventions are possible within the existing curriculum and what effects such implementation may have on other curricular demands. When an intervention is likely to interfere with staff members' ability to implement their instructional responsibilities, decisions must be made about how the intervention and instructional goals can be completed. Planning must also address the roles and responsibilities of different staff members. Finally, the increased monitoring requirements should be analyzed (Cooper, Heron, & Heward, 1987). The effects of intervention in all needed environments, the consistency of implementation, the occurrence of positive and negative side effects, the responses of the environment to the intervention, and its impact on other instructional activities must be monitored. Given the usual demands of most programs, the additional monitoring, though necessary, may present challenges. If the demands already placed on staff members are not considered, the reliability and validity of the monitoring system for the intervention is suspect.

Use of the Curriculum as an Adjunct to Other Interventions

As an adjunctive treatment, curricular modifications can be used to (1) minimize the possibility that curricular variables will set the occasion for problem behavior and (2) support adaptive responding and replacement behaviors.

The operational curriculum, as noted above, may contain variables that, while not controlling the problem behavior, set the occasion for its display or support it in other ways. The presence of these variables may make it more likely that the problem behavior will occur and may increase the probability that the intervention will fail. To prevent these outcomes, such curricular variables should be identified in the assessment activities and should be changed during intervention.

Another adjunctive role of the curriculum is to support adaptive responding and replacement behaviors. Programs intended to reduce problem behaviors should be accompanied by attempts to promote adaptive replacement behaviors (Lennox & Miltenberger, 1990). In fact, this strategy has been used as a primary intervention (Carr, 1988; Horner & Budd, 1985) and in conjunction with other treatment procedures. In much of the research evaluating aversive procedures, reinforcement for adaptive behavior was systematically included (Wolery et al., 1988). The intent of such programming is to transfer stimulus control from the problem behavior to the replacement behavior.

Use of the Curriculum as a Primary Intervention

Procedures for transferring stimulus control from the problem response to the replacement behavior may be the primary means of controlling the problem behavior. Also, a number of other curricular variables may serve as the primary intervention: changes in setting variables, such as manipulations in the physical space and related variables (e.g., noise levels, temperature, and lighting); materials; proximity to the teacher and peers; and the schedule of events and activities. Other variables are related more directly to changes in the instructional exchanges, including the demands placed on the learner, reinforcers and schedules of reinforcement, and instructional strategies. In these manipulations, the intervention should be based on an assessment of the contexts in which the problem behavior occurs and the relationships between those variables and its occurrence.

CURRICULAR INTERVENTIONS

Various curricular interventions are presented as potential options. The idiosyncratic nature of problem behavior means that assessment information should be used to design curricular modifications. Three categories of interventions are described: modifying the behaviors to be taught, manipulating contextual variables, and adjusting instructional exchanges. Research is cited to illustrate the various modifications rather than as a comprehensive review.

Modifying the Behaviors to Be Taught

Some curricular modifications focus on what is taught. These include teaching replacement behaviors, promoting adaptive and alternative response patterns, and teaching self-management skills. These modifications can be used as primary or adjunctive interventions.

Use of Replacement Behaviors

Teaching replacement behaviors to deal with problem responding is based on three assumptions: (1) The problem behavior fulfills some function (i.e., is maintained by its effect); (2) the replacement behavior can serve the same function (i.e., be functionally equivalent); and (3) the replacement behavior will compete favorably with the problem behavior in producing the effect (Horner, Sprague, O'Brien, & Heathfield, 1990).

The team must address at least three issues when selecting replacement behaviors and using curricular modifications to promote their occurrence. First, the function of the problem behavior must be identified. This is accomplished through assessment (e.g., Doss & Reichle, 1989; O'Neill, Horner, Albin, Storey, & Sprague, 1990; Wacker et al., 1990a).

Second, the team must select a replacement behavior. The replacement behavior must fulfill the same function (i.e., cause the same effect) as the problem behavior and must be usable in all contexts in which the problem behavior occurs (Horner & Billingsley, 1988). Also, people in the learner's environment (family members and service providers) must view it as an acceptable alternative to the problem behavior (Durand & Kishi, 1987). These persons should respond to the replacement behaviors as though they fulfilled the same function as the problem behavior. In some cases, learners may not use the replacement behavior in situations where the problem behavior occurs. In other cases, learners may use the replacement behavior, but it is not responded to by caregivers as fulfilling the same function. In either case, the caregivers must respond to the replacement behavior so that it will compete favorably with the problem behavior.

Also, the response efficiency of replacement behaviors should be analyzed. Response efficiency includes "(a) the physical effort (calories of energy) a response requires, (b) the schedule of reinforcement it receives, and (c) the latency between the presentation of a discriminative stimulus and obtaining the reinforcer" (Horner et al., 1990, p. 91). Ideally, the replacement behavior will require less effort than the problem behavior, access the same reinforcers on a similar or richer schedule, and result in a shorter latency between the stimuli that signaled the occurrence of the behavior and the receipt of reinforcement. Recent experimental analyses indicate that these dimensions are important. Specifically, problem behavior was less frequent when the replacement behavior required less rather than more effort, when the schedule of reinforcement was continuous as compared to intermittent, and when the latency between discriminative stimuli and reinforcement was short rather than long (Horner & Day, 1991).

Third, the team must design a "curriculum" that teaches the replacement behavior. How this is done depends, in large part, on the extent to which the replacement behavior already occurs and the conditions under which it occurs. These conditions are the antecedents (i.e., discriminative stimuli that cue the learner to perform the problem and replacement behaviors) and the consequences (i.e., reinforcers for the problem and replacement behaviors). Horner, O'Neill, and Flannery (1993) use the "competing behavior model" (Horner & Billingsley, 1988) to devise a curriculum based on the conditions in which the problem and potential replacement behaviors occur. They argue that the problem behavior and the potential replacement behavior may have (1) the same antecedents and the same consequences, (2) different antecedents and the same consequences, (3) the same antecedents and different consequences, or (4) different discriminative stimuli and different consequences. Based on an analysis of the antecedents and consequences of the problem and potential replacement behaviors, differential recommendations are made for intervention. Horner et al. (1993) describe considerations that should be made in developing such interventions. These are described in Box 5-2.

When the replacement behavior is not in the learner's repertoire, the curriculum must involve other strategies, including prompting, fading of prompts, and reinforcement. To ensure that the replacement behaviors serve the same function as the problem behaviors, they must come under the control of the stimuli that set the occasion for the problem response. This involves identifying the stimuli and using instruction to ensure that they will acquire control of the replacement behaviors.

Several studies have focused on "functional communication training," which is an attempt to teach learners communicative responses that fulfill the same function and are performed more efficiently than the problem behaviors. For example, if the problem behavior appears to serve the function of escaping from tasks, then the learners are taught to request assistance (Carr & Durand, 1985; Durand & Carr, 1987) or to request breaks from the task (Durand & Kishi, 1987; Horner & Day, 1991). If the problem behavior results in adult attention, then appropriate communicative means of securing attention are taught (Carr & Durand, 1985; Durand & Carr, 1991). If the problem behavior results in tangible reinforcers, then appropriate requesting behaviors are taught (Durand & Kishi, 1987; Horner & Budd, 1985). These replacement behaviors may be verbal (Carr & Durand, 1985), signed (Northup et al., 1991), or may be messages on alternative communication systems such as

> **Box 5-2**
>
> ## ISSUES TO CONSIDER IN USING REPLACEMENT BEHAVIORS
>
> 1. Identify when and under what conditions the learner performs potential replacement behaviors.
>   - If a potential replacement behavior is performed fluently and in conditions similar to the performance of the problem behavior, then it is a good candidate as a replacement behavior.
>   - If a potential replacement behavior is not performed fluently, then effective teaching strategies should be used to establish fluent performance.
> 2. Determine whether potential replacement and problem behaviors have similar antecedent stimuli.
>   - If the potential replacement and problem behaviors have different antecedent stimuli, then attempts should be made to remove the discriminative stimuli for the problem behavior.
>   - If the potential replacement and problem behaviors have the same antecedent stimuli, then prompts and supports should be added to promote the occurrence of the replacement behavior.
> 3. Determine whether potential replacement and problem behaviors have similar consequent event (i.e., reinforcers).
>   - If the consequent events are the same, ensure that the replacement behavior will be more efficient.
>   - If the consequent events are different, ensure that the reinforcers for the replacement behavior will be more powerful and/or will decrease the value of the reinforcer for the problem behavior.
>   - If the consequent events are different, use another replacement behavior that will access the same reinforcers.
> 4. Determine the role and impact of the setting events on potential replacement and problem behaviors.
>   - Develop a system for evaluating the effects of the setting events.
>   - Develop a plan for dealing with the effects of the setting events.

electronic devices (Horner et al., 1990). More efficient replacement behaviors appear to produce greater problem behavior reduction than less efficient replacement behaviors (e.g., pressing one key, compared to typing in a word or sentence) (Horner & Day, 1991). These replacement behaviors are thought to promote long-term maintenance and generalization, and some data appear to support this contention (Durand & Carr, 1991). Functional communication training has been used with a variety of responses, such as disruptive (Durand & Carr, 1991), stereotypical (Durand & Carr, 1987), and aggressive and self-injurious behaviors (Horner & Day, 1991; Wacker et al., 1990b). Other research has focused on teaching communicative responses for inappropriate verbal behaviors (e.g., echolalia). For example, the cues-pause-point training procedure has been used successfully to teach a variety of individuals to respond to trained and novel questions and to decrease the occurrence of echolalic behavior (e.g., Foxx, Faw, McMorrow, Kyle, & Bittle, 1988; McMorrow & Foxx, 1986).

Adaptive and Alternative Response Patterns

Some research has focused on teaching adaptive skills and has assessed the effects on problem behaviors. For example, Mace and Lalli (1991) evaluated two treatments (i.e., noncontingent attention and verbal prompts to initiate and maintain conversations) for the bizarre speech of a group home resident. Both treatments were effective, but the second was more useful because it provided the client with regular attention and promoted adaptive speech. Other studies have documented that specially designed "books" and prompts to be communicative produced increases in conversational skills and decreases in problem interactions (Hunt, Alwell, & Goetz, 1988; Hunt, Alwell, Goetz, & Sailor, 1990). Similarly, teaching learners problem-solving skills may lead to increases in adaptive interactional skills and decreases in problem behaviors (Park & Gaylord-Ross, 1989).

Other studies have focused on the effect of the availability of toys and instruction for play on problem behaviors. From these studies, it is apparent that: (1) for subjects who readily play, the presence of toys seems to be inversely related to the amount of stereotypical behavior (Greer, Becker, Saxe, & Mirabella, 1985); (2) for subjects who do not readily play, prompts and reinforcement to increase play decrease the frequency of stereotypical responding and inappropriate play (Greer et al., 1985; Singh & Millichamp, 1987; (3) increases in purposeful activity (e.g., manipulating materials) may decrease problem behaviors (Spangler & Marshall, 1983); (4) prompts to establish toy play can be used to increase social play, while maintaining suppressed levels of stereotypical responding and inappropriate play (Singh & Millichamp, 1987); (5) instruction in social play appears to generalize to persons who were not involved in the original training (Singh & Millichamp, 1987); (6) teaching sharing decreases aggression and taking others' materials without permission (Bryant & Budd, 1984); (7) organized games on playgrounds reduce inappropriate behaviors (Murphy, Hutchison, & Bailey, 1983); and (8) increasing children's interactions through affection training decreases social isolation during free play (McEvoy et al., 1988). However, for some subjects, increases in play may result in decreases, but not the elimination, of problem behaviors (Greer et al., 1985; Spangler & Marshall, 1983). Thus, active engagement may produce the desired decreases in problem behaviors.

A number of studies have shown that exercise regimes are related to reductions in the frequency of problem behaviors when measured later in the day (e.g., Bachman & Fuqua, 1983; Bachman & Sluyter, 1988). Although the reasons for these effects are not known, these findings, coupled with the positive health outcomes of exercise, suggest that this is a viable curricular modification (cf. Coleman & Whitman, 1984; Halle, Gabler-Halle, & Bemben, 1989).

Self-Management Skills

Some research focuses on teaching learners with disabilities to manage their own behavior. This involves teaching them to apply some process of behavioral control to their own behavior (Baer, 1984; Fowler, 1984). Self-management often includes one or more of the following components: (1) self-monitoring—recognizing that the behavior in question has occurred and then recording it in some manner; (2) self-evaluation or assessment—making a judgment (based on monitoring) as to whether a set criterion was achieved; (3) self-reinforcement—selecting and/or delivering reinforcers to oneself, usually at the person's discretion, which may or may not be when a specific level of behavior has occurred; and (4) self-instruction—using and fading verbalizations to direct and control one's own behavior.

Reviews of self-management (Browder & Shapiro, 1985; Hughes, Korinek, & Gorman, 1991), show several findings. First, self-management strategies have been taught to learners with a variety of disabilities from a broad age range. Second, these strategies have been used to teach adaptive skills and to reduce problem behaviors (Cooper et al., 1987). Third, self-management strategies can be used alone and with other treatments (Wolery et al., 1988). Fourth, these procedures can be used to promote maintenance and generalization to nontraining settings (Koegel & Koegel, 1990). However, in some cases, they may need to be supplemented with strategies such as recruiting feedback (Mank & Horner, 1987). Fifth, these strategies may be effective in some cases but less effective in others (Bornstein, 1985). Sixth, although procedures for using self-instruction strategies are described in many sources (Cooper et al., 1987; Wolery et al., 1988) and are considered relatively efficient (Fowler, 1984), much remains to be learned about their application to behavior problems and their effects on generalized self-control (Baer, 1984). Yet these strategies appear to be a viable curricular modification.

Summary

A major curricular modification focuses on what to teach, including teaching replacement responses for problem behaviors, promoting adaptive and alternative response patterns, and teaching self-management strategies. Because of the efficacy of these strategies, most intervention plans for reducing the occurrence of problem behavior should include these procedures. In many cases, they are sufficient alone; in other cases, they are valuable adjuncts to other treatments.

Manipulating Contextual Variables

Contextual variables are social and nonsocial factors that may be associated with the frequency of problem behavior. When they are related to the occurrence of problem behaviors, they should be removed, if possible. Similarly, when they are related to the nonoccurrence of a problem behavior, they should be present in intervention plans. Contextual variables may be idiosyncratic for each learner, and the function of problem behaviors may vary depending on the context (Haring & Kennedy, 1990). Thus, assessment is necessary. Variables related to problem behavior in some subjects are relevant because they provide information about which stimuli to assess for other subjects.

Nonsocial Variables

A number of distal and proximal setting events may be related to the occurrence of problem behavior (Wahler & Fox, 1981). For example, the annoying and deviant behavior of young boys occurred more in the afternoon (e.g., 3:30–5:00) than in the evening (e.g., 6:30–8:00), later rather than earlier in the week, and on days without precipitation. However, no statistically significant relationships to lunar phase or temperature were noted (Russell & Bernal, 1977). Other studies have noted increases in peer conflicts when children play in hot, unshaded areas as compared to cool, shaded areas (e.g., Body, 1955). In addition, crowded space has been related to increases in aggression (e.g., McAfee, 1987). However, such findings appear to interact with the number and types of toys available and with the existing classroom management system (Sainato & Carta, 1992). Similarly, the presence of an "enriched" environment (i.e., the addition of materials) produced increases in appropriate object manipulation and decreases in problem behaviors. These effects were also enhanced through differential reinforcement for appropriate behavior (Horner, 1980). High ambient noise levels appear to be related to increases in inappropriate activity levels (Whalen, Henker, Collins, Finck, & Dotemoto, 1979). Within classrooms, the frequencies of problem behaviors appear to vary depending on the activity and/or the setting (Charlop, Schreibman, Mason, & Vesey, 1983). These findings need qualification. First, they may be idiosyncratic for settings and learners. Thus, assessment of their effects is necessary. When the assessment information indicates a strong relationship, then manipulation of these variables is reasonable and indicated. Second, such variables may not eliminate problem behaviors but may decrease the likelihood of their occurrence. Thus, their manipulation should be supplemented with attempts to teach replacement behaviors and to promote incompatible adaptive responding. Third, some of these variables (e.g., time of day and precipitation) are not in the educator's control. Thus, their relationship to the problem behavior may signal the need for additional preventive efforts.

Teacher Interaction, Proximity, and Presence

Several studies have noted that more rather than less or no interaction with staff members results in decreases in self-injurious behavior (Burke, Burke, & Forehand, 1985), pica (Mace & Knight, 1986), and stereotypical behavior, particularly during teaching episodes (Wetzel, Taylor, & Lachowicz, 1991). Other studies show that these effects are complex. For example, Brusca, Nieminen, Carter, and Repp (1989) found the frequency of stereotypical behavior lower when staff interacted with students; however, the effects of particular types of activities were specific to individual students (i.e., some types of activities were related to decreases in stereotypical behavior in certain students, but not others). Further, the presence of certified teachers rather than teaching assistants was related to decreases in stereotypical behavior. Marholin and Steinman (1977) found that more disruptive behavior occurred when the teacher was absent from the room, but that reinforcement for accurate performance resulted in less disruptive behavior than reinforcement for on-task behavior. These conditional effects are supported by research indicating that eye contact differentially affects the likelihood of compliance (Hamlet, Axelrod, & Kuerschner, 1984), and that reprimands provided when the adult is near to (e.g., 1 meter away) rather than far from (e.g., 7 meters away) the child are more likely to be effective (Van Houten, Nau, MacKenzie-Keating, Sameoto, & Colaveechia, 1982). These and other studies indicate that professionals should interact positively and frequently with learners who have disabilities, and that assessment activities should address the effects of interaction patterns. As Brusca el al. (1989) indicate, manipulating interactions is a positive means of dealing with problem behavior.

Activities and Choices

The nature and scheduling of activities are important contextual variables (cf. Brown, 1991). As noted, varied as opposed to constant activities appear to result in greater learning and more attention to task (Dunlap, 1984; Dunlap & Koegel, 1980). Winterling, Dunlap, and O'Neill (1987) replicated this earlier research and found that (1) more rapid acquisition of target skills occurred in the varied task condition, and (2) the frequency of problem behavior decreased in the varied task condition.

Wong et al. (1987) evaluated the effects of specific types of activities by comparing an unstructured leisure time with individually selected activities based on learners' preferences. Problem behavior occurred less frequently when learners were allowed to engage in individually selected, compared to free-choice, leisure activities. In a series of studies, Koegel, Dyer, and Bell (1987) evaluated the effects of children's preferences for types of activities on their social avoidance and responsiveness. Less social avoidance occurred when adults prompted engagement in child-preferred, compared to non-preferred, activities, and when the prompts were removed, high levels of interaction were maintained without social avoidance. Dyer, Dunlap, and Winterling (1990) evaluated the effects of learners' overt choices on problem behavior by providing learners with choices of tasks and reinforcers. Having choices of tasks and reinforcers produced less problem behavior than did a condition in which no choices were provided. Interestingly, the amount of correct responding did not differ across conditions.

These studies appear to indicate that the nature of the activities, the learners' preferences, and the choices may differentially affect the occurrence of problem behaviors. Other studies have noted that opportunities to engage in preferred activities or having choices about activities resulted in increased attention to tasks (Parsons, Reid, Reynolds, & Bumgarner, 1990), and that staff can be trained to provide learners with more choices (Parsons & Reid, 1990). For a discussion of the rationale for allowing choices and of related issues, see Bannerman, Sheldon, Sherman, and Harchik (1990), Guess, Benson, and Siegel-Causey (1985), and Shevin and Klein (1984).

Social Role of Learners

Clearly, peers can be effective models during small-group instruction, for appropriate social behavior, and for other important skills (Greer, Dorow, Williams, McCorkle, & Asnes, 1991). However, other manipulations of social roles are of potential value. Sainato, Maheady, and Shook (1986) assigned the role of classroom "manager" to young children who were socially withdrawn. As a manager, the child assisted in feeding the classroom pet, collecting lunch money, and other "jobs." Acting as a manager resulted in increases in positive social interactions initiated by peers and the target child. Although negative behavior occurred at low levels before the intervention, it is a viable strategy for dealing with social isolation and perhaps other interactive problems. In a series of studies, Fowler and her colleagues evaluated the effects of peer monitoring of interactive difficulties. In general, these studies indicate that token systems initially used by adults can be implemented by peers or the target child without a loss of effectiveness (Dougherty, Fowler, & Paine, 1985; Smith

& Fowler, 1984). Also, with training, peers effectively implemented the system without prior experience of observing adults use it (Smith & Fowler, 1984). When children who displayed negative interactive behavior served as monitors of their peers, there was a decrease in the frequency of their own problem behaviors (Fowler, Dougherty, Kirby, & Kohler, 1986). Comparisons of the two roles (i.e., monitor or earner) produced equal decreases in problem behavior when used with a group contingency system (Stern, Fowler, & Kohler, 1988).

Thus, the manipulation of learners' roles in group settings may result in increases in positive social interactions and decreases in social withdrawal, negative interactions, and disruptive behaviors. Although these studies typically occurred in the context of ongoing management systems, they discuss positive manipulations of the social context that appear defensible and appropriate. Several sources provide information on the role of peers in changing learners' prosocial behavior (Kohler & Strain, 1990; Odom, McConnell, & McEvoy, 1992).

Summary

Clearly, some social and nonsocial contextual variables appear to be related to the frequency of problem behaviors. In many cases, the effects of these variables are idiosyncratic for learners and contexts; thus, assessment is appropriate. When possible, these variables should be manipulated during interventions for problem behavior. In some cases, the manipulation of these variables results in solutions to the problem situation; in others, they are likely to produce reductions but may need to be supplemented with other interventions, such as teaching replacement behaviors and differential reinforcement.

Adjusting Instructional Exchanges

Several teaching practices are associated with positive outcomes for learners: managing instructional time, managing behavior, presenting instruction, monitoring students' performance, and providing feedback to students (Stevens & Rosenshine, 1981; Wolery et al., 1992). Implications for the control of problem behaviors are described below.

Managing Instructional Time

Agreement exists that instructional time should be filled with meaningful tasks. These require specifying curricular objectives (Bailey & Wolery, 1989), teaching useful skills (Dunlap et al., 1990), promoting learners' engagement

(McWilliam, 1991), ensuring smooth transitions (Strain & Sainato, 1987), engaging in creative scheduling (Brown, 1991), structuring the environment to support adaptive rather than problem responding (Stainback et al., 1987), ensuring frequent teacher-child interactions (Brusca et al., 1989), and attending to learners' preferences and providing choices about activities and reinforcers (Dyer et al., 1990). These curricular manipulations serve primarily preventive functions. However, if the assessment information indicates that the instructional context is not characterized by these features, then they should be put in place before other intervention efforts are devised.

Managing Student Behavior

The focus of this chapter is this function, but emphasis in the effective teaching literature is on stating expectations and rules clearly and preventing the occurrence of problem behavior through vigilant surveillance and rapid responding to the precursors of problem episodes.

Presenting Instructional Stimuli

Variables related to presenting instruction include teaching tasks that match the learners' current abilities, reviewing previously acquired skills, presenting tasks clearly, and providing instruction at an appropriately brisk pace (Wolery et al., 1992). Each of these variables may be related to the frequency of problem behaviors. For example, numerous studies document that difficult tasks (i.e., those that may not match the learners' abilities) are related to increases in problem behaviors (e.g., Carr & Durand, 1985). Similarly, slow instructional presentation appears to be related to decreases in attention-to-task behaviors, while more rapid presentation results in better learning and greater attention (e.g., Carnine, 1976). Further, these variables may interact to influence the frequency of behavior. For example, Gaylord-Ross, Weeks, and Lipner (1980) found that the frequency of self-injurious behavior appeared to interact with the nature of the task and with the frequency with which adults provided commands. Manipulating the frequency of commands was related to the occurrence of self-injury in some tasks.

When task difficulty is related to the occurrence of problem behaviors, the use of errorless learning procedures (i.e., stimulus modification strategies; cf. Wolery et al., 1992) may produce decreases in errors and problem behaviors for some but not all students (Weeks & Gaylord-Ross, 1981). Iwata, Pace, Kalsher, Cowdery, and Cataldo (1990) noted that some learners' self-injurious behaviors were maintained by escape from tasks (i.e., were negatively reinforced). For this reason, these authors initiated a procedure that involved

physically prompting learners when problem behaviors occurred; this procedure was an extinction procedure (i.e., the self-injurious behaviors no longer
produced escape). It was effective in establishing increased compliance with
task directions and with reductions in the problem behaviors. This study was
not designed to evaluate the use of response-prompting procedures (cf.
Wolery et al., 1992). However, analysis of such procedures is appropriate. For
example, one learner in a study by Steege, Wacker, Berg, Cigrand, and Cooper
(1989) showed high levels of self-injury in solitary conditions (i.e., when toi-
leting and when positioned in a standing box), but not during instruction in
which prompting and reinforcement were used. For another subject, the use
of prompts was not effective until specifically identified reinforcers were used
(Steege et al., 1989).

A comprehensive investigation of curricular modifications was conducted
by Dunlap, Kern-Dunlap, Clarke, and Robbins (1991). Based on an assessment,
they concluded that the student was better behaved under certain conditions.
From the assessment results, a set of guidelines for structuring the student's day
were generated. These guidelines (and consultation with the research staff on
their use) were used. The data indicate that on-task behavior and appropriate
social behavior increased with the implementation of the curricular modifications, and that disruptive behavior and inappropriate vocalizations decreased.
This study serves as a model for (1) conducting assessments in an educational
setting, (2) devising multicomponent curricular modifications based on assessment results, and (3) monitoring the effects of those manipulations.

Monitoring Students' Performance

Frequent monitoring of performance is conducted to (1) identify learners
who are not making adequate progress and (2) provide information for making decisions about adjusting instruction (Bailey & Wolery, 1992). Several
applications exist for controlling problem behavior. First, if students are in
programs in which they are not making progress and are receiving lean schedules of reinforcement, many of them will engage in problem behavior.
Frequent monitoring will identify such programs and will allow decisions to
be made to revise them. Second, monitoring performance may serve as a
check on the adequacy of the assessment activities. When the assessment
information is incorrect (i.e., the identified skills are too easy or too difficult
to learn), the likelihood of inattention and inappropriate behaviors is
increased. Thus, frequent monitoring can identify problems in instructional
programs that may lead to problem behavior. Third, the frequent monitoring
of curricular outcomes in all relevant contexts provides information on the
effectiveness of the interventions in changing problem behaviors (e.g., the

extent to which replacement behaviors are competing favorably with the problem behaviors).

Providing Feedback to Students

The term *feedback,* as used in the effective teaching literature, refers to a number of strategies, such as providing information on results, reinforcing correct performance, and correcting errors. Although the use of reinforcement is often not viewed as a curricular modification, the selection and use of reinforcers are central to the instructional process. Thus, reinforcement deserves consideration as a curricular modification for problem behaviors.

The contingent use of reinforcers produces greater learning than not using reinforcers or not using them contingently (Cooper et al., 1987). Of interest is whether the reinforcement of correct performance decreases problem behaviors. Four findings are apparent: (1) For some students, reinforcement of correct performance with common reinforcers results in decreases in problem behavior (Dyer, 1987); (2) for other students, reinforcement for correct performance does not produce decreases in problem behavior unless the reinforcers are specially and individually selected (Dyer, 1987; Steege et al., 1989); (3) allowing children to choose a reinforcer before an activity decreases problem behavior (Mason et al., 1989); and (4) using varied reinforcers appears to increase acquisition and decrease off-task behavior (Egel, 1981). Thus, correct responses should result in reinforcement with individually selected reinforcers.

Learners' preferences for stimuli have been assessed by presenting a number of stimuli and noting the learners' responses. *Preference* is defined as movement toward a stimulus within a given number of seconds after presentation (Pace, Ivancic, Edwards, Iwata, & Page, 1985). Preference stimuli appear to function as reinforcers when they are used contingently (Pace et al., 1985). Further, stimuli that learners prefer are more powerful reinforcers than stimuli that they do not prefer (Green, Reid, Canipe, & Gardner, 1991). Testing learners' preferences systematically appears to be a better means of identifying reinforcers than asking caregivers to identify stimuli they think will be reinforcers (Green et al., 1988). For some learners, these preferences appear to last over time (Green et al., 1991). For students who have severe physical limitations, microswitches have been used to identify preferred stimuli (Leatherby, Gast, Wolery, & Collins, 1992). For some students, the stimuli that are preferred are sensory stimuli (e.g., vibration, particular textures of stimuli, and auditory and vestibular stimuli) (Mason et al., 1989). The power of such sensory stimuli appears to be comparable to that of more traditional stimuli (e.g., food and praise) (Ferrari & Harris, 1981). Thus, assessment identifies learners' preferences for stimuli that will function as reinforcers.

Reinforcers may also be identified through applications of the Premack principle; that is, learners' high-probability behaviors are used as reinforcers or as a basis for devising reinforcers. Wolery (1978) noted learners' stereotypical behavior and devised reinforcers that appeared to provide similar sensory input. Such stimuli functioned as powerful reinforcers. Hung (1978) provided learners with tokens for adaptive behavior and allowed the learners to exchange the tokens for opportunities to engage in stereotypical behavior. The result was increases in adaptive behavior. Sugai and White (1986) allowed a student to maintain contact with an object used during stereotypical behavior only when adaptive behavior was displayed. The object was removed when the student engaged in stereotypical or off-task behavior. Again, the result was increases in adaptive behavior. Wolery, Kirk, and Gast (1985) allowed students to engage in stereotypical behavior contingent on correct responses, and they measured the amount of stereotypical behavior during sessions before and after instruction. The stereotypical behavior functioned as a reinforcer, and no increase in the stereotypical behavior occurred.

Foxx, McMorrow, Fenlon, and Bittle (1986) reinforced a learner with opportunities to engage in the stereotypical manipulation of rice, contingent on specific and gradually increasing durations of not engaging in genital stimulation. Also, they reinforced the stereotypical rice play with edibles, and later, they withheld the edibles to produce extinction of the stereotypical rice play. The genital stimulation was substantially reduced, but withdrawal of the edibles did not produce extinction of the stereotypical rice play. In a series of experiments, Charlop, Kurtz, and Casey (1990) compared conditions: (1) contingent opportunities to engage in aberrant behavior (e.g., stereotypical behavior and echolalia); (2) contingent access to edibles; and (3) varied, which involved contingent access to food and aberrant behavior. In general, contingent opportunities to engage in problem behavior functioned as more powerful reinforcers than edibles, and no increases in the aberrant behavior were found. In a slightly different approach, Durand, Crimmins, Caulfield, and Taylor (1989) identified the factors (i.e., social attention or escape from tasks) that appeared to maintain learners' problem behaviors (e.g., aggression, self-injury, and tantrums). They then used this information to devise reinforcers for correct task performance; praise and/or brief periods of escape from tasks were used as consequences. The results indicated that: (1) for learners whose aberrant behaviors were maintained by social attention, praise (but not escape from tasks) produced increases in correct performance; (2) for learners whose problem behaviors were maintained by escape from tasks, escape (but not praise) produced increases in correct performance; (3) for some students whose problem behaviors were maintained by social attention, access to praise for correct performance resulted in decreases in problem behaviors; and (4) for some students whose problem behaviors were maintained by escape, access to escape for correct performance produced decreases in the problem behaviors.

Regardless of the reinforcer used or the manner in which it is identified, numerous applications of reinforcement have been employed to treat problem behaviors. Although a review of such procedures is beyond the scope of this chapter, several deserve mention. Differential reinforcement of other behavior, of low rates of behavior, and of incompatible behavior has been applied to several problem behaviors (O'Brien & Repp, 1990). Other applications include playing the "good behavior game" (e.g., Fishbein & Wasik, 1981), establishing token economies (Kazdin, 1982), contingency contracting (Kelly & Stokes, 1982), using correspondence training (Baer, 1990), delaying reinforcement to promote generalization (Dunlap, Koegel, Johnson, & O'Neill, 1987), thinning the reinforcement schedule and using postsession contingencies to promote responding in unsupervised settings (Dunlap, Plienis, & Williams, 1987), teaching children to recruit reinforcement and feedback (Stokes, Fowler, & Baer, 1978), and using daily reports to parents and contingent access to reinforcers at home to produce improvements in behavior at school (Schumaker, Hovell, & Sherman, 1977).

Some attention has been focused on exactly which behaviors are reinforced. Specifically, contingent reinforcement of compliance appears to be related to decreases in other problem behaviors. However, this effect on various problem behaviors appears idiosyncratic for each learner (Cataldo, Ward, Russo, Riordan, & Bennett, 1986). A similar application has been called *behavioral momentum,* which involves reinforcing learners for complying with a series of rapidly presented requests with which compliance is likely and then immediately presenting a request that is likely to result in noncompliance. Such arrangements increase compliance (Mace et al., 1988; Singer, Singer, & Horner, 1987). This strategy has also been used to reduce disruptive stereotypical behavior that appeared to be maintained by escape from task demands (Mace & Belfiore, 1990). A variation of this procedure includes reinforcing the series of requests before an instructional session and interspersing such requests throughout instructional sessions that were likely to result in problem behaviors (Horner, Day, Sprague, O'Brien, & Heathfield, 1991). This procedure resulted in decreases in aggression and self-injury during instruction.

Other researchers have evaluated the use of negative reinforcement in instructional and behavior control programs. Foxx (1984) compared the effect of positive reinforcement and the effect of positive and negative reinforcement on learners' discrimination learning. The positive reinforcers in both conditions were praise and edibles; the negative reinforcement was hand-over-hand guidance contingent on no response within two seconds of the instructor's task direction. The positive plus negative reinforcement increased learners' correct compliance with task commands. Hughes, Wolery, and Neel (1983) used verbal "nags" contingent on off-task behaviors and produced increases in task performance and decreases in off-task behaviors. Steege et al. (1990) also used negative reinforcement to treat self-injurious behavior that appeared to produce escape from task demands. As a treatment, students were taught to activate a microswitch that signaled "stop." This produced a brief escape from the task and resulted in a decrease in the frequency of self-injury. For a complete discussion of negative reinforcement, see Iwata (1987).

Summary

In terms of instructional exchanges, several curricular modifications are possible. These include the appropriate management of instructional time, the manner in which instructional strategies are used, the continuous monitoring of learners' performance, and the provision of feedback on learners' performance. These modifications (except for monitoring) appear to be viable primary and secondary interventions that address learners' behavior problems.

CONCLUSIONS

Curricular modifications are a primary component of state-of-the-art practices in dealing with problem behavior. Two definitions of the curriculum were presented. One definition includes the usual notion of curriculum; that is, specifying and ordering all teachable behaviors, using assessment to identify which behaviors to teach, employing instructional methods to promote the acquisition and use of skills, and ensuring that these three elements are grounded in compatible conceptual systems. The second definition focuses on an analysis of what actually occurs with the learner. Four roles of the curriculum in designing intervention plans for problem behavior were described: using the curriculum (1) as prevention, (2) as the context for other interventions, (3) as an adjunctive intervention, and (4) as the primary intervention.

This chapter has also described specific curricular modifications that can be used to deal with problem behaviors, and it cited illustrative literature to support their use. These modifications include teaching replacement behaviors, promoting adaptive responding that is incompatible with problem behavior, and teaching self-management behaviors. Also, contextual variables can be manipulated: nonsocial variables, teacher interaction variables, providing choices of curricular activities, and using specialized roles for learners. Finally, the chapter has described manipulations of the major teaching functions, such as managing instructional time, presenting instructional strategies, and providing feedback to learners.

REFERENCES

Bachman, J. E., & Fuqua, R. W. (1983). Management of inappropriate behaviors of trainable mentally impaired students using antecedent exercise. *Journal of Applied Behavior Analysis, 16,* 477–484.

Bachman, J. E., & Sluyter, D. (1988). Reducing inappropriate behaviors of developmentally disabled adults using antecedent aerobic dance exercises. *Research in Developmental Disabilities, 2,* 73–83.

Baer, D. M. (1984). Does research on self-control need more control. *Analysis and Intervention in Developmental Disabilities, 4,* 211–218.

Baer, R. A. (1990). Correspondence training: Review and current issues. *Research in Developmental Disabilities, 11,* 379–393.

Bailey, D. B., & Wolery, M. (1989). *Assessing infants and preschoolers with handicaps.* Columbus, OH: Merrill.

Bailey, D. B., & Wolery, M. (1992). *Teaching infants and preschoolers with disabilities* (2nd ed.). Columbus, OH: Macmillan.

Bannerman, D. J., Sheldon J. B., Sherman, J. A., & Harchik, A. E. (1990). Balancing the right to habilitation with the right to personal liberties: The rights of people with developmental disabilities to eat too many doughnuts and take a nap. *Journal of Applied Behavior Analysis, 23,* 78–89.

Billingsley, F. F., White, O. R., & Munson R. (1980). Procedural reliability: A rationale and an example. *Behavioral Assessment, 2,* 229–241.

Body, M. K. (1955). Patterns of aggression in nursery school. *Child Development, 26,* 3–11.

Bornstein, P. H. (1985). Self-instruction training: A commentary and state-of-the-art. *Journal of Applied Behavior Analysis, 18,* 69–72.

Browder, D. M. (1987). *Assessment of individuals with severe handicaps: An applied behavior approach to life skills assessment.* Baltimore: Paul E. Brookes.

Browder, D. M., & Shapiro, E. S. (1985) Applications of self-management to individuals with severe handicaps: A review. *Journal of the Association for Persons with Severe Handicaps, 10,* 200–208.

Brown, F. (1991). Creative daily scheduling: A nonintrusive approach to challenging behaviors in community residences. *Journal of the Association for Persons with Severe Handicaps, 16,* 75–84.

Brusca, R. M., Nieminen, G. S., Carter, R., & Repp, A. C. (1989). The relationship of staff contact and activity to the stereotypy of children with multiple disabilities. *Journal of the Association for Persons with Severe Handicaps, 14,* 127–136.

Bryant, L. E., & Budd, K. S. (1984). Teaching behaviorally handicapped preschool children to share. *Journal of Applied Behavior Analysis, 17,* 45–56.

Burke, M. M., Burke, D., & Forehand, R. (1985). Interpersonal antecedents of self-injurious behavior in retarded children. *Education and Training in Mental Retardation, 20,* 204–208.

Carnine, D. W. (1976). Effects of two teacher-presentation rates on off-task behavior, answering correctly, and participation. *Journal of Applied Behavior Analysis, 9,* 199–206.

Carr, E. G. (1988). Functional equivalence as a mechanism of response general-ization. In R. H. Horner, G. Dunlap, & R. L. Koegel (Eds.), *Generalization and maintenance: Life-style changes in applied settings* (pp. 221–241). Baltimore: Paul E. Brookes.

Carr E. G., & Durand, V. M. (1985). Reducing behavior problems through functional communication training. *Journal of Applied Behavior Analysis, 18,* 111–126.

Carr, E. G., Taylor, J. C., & Robinson, S. (1991). The effects of severe behavior prob-lems in children on the teaching behavior of adults. *Journal of Applied Behavior Analysis, 24,* 523–535.

Casey, L. (1978). Development of communication behavior in autistic children: A par-ent program using manual signs. *Journal of Autism and Childhood Schizophrenia, 8,* 45–59.

Cataldo, M. F., Ward, E. M., Russo, D. C., Riordan, M., & Bennett, D. (1986). Compliance and correlated problem behavior in children: Effect of contingent and noncontingent reinforcement. *Analysis and Intervention in Developmental Disabilities, 6,* 265–282.

Charlop, M. H., Kurtz, P. F., & Casey, F. G. (1990). Using aberrant behaviors as reinforcers for autistic children. *Journal of Applied Behavior Analysis, 23,* 163–181.

Charlop, M. H., Schreibman, L., Mason, J., & Vesey, W. (1983). Behavior-setting inter-actions of autistic children: A behavioral mapping approach to assessing class-room behaviors. *Analysis and Intervention in Developmental Disabilities, 3,* 359–373.

Coleman, R. S., & Whitman, T. L. (1984). Developing, generalizing, and maintaining physical fitness in mentally retarded adults: Toward a self-directed program. *Analysis and Intervention in Developmental Disabilities, 4,* 109–127.

Cooper, J. O. (1981). *Measuring behavior* (2nd ed.). Columbus, OH: Merrill.

Cooper, J. O., Heron, T. E., & Heward, W. L. (1987). *Applied behavior analysis.* Colum-bus, OH: Merrill.

DeLuke, S. V., & Knoblock, P. (1987). Teacher behavior as preventive discipline. *Teaching Exceptional Children, 19*(4), 18–24.

Doss, S., & Reichle, J. (1989). Establishing communicative alternatives to the emission of socially motivated excess behavior: A review. *Journal of the Association for Persons with Severe Handicaps, 14,* 101–112.

Dougherty, B. S., Fowler, S. A., & Paine, S. C. (1985). The use of peer monitors to reduce negative interaction during recess. *Journal of Applied Behavior Analysis, 18,* 141–153.

Dunlap, G. (1984). The influence of task variation and maintenance tasks on the learning and affect of autistic children. *Journal of Experimental Child Psychology, 37,* 41–64.

Dunlap, G., Johnson, L. F., & Robbins, F. R. (1990). Preventing serious behavior prob-lems through skill development and early intervention. In A. C. Repp & N. N. Singh (Eds.), *Perspectives on the use of nonaversive and aversive interventions for persons with developmental disabilities* (pp. 273–286). Sycamore, IL: Sycamore Press.

Dunlap, G., Kern-Dunlap, L., Clarke, S., & Robbins, F. R. (1991). Functional assessment, curricular revision, and severe behavior problems. *Journal of Applied Behavior Analysis, 24,* 387–397.

Dunlap, G., & Koegel, R. L. (1980). Motivating autistic children through stimulus variation. *Journal of Applied Behavior Analysis, 13,* 619–627.

Dunlap, G., Koegel, R. L., Johnson, J., & O'Neill, R. E. (1987). Maintaining performance of autistic clients in community settings with delayed contingencies. *Journal of Applied Behavior Analysis, 20,* 185–191.

Dunlap, G., Plienis, A. J., & Williams, L. (1987). Acquisition and generalization of unsupervised responding: A descriptive analysis. *Journal of the Association for Persons with Severe Handicaps, 12,* 274–279.

Dunst, C. J. (1981). *Infant learning: A cognitive-linguistic intervention strategy.* Hingham, MS: Teaching Resources.

Durand, V. M., & Carr, E. G. (1987). Social influences on self-stimulatory behavior: Analysis and treatment applications. *Journal of Applied Behavior Analysis, 20,* 119–132.

Durand, V. M., & Carr, E. G. (1991). Functional communication training to reduce challenging behavior: Maintenance and application in new settings. *Journal of Applied Behavior Analysis, 24,* 251–264.

Durand, V. M., Crimmins, D. B., Caulfield, M., & Taylor, J. (1989). Reinforcer assessment: 1. Using problem behavior to select reinforcers. *Journal of the Association for Persons with Severe Handicaps, 14,* 113–126.

Durand, V. M., & Kishi, G. (1987). Reducing severe behavior problems among persons with dual sensory impairments: An evaluation of a technical assistance model. *Journal of the Association for Persons with Severe Handicaps, 12,* 2–10.

Dyer, K. (1987). The competition of autistic stereotyped behavior with usual and specially assessed reinforcers. *Research in Developmental Disabilities, 8,* 607–626.

Dyer, K., Dunlap, G., & Winterling, V. (1990). Effects of choice making on the serious problem behaviors of students with severe handicaps. *Journal of Applied Behavior Analysis, 23,* 515–524.

Egel, A. L. (1981). Reinforcer variation: Implications for motivating developmentally disabled children. *Journal of Applied Behavior Analysis, 14,* 345–350.

Fagen, S. A., & Hill J. M. (1987). Teaching acceptance of frustration. *Teaching Exceptional Children, 19,* 49–51.

Ferrari, M., & Harris, S. L. (1981). The limits and motivating potential of sensory stimuli as reinforcers for autistic children. *Journal of Applied Behavior Analysis, 14,* 339–343.

Fishbein, J. E., & Wasik, B. H. (1981). Effect of the good behavior game on disruptive library behavior. *Journal of Applied Behavior Analysis, 14,* 89–93.

Fowler, S. A. (1984). Introductory comments: The pragmatics of self-management for the developmentally disabled. *Analysis and Intervention in Developmental Disabilities, 4,* 85–89.

Fowler, S. A., Dougherty, B. S., Kirby, K. C., & Kohler, F. W. (1986). Role reversals: An analysis of therapeutic effects achieved with disruptive boys during their appointments as peer monitors. *Journal of Applied Behavior Analysis, 19,* 437–444.

Foxx, R. M. (1984). The use of a negative reinforcement procedure to increase the performance of autistic and mentally retarded children on discrimination training tasks. *Analysis and Intervention in Developmental Disabilities, 4,* 253–265.

Foxx, R. M., Faw, G. D., McMorrow, M. J., Kyle, M. S., & Bittle, R. G. (1988). Replacing maladaptive speech with verbal labeling responses: An analysis of generalized responding. *Journal of Applied Behavior Analysis, 21,* 411–417.

Foxx, R. M., McMorrow, M. J., Fenlon, S., & Bittle, R. G. (1986). The reductive effects of reinforcement procedures on the genital stimulation and stereotypy of a mentally retarded adolescent male. *Analysis and Intervention in Developmental Disabilities, 6,* 239–248.

Gaylord-Ross, R. J., Weeks, M., & Lipner, C. (1980). An analysis of antecedent, response, and consequence events in the treatment of self-injurious behavior. *Education and Training of the Mentally Retarded, 15,* 35–42.

Green, C. W., Reid, D. H., Canipe, V. S., & Gardner, S. M. (1991). A comprehensive evaluation of reinforcer identification processes for persons with profound multiple handicaps. *Journal of Applied Behavior Analysis, 24,* 537–552.

Green, C. W., Reid, D. H., White L. K., Halford, R. C., Brittain, D. P., & Gardner, S. M. (1988). Identifying reinforcers for persons with profound handicaps: Staff opinion versus systematic assessment of preferences. *Journal of Applied Behavior Analysis, 21,* 31–43.

Green, G. (1990). Least restrictive use of reductive procedures: Guidelines and competencies. In A. C. Repp & N. N. Singh (Eds.), *The use of nonaversive and aversive interventions for persons with developmental disabilities* (pp. 479–493). Sycamore, IL: Sycamore Press.

Greer, R. D., Becker, B. J., Saxe, C. D., & Mirabella, R. F. (1985). Conditioning histories and setting stimuli controlling engagement in stereotypy or toy play. *Analysis and Intervention in Developmental Disabilities, 5,* 269–284.

Greer, R. D., Dorow, L., Williams, G., McCorkle, N., & Asnes, R. (1991). Peer-mediated procedures to induce swallowing and food acceptance in young children. *Journal of Applied Behavior Analysis, 24,* 783–790.

Guess, D., Benson, H. A., & Siegel-Causey, E. (1985). Concepts and issues related to choice-making and autonomy among persons with severe disabilities. *Journal of the Association for Persons with Severe Handicaps, 10,* 79–86.

Halle, J. W., Gabler-Halle, D., & Bemben, D. (1989). Physical fitness and integration of children with moderate and severe disabilities. *Journal of the Association for Persons with Severe Handicaps, 14,* 48–57.

Hamlet, C. C., Axelrod, S., & Kuerschner, S. (1984). Eye contact as an antecedent to compliant behavior. *Journal of Applied Behavior Analysis, 17,* 553–557.

Haring, T. G., & Kennedy, C. H. (1990). Contextual control of problem behavior in students with severe disabilities. *Journal of Applied Behavior Analysis, 23,* 235–243.

Heller, M. S., & White, M. A. (1975). Teacher approval and disapproval on ability groupings. *Journal of Educational Psychology, 67,* 795–800.

Horner, R. D. (1980). The effects of an environmental "enrichment" program on the behavior of institutionalized profoundly retarded children. *Journal of Applied Behavior Analysis, 13,* 473–491.

Horner, R. H., & Billingsley, F. F. (1988). The effect of competing behavior on the generalization and maintenance of adaptive behavior in applied settings. In R. H. Horner, G. Dunlap, & R. L. Koegel (Eds.), *Generalization and maintenance: Lifestyle changes in applied settings* (pp. 197–220). Baltimore: Paul E. Brookes.

Horner, R. H., & Budd, C. M. (1985). Teaching manual sign language to a nonverbal student: Generalization of sign use and collateral reduction of maladaptive behavior. *Education and Training of the Mentally Retarded, 20,* 39–47.

Horner, R. H., & Day, H. M. (1991). The effects of response efficiency on functionally equivalent competing behaviors. *Journal of Applied Behavior Analysis, 24,* 719–732.

Horner, R. H., Day, H. M., Sprague, J. R., O'Brien, M., & Heathfield, L. T. (1991). Interspersed requests: A nonaversive procedure for reducing aggression and self-injury during instruction. *Journal of Applied Behavior Analysis, 24,* 265–278.

Horner, R. H., O'Neill, R. E., & Flannery, K. B. (1993). Building effective behavior support plans from functional assessment information. In M. E. Snell (Ed.), *Systematic instruction of persons with severe handicaps* (4th ed.). Columbus, OH: Macmillan.

Horner, R. H., Sprague, J. R., O'Brien, M., & Heathfield, L. T. (1990). The role of response efficiency in the reduction of problem behaviors through functional equivalence training: A case study. *Journal of the Association for Persons with Severe Handicaps, 15,* 91–97.

Hughes, C. A., Korinek, L., & Gorman, J. (1991). Self-management for students with mental retardation in public school settings: A research review. *Education and Training in Mental Retardation, 26,* 271–291.

Hughes, V., Wolery, M., & Neel, R. S. (1983). Teacher verbalizations and task performance with autistic children. *Journal of Autism and Developmental Disorders, 15,* 305–316.

Hung, D. W. (1978). Using self-stimulation as reinforcement for autistic children. *Journal of Autism and Childhood Schizophrenia, 8,* 355–366.

Hunt, P., Alwell, M., & Goetz, L. (1988). Acquisition of conversation skills and the reduction of inappropriate social interaction behaviors. *Journal of the Association for Persons with Severe Handicaps, 13,* 20–27.

Hunt, P., Alwell, M., Goetz, L., & Sailor, W. (1990). Generalized effects of conversation skill training. *Journal of the Association for Persons with Severe Handicaps, 13,* 250–260.

Iwata, B. A. (1987). Negative reinforcement in applied behavior analysis: An emerging technology. *Journal of Applied Behavior Analysis, 20,* 361–378.

Iwata, B. A., Pace, G. M., Kalsher, M. J., Cowdery, G. E., & Cataldo, M. F. (1990). Experimental analysis and extinction of self-injurious escape behavior. *Journal of Applied Behavior Analysis, 23,* 11–27.

Kazdin, A. E. (1982). The token economy: A decade later. *Journal of Applied Behavior Analysis, 15,* 431–445.

Kelly, M. L., & Stokes, T. F. (1982). Contingency contracting with disadvantaged youths: Improving classroom performance. *Journal of Applied Behavior Analysis, 15,* 447–454.

Koegel, R. L., Dyer, K., & Bell, L. K. (1987). The influence of child-preferred activities on autistic children's social behavior. *Journal of Applied Behavior Analysis, 20,* 243–252.

Koegel, R. L., & Koegel, L. K. (1990). Extended reductions in stereotypic behavior of students with autism through a self-management treatment package. *Journal of Applied Behavior Analysis, 23,* 119–127.

Kohler, F. W., & Strain, P. S. (1990). Peer-assisted interventions: Early promises, notable achievements, and future aspirations. *Clinical Psychology Review, 10,* 441–452.

Kozloff, M. (1995). *Principles of developmental-functional assessment and program planning.* Baltimore: Paul E. Brookes.

Leatherby, J. G., Gast, D. L., Wolery, M., & Collins, B. C. (1992). Assessment of reinforcer preference in multi-handicapped students. *Journal of Developmental and Physical Disabilities, 4,* 15–36.

Lennox, D. B., & Miltenberger, R. G. (1990). On the conceptualization of treatment acceptability. *Education and Training in Mental Retardation, 25,* 211–224.

Mace, F. C., & Belfiore, P. (1990). Behavioral momentum in the treatment of escape-motivated stereotypy. *Journal of Applied Behavior Analysis, 23,* 507–514.

Mace, F. C., Hock, M. L., Lalli, J. S., West, B. J., Belfiore, P., Pinter, E., & Brown, D. K. (1988). Behavioral momentum in the treatment of noncompliance. *Journal of Applied Behavior Analysis, 21,* 123–141.

Mace, F. C., & Knight, D. (1986). Functional analysis and treatment of severe pica. *Journal of Applied Behavior Analysis, 19,* 411–416.

Mace, F. C., & Lalli, J. S. (1991). Linking descriptive and experimental analysis in the treatment of bizarre speech. *Journal of Applied Behavior Analysis, 24,* 553–562.

Mank, D. M., & Horner, R. H. (1987). Self-recruited feedback: A cost-effective procedure for maintaining behavior. *Research in Developmental Disabilities, 8,* 91–112.

Marholin, D., & Steinman, W. M. (1977). Stimulus control in the classroom as a function of the behavior reinforced. *Journal of Applied Behavior Analysis, 10,* 465–478.

Mason, S. A., McGee, G. C., Farmer-Dougan, V., & Risley, T. R. (1989). Practical strategy for ongoing reinforcer assessment. *Journal of Applied Behavior Analysis, 20,* 45–68.

McAfee, J. K. (1987). Classroom density and the aggressive behavior of handicapped children. *Education and Treatment of Children, 10,* 134–145.

McEvoy, M. A., Nordquist, V. M., Twardosz, S., Heckman, K. A., Wehby, J. H., & Denny, R. K. (1988). Promoting autistic children's peer interaction in an integrated early childhood setting using affection activities. *Journal of Applied Behavior Analysis, 21,* 193–200.

McMorrow, M. J., & Foxx, R. M. (1986). Some direct and generalized effects of replacing an autistic man's echolalia with correct responses to questions. *Journal of Applied Behavior Analysis, 12,* 289–297.

McWilliam, R. A. (1991). Targeting teaching at children's use of time: Perspectives on preschoolers' engagement. *Teaching Exceptional Children, 23,* 42–43.

McWilliam, R. A., & Bailey, D. B. (1992). Promoting engagement. In D. B. Bailey & M. Wolery (Eds.), *Teaching infants and preschoolers with disabilities* (2nd ed., pp. 229–255). Columbus, OH: Macmillan.

Mercer, C. D., & Mercer, A. R. (1989). *Teaching students with learning problems* (3rd ed.). Columbus, OH: Merrill.

Murphy, H. A., Hutchison, J. M., & Bailey, J. S. (1983). Behavioral school psychology goes outdoors: The effect of organized games on playground aggression. *Journal of Applied Behavior Analysis, 16*, 29–35.

Northup, J., Wacker, D., Sasso, G., Steege, M., Cigrand, K., Cook, J., & DeRaad, A. (1991). A brief functional analysis of aggressive and alternative behavior in an outclinic setting. *Journal of Applied Behavior Analysis, 24*, 509–522.

O'Brien, S., & Repp, A. C. (1990). Reinforcement-based reductive procedures: A review of 20 years of their use with persons with severe or profound retardation. *Journal of the Association for Persons with Severe Handicaps, 15*, 148–159.

Odom, S. L., McConnell, S. R., & McEvoy, M. A. (1992). *Social competence of young children with disabilities: Issues and strategies for intervention.* Baltimore: Paul E. Brookes.

O'Neill, R. E., Horner, R. H., Albin, R. W., Storey, K., & Sprague, J. R. (1990). *Functional analysis of problem behavior: A practical assessment guide.* Sycamore, IL: Sycamore Press.

Pace, G. M., Ivancic, M. T., Edwards, G. L., Iwata, B. A., & Page, T. J. (1985). Assessment of stimulus preference and reinforcer value with profoundly retarded individuals. *Journal of Applied Behavior Analysis, 18*, 249–255.

Park, H. S., & Gaylord-Ross, R. (1989). A problem-solving approach to social skills training in employment settings with mentally retarded youth. *Journal of Applied Behavior Analysis, 22*, 373–380.

Parsons, M. B., & Reid, D. H. (1990). Assessing food preferences among persons with profound mental retardation: Providing opportunities to make choices. *Journal of Applied Behavior Analysis, 23*, 183–195.

Parsons, M. B., Reid, D. H., Reynolds, J., & Bumgarner, M. (1990). Effects of chosen versus assigned jobs on the work performance of persons with severe handicaps. *Journal of Applied Behavior Analysis, 23*, 253–258.

Russell, M. B., & Bernal, M. E. (1977). Temporal and climatic variables in naturalistic observations. *Journal of Applied Behavior Analysis, 10*, 399–405.

Sainato, D. M., & Carta, J. J. (1992). Classroom influences on the development of social competence of young children with disabilities. In S. L. Odom, S. R. McConnell, & M. McEvoy (Eds.), *Peer-related social competence of young children with disabilities* (pp. 93–109). Baltimore: Paul E. Brookes.

Sainato, D. M., Maheady, L., & Shook, G. I. (1986). The effects of a classroom manager role on the social interaction patterns and social status of withdrawn kindergarten students. *Journal of Applied Behavior Analysis, 19*, 187–195.

Schumaker, J. B., Hovell, M. F., & Sherman, J. A. (1977). An analysis of daily report cards and parent-managed privileges in the improvement of adolescents' classroom performance. *Journal of Applied Behavior Analysis, 10*, 449–464.

Shevin, M., & Klein, N. K. (1984). The importance of choice-making skills for students with severe disabilities. *Journal of the Association for Persons with Severe Handicaps, 9*, 159–166.

Singer, G. H. S., Singer, J., & Horner, R. H. (1987). Using pretask requests to increase the probability of compliance for students with severe disabilities. *Journal of the Association for Persons with Severe Handicaps, 12,* 287–291.

Singh, N. N., & Millichamp, C. J. (1987). Independent and social play among profoundly mentally retarded adults: Training, maintenance, generalization, and long-term follow-up. *Journal of Applied Behavior Analysis, 20,* 23–34.

Smith, L. K. C., & Fowler, S. A. (1984). Positive peer pressure: The effects of peer monitoring on children's disruptive behavior. *Journal of Applied Behavior Analysis, 17,* 213–227.

Snell, M. E. (1987). *Systematic instruction of persons with severe handicaps.* Columbus, OH: Merrill.

Spangler, P. F., & Marshall, A. M. (1983). The unit play manager as facilitator of purposeful activities among institutionalized profoundly and severely retarded boys. *Journal of Applied Behavior Analysis, 61,* 345–349.

Stainback, W., Stainback, S., & Froyen, L. (1987). Structuring the classroom to prevent disruptive behaviors. *Teaching Exceptional Children, 19,* 12–16.

Steege, M. W., Wacker, D. P., Berg, W. K., Cigrand, K. C. & Cooper, L. J. (1989). The use of behavioral assessment to prescribe and evaluate treatments for severely handicapped children. *Journal of Applied Behavior Analysis, 22,* 23–33.

Steege, M. W., Wacker, D. P., Cigrand, K. C., Berg, W. K., Novak, C. G., Reimers, T. M., Sasso, G. M., & DeRaad, A. (1990). Use of negative reinforcement in the treatment of self-injurious behavior. *Journal of Applied Behavior Analysis, 23,* 459–467.

Stern, G. W., Fowler, S. A., & Kohler, F. W. (1988). A comparison of two intervention roles: Peer monitor and point earner. *Journal of Applied Behavior Analysis, 21,* 103–109.

Stevens, R., & Rosenshine, B. (1981). Advances in research on teaching. *Exceptional Education Quarterly, 2*(1), 1–9.

Stokes, T. F., Fowler, S. A., & Baer, D. M. (1978). Training preschool children to recruit natural communities of reinforcement. *Journal of Applied Behavior Analysis, 11,* 285–303.

Strain, P. S., & Sainato, D. M. (1987). Preventive discipline in early childhood. *Teaching Exceptional Children, 19,* 26–30.

Sugai, G. M., & White, W. (1986). The effect of self-stimulation as a reinforcer on the vocational work rates with severely handicapped students. *Journal of Autism and Developmental Disorders, 16,* 459–471.

Swanson, H. L., & Watson, B. L. (1989). *Educational and psychological assessment of exceptional children* (2nd ed.). Columbus, OH: Merrill.

Thomas, J. D., Presland, I. E., Grant, M. D., & Glynn, T. L. (1978). Natural rates of teacher approval and disapproval in grade 7 classrooms. *Journal of Applied Behavior Analysis, 11,* 91–94.

Van Houten, R., Nau, P. A., MacKenzie-Keating, S. E., Sameoto, D., & Colaveechia, B. (1982). An analysis of some variables influencing the effectiveness of reprimands. *Journal of Applied Behavior Analysis, 15,* 65–83.

Wacker, D., Steege, M., Northup, J., Reimers, T., Berg, W., & Sasso, G. (1990a). Use of functional analysis and acceptability measures to assess and treat severe behavior problems: An outpatient clinic model. In A. C. Repp & N. N. Singh (Eds.),

Perspectives on the use of nonaversive and aversive interventions for persons with developmental disabilities (pp. 349–359). Sycamore, IL: Sycamore Press.

Wacker, D., Steege, M. W., Northup, J., Sasso, G., Berg, W., Reimers, T., Cooper, L., Cigrand, K., & Donn, L. (1990b). A component analysis of functional communication training across three topographies of severe behavior problems. *Journal of Applied Behavior Analysis, 23,* 417–429.

Wahler, R. G., & Dumas, J. E. (1986). Maintenance factors in coercive mother-child interactions: The compliance and predictability hypothesis. *Journal of Applied Behavior Analysis, 19,* 13–22.

Walher, R. G., & Fox, J. J. (1981). Setting events in applied behavior analysis: Toward a conceptual and methodological expansion. *Journal of Applied Behavior Analysis, 14,* 327–338.

Weeks., M., & Gaylord-Ross, R. (1981). Task difficulty and aberrant behavior in severely handicapped students. *Journal of Applied Behavior Analysis, 14,* 449–463.

Wetzel, M. C., Taylor, M. J., & Lachowicz, J. M. (1991). Ecological assessment of disabling stereotyped behavior in a workday training program. *Education and Training in Mental Retardation, 26,* 223–231.

Whalen, C. K., Henker, B., Collins, B. E., Finck, D., & Dotemoto, S. (1979). A social ecology of hyperactive boys: Medication effects in structured classroom environments. *Journal of Applied Behavior Analysis, 12,* 65–81.

Wilcox, B., & Bellamy, G. T. (1987). *The activities catalog: An alternative curriculum for youth and adults with severe disabilities.* Baltimore: Paul E. Brookes.

Winterling, V., Dunlap, G., & O'Neill, R. E. (1987). The influence of task variation on the aberrant behaviors of autistic students. *Education and Treatment of Children, 10,* 105–119.

Winton, P. J. (1988). The family-focused interview: An assessment measure and goal-setting mechanism. In D. B. Bailey & R. J. Simeonsson (Eds.), *Family assessment in early intervention* (pp. 185–205). Columbus, OH: Merrill.

Wolery, M. (1978). Self-stimulatory behavior as a basis for devising reinforcers. *American Association for the Education of the Severely and Profoundly Handicapped Review, 3,* 23–29.

Wolery, M., Ault, M. J., & Doyle, P. M. (1992). *Teaching students with moderate and severe disabilities: Use of response prompting procedures.* White Plains, NY: Longman.

Wolery, M., Bailey, D. B., & Sugai, G. M. (1988). *Effective teaching: Principles and procedures of applied behavior analysis with exceptional students.* Boston: Allyn & Bacon.

Wolery, M., Fleming, L. A. (1992). Preventing and responding to problem situations. In D. B. Bailey & M. Wolery (Eds.), *Teaching infants and preschoolers with disabilities* (2nd ed., pp. 363–406). Columbus, OH: Macmillan.

Wolery, M., Kirk, K., & Gast, D. L. (1985). Stereotypic behavior as a reinforcer: Effects and side effects. *Journal of Autism and Developmental Disorders, 15,* 149–161.

Wong, S. E., Terranova, M. D., Bowen, L., Zarate, R., Massel, H. K., & Liberman, R. P. (1987). Providing independent recreational activities to reduce stereotyped vocalizations in chronic schizophrenics. *Journal of Applied Behavior Analysis, 20,* 77–81.

Chapter
6

Developing Functional Communication Skills: Alternatives to Severe Behavior Problems

KATHLEEN DYER AND ERIC V. LARSSON

INTRODUCTION

Severe behavior disorders, such as aggression, self-injury, and destruction, severely limit the extent to which an individual can enjoy a normal life in the community. Since the mid-1980s, a promising new treatment approach to these disorders has been developed based on the pioneering work of Carr and Durand (1985). These authors proposed the idea that many aberrant behaviors have a communicative function. That is, an individual may engage in a tantrum to communicate the need for attention, or in aggression to communicate the desire to escape a long, frustrating work assignment. This idea was confirmed when these researchers taught individuals with aberrant behavior to communicate requests for attention and breaks from work in socially appropriate ways. After the individuals learned these new communicative responses, the aberrant behaviors were eliminated. This groundbreaking research has stimulated a whole new treatment approach called *functional communication training*. We will discuss a variety of issues and procedures related to this treatment approach. The research demonstrating the effects and value of functional communication training will be reviewed. Then, specific procedures for assessing the communicative functions of aberrant behavior will be discussed. Finally, specific functional communication training strategies will be delineated.

RESEARCH ON FUNCTIONAL COMMUNICATION TRAINING

While a variety of treatment strategies for severe behavior disorders have been applied with some degree of success, the skills acquisition approach is heuristically and empirically the most promising. The skills-based approach exemplifies the spirit of the highly valued proactive approach to the development of independence (Accreditation Council on Services for People with Developmental Disabilities, 1990). Here, the development of skills that support independence, rather than a simple reduction of problems, is the focus of treatment services.

In particular, the purpose of this section is to review the effects and value of functional communication training in accomplishing this goal. This approach is based on the concept of *functional equivalence* (Carr, 1988). This concept can be summarized as follows: Once a function of a disorder is identified, an alternative socially desirable behavior can be identified that will also serve the same function. If a disorder serves to communicate a need (i.e., to request a given reinforcer from staff), then a more typical communicative response can also serve to request that need. Practically, if the disorder currently results in access to a reinforcing consequence, then an alternative communication skill can also result in access to the consequence. With various practical features, this communication skill will then replace the disorder, and the disorder will be remediated. This is the approach to be discussed here. This approach has also been termed *differential reinforcement of communicative behavior* (DRC) (Carr, Robinson, Taylor, & Carlson, 1990).

The initial step in training is to conduct a functional analysis (Baer, Wolf, & Risley, 1968). Quite a variety of published reports illustrate the potential results of the analysis (e.g., Iwata, Dorsey, Slifer, Bauman, & Richman, 1982). The functional analysis identifies adaptive communication skills that will facilitate functioning in all target environments for the individual. For example, four motivating conditions—DRO (differential reinforcement of other behavior), attention reinforcement, escape from demands, and being left alone—were analyzed by providing several alternating 10-minute periods of each condition in an analog setting (Steege, Wacker, Berg, Cigrand, & Cooper, 1989). Escape from demands was found to be the critical motivator for self-injurious biting during grooming in two different individuals. After this finding, each of the nonvocal individuals was taught to press a microswitched device to play the message "stop," which was negatively reinforced with 10 seconds of time-out from grooming. If the biting did occur, the individuals were physically guided to continue grooming. This approach resulted in gradual reductions of biting across 3 to 15 sessions until biting rarely occurred.

Other studies have replicated the essential features of such an approach (Iwata, Pace, Cowdery, Kalsher, & Cataldo, 1990). An essential feature of the functional communication approach is that the adaptive skill that is taught should be taught in a truly functional manner. For example, one individual was taught to request help rather than produce stereotyped speech during difficult tasks. Here, the level of stereotyped speech increased when the help request was simply reinforced with social praise (Durand & Crimmins, 1987). However, when the help request was reinforced with assistance, the level of stereotyped speech decreased to near zero.

Functional communication training has also resulted in the rapid suppression of severe aggression, self-injurious behavior, and tantrums in four children (Carr & Durand, 1985). This was a significant finding, for a presumed limitation of the functional communication approach is that it may require extensive training before proving successful and thus may not reduce reliance on more restrictive techniques. In analog assessments of easy versus difficult tasks and levels of reinforcing attention, either escape from demands or reinforcing attention was found to motivate the aberrant behaviors in different individuals. Teaching the appropriate individual either to request social attention or to request assistance resulted in substantial reduction within 10 to 20 minutes. Similar results were obtained when the self-stimulatory behavior of four individuals was analyzed and found to be maintained by escape from difficult tasks (Durand & Carr, 1987). Teaching the individuals to request help resulted in an immediate reduction in self-stimulation.

The functional analysis has also been successful when conducted through interviewing staff rather than through experimental analysis. Here, structured interviews using the Motivation Assessment Scale (Durand, 1990) suggested that the dangerous aggressive and self-injurious behaviors of five individuals were controlled variously by escape from demands, by reinforcing attention, and by reinforcing tangible items. Four of the five individuals with multiple disabilities were taught to nonvocally request the relevant event by handing tokens to the staff. Significant improvements were found. An additional significant feature of this study was that the adults had met with previous failures to benefit from communication training, but a successful modality could still be identified.

One concern in this approach is that, when it is found that escape from demands is the motivating condition, the functional equivalent (e.g., requesting breaks) may result in lack of progress or effort. One study addressed this potential side effect by teaching two individuals in a work setting to request breaks rather than engage in aggression and self-injury (Bird, Dores, Moniz, & Robinson, 1989). The results were that work productivity actually improved after the functional equivalent (request for break) was taught. More research is certainly needed to identify whether such an effect on work productivity would be typical if individuals are taught to request breaks during work periods.

In some circumstances, the functional analysis may need to be fine-grained before the essential function of the aberrant behavior is discovered. For example, an analysis showing that the behavior is maintained because it results in attention may need to identify the source of this attention. In one case, it was found that peer attention rather than adult attention was the motivation for the disruptive behavior of three adolescents (Hunt, Alwell, & Goetz, 1988). Teaching peer-conversation skills to the individuals served to replace the function of the disruptive behavior. A recent study provides an excellent example of a careful development of experimental conditions based on extensive structured interviews and naturalistic observation (Dunlap, Kern-Dunlap, Clarke, & Robbins, 1991). The analog study then produced a fine-grained set of recommended curricular revisions.

While a functionally equivalent communicative response may be identified for each disorder, the simple training of the communicative response may not reduce the incidence of the disorder (Wacker et al., 1990). In this study, for example, a functional analysis showed clear functions for the self-injurious behavior, the self-stimulatory behavior, and the aggression of three individuals. The interventions were functional communication training as well as time-out, DRO, or graduated physical guidance, whichever was relevant to the functions of the behavior. In each case, the intervention package was successful. However, a subsequent component experimental analysis found that neither the functional communication training nor the accompanying procedures, when used in isolation, were sufficient to maintain the previously low levels of the aberrant behavior.

Several features of a disorder and its functional equivalent may determine such an effect. First, where the functional equivalence is based on obtaining the same reinforcer, even if the adaptive equivalent is just as effective as the disorder, it is unlikely to replace the disorder. The adaptive equivalent is more likely to replace the disorder if it is more reliably followed by the reinforcer, if it is more quickly followed by the reinforcer, or if it is a more fluent response (i.e., if the topography of the response has a shorter latency in context or if the topography is more easily produced). The disorder may also have a history of an intermittent schedule of reinforcement, which makes it highly resistant to change. Here, despite the above features, the disorder will continue to have a given probability of occurrence. Further, the adaptive equivalent may not have been adequately established in all contexts where the disorder occurs. In order to ensure replacement of the disorder, direct consequences for the disorder often need to be programmed (Wacker et al., 1990).

A strength of the functional analysis is that it presents the opportunity to identify the natural reinforcers existing in the ecology of the treatment environment. When skills training addresses the natural reinforcers, then the skills taught are most likely to be maintained when staff implementation fails. A further complication, however, is that the success of the skills training often results in moving the individual into less restrictive placements. When this occurs, a functional analysis of the future environment is necessary to extend the maintenance to the novel contingencies (Anderson & Schwartz, 1986). Ideally, the communicative response will be so robust that it will not require modification or assistance when used by strangers. Therefore, a priority is to use modes of communication that are readily understood by the untrained public. Functional communication (along with generalized independent play and work skills) is perhaps one of the easiest such skills to maintain.

ASSESSING COMMUNICATIVE FUNCTIONS OF ABERRANT BEHAVIOR

In this section, we delineate specific procedures for implementing a functional communication training program. The first procedure to be discussed is how to conduct an initial and ongoing assessment of the communicative strategies used by the person with the problem behavior. These assessments aim to (1) create hypotheses about the communicative functions of aberrant behavior; (2) determine the availability of appropriate communicative skills that can be used to replace the aberrant behavior; and (3) aid in monitoring the effectiveness of ongoing functional communication training strategies. The steps we cover for the assessment process are listed in Box 6-1.

An interview with caregivers and/or teachers is an efficient first step in gathering information about how the person with disabilities behaves in a variety of situations. An interviewer who has had extensive contact with the individual may administer the interview questions to herself or himself as a way of structuring her or his thinking about how the individual communicates. The interview can help pinpoint variables that may contribute to the aberrant behavior, providing the interviewer with situations on which to focus the observation portion of the assessment.

A communication interview can be used to identify communicative behaviors (means) and their situational uses (functions) (Peck & Schuler, 1987). The communicative means include aberrant behaviors such as aggression and self-injury, prelinguistic behavior such as gaze and pointing, and conventional symbolic behavior such as speech, sign language, and the use of a communication board. The interviewer then poses questions to determine the possible functions of the aberrant behavior. A review of the literature and the results of our clinical practice have yielded quite a variety of potential functions of behaviors. Some of these functions are listed in Box 6-2. For example, the caregiver may report that if a favorite food is removed, the individual initially begins to cry, and if the food is not returned, the crying escalates into a tantrum. Thus, the function of tantrum behavior may be to resist the withdrawal of preferred activities. The communication interview also provides information regarding the use of adaptive, conventional communication

**Box
6-2**

POTENTIAL FUNCTIONS OF ABERRANT BEHAVIORS

1. Response to prevention of access.
2. Sensory reinforcement/self-stimulation.
3. Reduction of pain/response to pain.
4. Anxiety reduction.
5. Direct (nonescape) response to stimulation.
6. Escape from boring environment.
7. Escape from aversive setting.
8. Escape from an immediate instruction.
9. Oppositional response to instruction.
10. Escape from an ongoing task.
11. Simple frustration resulting from inability to do a task.
12. Gain of attention from staff.
13. Gain of attention from peer.
14. Competition with peer.
15. Imitation of peer.
16. Production of apparent pain in peer or staff (tease, torment).
17. Request for a tangible reinforcer in response to deprivation.
18. Request for a tangible reinforcer in response to preference.
19. Request for an activity in response to deprivation.
20. Request for an activity in response to preference.
21. Resistance to withdrawal of preferred activity.
22. Response to exhaustion of item.

strategies. For example, a person who communicates protest by aggressive behavior may also communicate by one-word utterances in other contexts. This information is useful in subsequent treatment planning, so that the person can be trained to use a one-word response (e.g., *no*) to communicate an appropriate protest. However, if the individual has exhibited only gestural communication in other contexts, subsequent treatment planning may involve teaching a protest response that involves a gestural response, such as handing back the nonpreferred activity.

In addition to asking questions regarding communicative means and functions, it is important to ask questions regarding the specific nature of the aberrant behaviors. In an excellent assessment instrument developed by O'Neill, Horner, Albin, Storey, and Sprague (1990), the interviewer asks questions to determine the topography, frequency, and intensity of the aberrant behaviors. Thus, self-injurious behavior can be more specifically defined as hitting the ears with the fists, occurring approximately 100 times per day, the result of the hitting being redness and bruises. The interview can also reveal if the aberrant behaviors occur in a predictable sequence, so that the behaviors can be viewed as belonging in a single response class (e.g., crying always occurs before tantrums; aggression occurs with loud vocalizations). This sequencing is also important in subsequent treatment planning, in that the practitioner can be sure to target all of the related behaviors in treatment.

The interview developed by O'Neill et al. (1990) also presents questions pertaining to possible "ecological" variables contributing to the behavior; that is, events that do not occur immediately before the behavior but may have some impact on it. These variables include (1) medications, (2) medical complications, (3) sleep cycles, (4) diet, (5) daily schedule, (6) predictability of events, (7) activities, (8) density of people, and (9) staffing patterns. Finally, questions are asked pertaining to setting events that may predict the occurrence of behavior, including time of day, physical setting, social control, and activity.

Another type of assessment is the rating scale, on which the interviewee is asked to rate how often an aberrant behavior occurs under certain conditions (e.g., ranging from never to always). The most widely used rating scale for this purpose is the Motivation Assessment Scale (Durand, 1990), which presents a series of questions that ascertain whether the aberrant behavior functions to (1) gain attention (e.g., "Does this person seem to do the behavior to get you to spend time with him or her?"); (2) escape or avoid situations (e.g., "Does the behavior stop occurring shortly after you stop working or making demands of this person?"); (3) gain access to tangible consequences (e.g., "Does the behavior ever occur to get a toy, food, or activity that this person has been told that he or she can't have?"); and (4) gain sensory input (e.g., "Would the behavior occur repeatedly in the same way, for very long periods of time, if no one was around?").

Information from interviews and rating scales provides direction for subsequent observational assessments by specifying the topography of the aberrant behavior and by indicating situations in which the aberrant behavior is likely to occur. One type of observational protocol is the A-B-C form (Bijou, Peterson, & Ault, 1968), on which there are spaces for the observer to record the antecedent conditions occurring immediately before the behavior (A), the behavior (B), and the consequent events occurring immediately after the behavior (C). For example, every time a student exhibits a tantrum, the teacher would record "tantrum" in the B column, the event immediately preceding the tantrum in the A column (e.g., "presentation of work"), and the event occurring immediately after the tantrum in the C column (e.g., "removal of work"). A-B-C charts may be excellent in providing information when completed by highly trained observers, although they often fall short if completed by teachers and/or caregivers, who often fail to provide enough detail, recording responses such as "nothing" or "lunchtime" for events occurring before and after the aberrant behavior (Durand, 1990).

To ameliorate this problem, a more detailed observation protocol, the Functional Analysis Observation Form (O'Neill et al., 1990), provides the specific antecedent (e.g., demand, alone) and consequent (e.g., attention, self-stimulation) events on the form. In addition, spaces are provided for information on specific target behaviors, setting events, and consequences for problem behavior. One problem that we have encountered in using the Functional Analysis Observation Form is that some aberrant behaviors occur at low and/or sporadic rates. Therefore, the behavior may not occur during several observation periods. In this case, we suggest that the staff member conduct a scatter plot analysis (Touchette, MacDonald, & Langer, 1985). To conduct this analysis, the staff member is supplied with a data sheet that is blocked off in relatively long time intervals (e.g., one-half hour). The staff member can then record whether aberrant behavior occurred (1) a small number of times (e.g., fewer than two); (2) a large number of times (e.g., more than two); or (3) not at all. This relatively easy data-collection procedure, carried out over a seven-day period, can reveal times when and situations in which the problem behavior is likely to occur. The staff member can subsequently target more thorough observations with the Functional Analysis Observation Form during these times and situations.

In the majority of cases, the interview and observation will provide enough information for the design of an effective treatment plan. However, if the information is unclear, or if the problem behavior occurs at a very low rate and/or at unpredictable times, the assessor may want to conduct environmental manipulations to obtain a clearer picture of the functions of the aberrant behavior.

One type of environmental manipulation is the analog assessment, in which a highly trained staff member sets up situations that may evoke problem behavior, such as (1) adult attention or lack of it, (2) nonpreferred and/or difficult tasks, (3) sensory consequences, and (4) desire for tangible consequences (Carr & Durand, 1985; Durand & Crimmins, 1988; Iwata et al., 1982). For example, if it was hypothesized that aggression functioned as escape from difficult tasks, the assessor would set up a series of sessions in which difficult tasks were presented and would alternate these with sessions in which easy tasks were presented. If aggressive behavior occurred at a consistently higher rate during the difficult tasks, the hypothesis would be supported that aggression functioned to allow escape from difficult tasks.

Another type of assessment through environmental manipulation is proposed by Dunlap et al. (1991). These authors suggest conducting the manipulations in the context of regular daily routines after a thorough preassessment has been conducted in the form of interviews and questionnaires. This method allows assessment of aberrant behavior in the specific situations in which the behavior was reported to occur in terms of setting and specificity of the environmental antecedent(s). For example, rather than assessing whether problem behavior functions to allow escape under the global category of "presentation of tasks," this hypothesis can be more precisely tested in conditions in which specific task attributes (e.g., fine motor tasks) serve as an antecedent to aberrant behavior. This method also allows the opportunity to assess situations in which *reduced* levels of the behavior occur. Specifically, in the Dunlap et al. (1991) study, the teachers reported that the subject of their study was *better* behaved when engaged in (1) gross motor tasks, (2) brief tasks, (3) functional activities, and (4) situations in which she had a choice of activities. Therefore, the environmental manipulations involved rapidly changing the conditions (e.g., fine vs. gross motor tasks) across the day, and measuring the levels of aberrant behavior in those conditions. This type of assessment directly suggests curricular modifications to reduce aberrant behavior, such as having the student communicate choice-making options. In addition, Durand (1990) suggests that, through the process of this type of assessment, caregivers can directly experience the positive effects of witnessing the reduction of the aberrant behavior while manipulating these variables and will thus be more likely to incorporate these changes into their curriculum.

After a battery of assessments has been completed and a functional communication training plan is devised, it is necessary to conduct ongoing assessment in the natural setting to ensure the effectiveness of the treatment plan by using repeated measures (Barlow & Hersen, 1984). This ongoing assessment provides a vehicle to determine if the treatment is effective and, if not, to make the necessary adjustments.

In summary, when developing functional communication skills, it is important to answer the following questions during initial and ongoing assessments: (1) What is the function(s) of the aberrant behavior? (2) What are the appropriate communicative behaviors? (3) What is the specific nature of the aberrant behavior and the communicative behavior? (4) What are the ecological events contributing to the behavior? and (5) What are the setting events contributing to the aberrant behavior? The form of these assessments may be interviews, rating scales, direct observation, environmental manipulations, and repeated measures of interventions. It is recommended that the interview and direct observation portions of the assessment be balanced, as caregivers and teachers who have extensive contact with the individual can provide rich descriptions of communicative repertoires in a short period of time. These reports can be confirmed and elaborated on by use of the direct observation procedures, and more elusive patterns of responding can be assessed with environmental manipulations. Finally, these hypotheses can be confirmed by ongoing data collection, and adjustments to the training program can be made if necessary.

DESIGNING A PROGRAM IN FUNCTIONAL COMMUNICATION TRAINING

Information from the assessment process is used in the development of a program of functional communication training. The assessment should reveal situations in which the individual exhibits aberrant behavior. It is important to note that not all aberrant behavior is responsive to functional communication training. That is, some behaviors may be affected by the ecological variables delineated in the interview designed by O'Neill et al. (1990). These include medications, diet, sleep cycles, and medical complications. The behaviors may also be affected by complex setting factors that may be difficult for the individual to control through spontaneous communication, such as the predictability of events and the density of people. If the assessment reveals that these factors may be contributing to aberrant behavior, curricular revisions to modify these setting events may be a more efficient treatment strategy (Dunlap et al., 1991).

Results of controlled research studies, as well as extensive observations in our own setting, reveal that aberrant behavior that is responsive to functional communication training typically occurs in one or more of the following situations: (1) when the individual desires the attention of a person; (2) when the individual is having difficulty with a task; (3) when the individual is presented with a nonpreferred activity or food; (4) when the individual wants a break from an activity; (5) when the individual wants an activity; and (6) when the individual is misunderstood. Before we discuss how to teach functional communication skills in each of these situations, specific training principles that are common to all programs in functional communication training are described.

Basic Training Principles

The following principles were drawn from a wealth of literature documenting their effectiveness. The procedures were also used in the successful training in functional communication skills of over 200 individuals with aberrant behaviors over a six-year period at the May Institute.

1. *Select a communicative response that is appropriate to the individual's level of functioning and that can be used in the least restrictive environment.*

Dyer, Santarcangelo, and Luce (1987) found that response forms that are appropriate to the individual's developmental level are easier to teach. For example, if the individual communicates primarily with two-word utterances, the target responses should also be in the form of two-word utterances (e.g., "Want help"), and the individual should not be prompted to expand his or her utterance length (e.g., "I want help, please").

If the individual cannot speak, or if his or her speech is understood only by familiar listeners, then an augmentative system should be used, in the form of gestures, sign language, and/or a communication device. The election decision matrix developed by Shane and Bashir (1980) delineates objective criteria for deciding whether to use an augmentative system. Further, other authors suggest that individuals at the Stage 4 level of sensorimotor development (approximately 9 to 18 months) can use rudimentary communicative devices that involve symbolic communication (Reichle & Yoder, 1985). Individuals functioning below this level should be taught presymbolic communication skills such as gestures or the use of simple microswitch devices.

The decision to use sign language or a communication device depends on a number of factors, the most important being which mode the individual learns most easily. A second factor in this decision is whether the people in the individual's environment know sign language. Even if they do, it is important to remember that the majority of people in the community do not know sign language, and therefore, the risk of being misunderstood in these situations is great (Rotholz, Berkowitz, & Burberry, 1989). Therefore, strategies that use communication devices as a backup system are discussed below.

2. *Train the initial response by using massed trials in a discrete trial format.* When first teaching the skill, it is advisable to teach the appropriate behavior by using discrete trial technology (cf. Koegel & Schreibman, 1982). The steps of a discrete trial are as follows:

1. The teacher (parent) presents a clear stimulus (cue or instruction) to the individual who is quietly attending to the teacher or the task at hand.
2. The stimulus may be followed by a prompt to evoke the desired response.
3. The individual responds correctly or incorrectly.
4. The teacher provides a consequence that is immediate, easily discriminable, contingent, and consistent.
5. There is a brief interval before the next trial begins.

Initial training sessions should consist of rapid presentations of 10 to 20 opportunities to learn the response, with no more than 4 seconds between each opportunity (Koegel, Dunlap, & Dyer, 1980). This structured training allows rapid acquisition of the appropriate response, which should be generalized to natural contexts in later phases of training.

3. *If the individual does not spontaneously use the appropriate communicative response, use prompt-fading techniques.* One type of prompting hierarchy that can be used to guide the individual to make the appropriate response is the system of least-intrusive prompts (cf. Snell, 1983). This involves first presenting the training trial. If the individual does not respond independently, the teacher provides more assistance (e.g., a verbal prompt). If, after a short latency, the individual does not respond, the teacher provides even more assistance (e.g., a model). This is followed by even more intrusive prompting (e.g., a physical prompt) if a correct response is not achieved. The teacher continues to use this procedure until a correct response is achieved. Thus, on every teaching trial, the individual has the opportunity to perform the response without prompting.

Another prompting procedure is graduated guidance, in which the teacher employs prompts of decreasing intrusiveness. This procedure is particularly effective when teaching an individual a protest response. For example, the teacher begins with a full physical prompt (e.g., hand-over-hand prompting to point to *no* on a communication board) and then fades to partial physical prompts (e.g., lightly guiding the individual's hand to point to the communication board). The teacher then shadows the response (e.g., keeping his or her hands within an inch of the student's hands) and finally removes the prompts altogether.

4. *If possible, train in the setting where the skill will eventually be used.* Individuals with severe behavior disorders often have difficulty generalizing the skills they have learned from a training setting to a new, nontraining environment (Rincover & Koegel, 1975). Therefore, if possible, train the skill in the environment(s) where the individual will eventually use the response (Durand, 1990).

5. *Have the individual's caregivers and teachers conduct the training.* Another strategy that enhances generalization is having the teachers and caregivers do the training. However, they often need administrative support and direct training on intervention strategies (Dyer & Kohland, 1991; Dyer, Williams, & Luce, 1991). This training should involve an in-service review of the procedures, modeling of the procedures, and feedback regarding the correct implementation of the training program. The trainer should also elicit input and ideas from the caregiver regarding how the training should be carried out in the context of the regular daily routine (Peck, Killen, & Baumgart, 1989). After initial modeling and feedback sessions are completed, the trainer can make periodic observations to monitor the intervention and can suggest necessary changes in the program. It is recommended that the caregivers collect ongoing data to assist in this monitoring process.

6. *Use natural antecedents and student-selected consequences.* When conducting training, set up the environment with the exact stimuli that elicit the

aberrant behavior, and train the student in the appropriate communicative response in the presence of those stimuli. For example, if the individual consistently exhibits aggression when presented with a particular task, teach that individual an appropriate method of protesting in the presence of the same task (e.g., by handing it back). Carr (1982) suggested that this type of programming may result in successful generalization because communicative responses are brought under the stimulus control of naturally occurring stimuli rather than more specific prompts such as adult instructions.

Implicit in functional communication training is the idea that the student selects the consequences. In the initial stages of training, the appropriate communicative behavior is directly reinforced with the event that the individual has requested. If a break has been requested, a break should be given. If a tangible reinforcer, such as food, has been requested, the food should be delivered immediately.

7. *Require a high training criterion of the new communicative response.* During all phases of training, require the individual to produce the appropriate communicative response before moving to the next phase of training. For example, we recommend that, during structured training sessions, the individual correctly respond to at least 80% of the opportunities presented to her or him across three consecutive days. Further, we recommend that, when assessing generalization of the response to new, untrained situations, the criterion should be 80% correct responses to at least 10 opportunities in these untrained contexts. If the individual does not reach this criterion, it is recommended that training be conducted in this new context. Finally, maintenance of the response can be assessed by collecting data on the individual's communicative responses once a week for several weeks. If at any time the individual falls below the 80% training criterion, provide booster training sessions on the appropriate use of the communicative response.

8. *Maintain the skill by fading the reinforcement schedule.* One of the most frequently stated concerns of parents and teachers about the functional communication training approach is that it is not realistic to reinforce the individual every time a request is made. That is, if the individual were allowed to protest all tasks, learning would not occur in the classroom. If the individual were reinforced every time food was requested, obesity might result. We have found that, in some cases, this simply does not occur. When we taught children who had previously been stealing food to request it, the frequency of requests dropped to a low rate, even though we reinforced every request with food (Hall, Camp, & Dyer, 1987). However, with other individuals, contingencies need to be specifically programmed if the appropriate response is to be maintained in the natural environment. One method is to use intermittent reinforcement schedules (Koegel & Rincover, 1977). That is, after reinforcing the individual for every appropriate communicative response, the reinforce-

ment schedule can be faded to reinforcing every other response. For example, if the individual protests a task, the teacher might say, "That's nice telling me you don't want to do this, but I would like you to do it anyway." Then, the next time the individual protested the task, the teacher would remove it. Similarly, if the individual asked for ice cream, the teacher might say, "Not right now," and then give the individual ice cream the next time it was requested. After the appropriate response is maintained on the schedule of reinforcement, the schedule can be further faded to every third response, and finally to every fourth response.

Another method of fading the reinforcement is to increase the amount of time between the time the individual makes the request and the time she or he receives the reinforcer. For example, if the individual requests a break, the teacher might say, "Just work for a little more time, and then you can have a break." The teacher would then provide the break after 5 seconds of appropriate work after the request and would then gradually increase the time by 5-second increments over successive requests. The individual who engaged in aberrant behavior during the waiting period would not be reinforced. This method of gradually increasing the amount of time the individual has to maintain appropriate behavior before receiving the reinforcer is helpful in ensuring the maintenance of appropriate behavior for gradually longer periods of time (Dunlap, Koegel, Johnson, & O'Neill, 1987).

9. *Generalize the newly acquired skill by using naturalistic communication training strategies.* After the individual has acquired the new communicative response through the use of massed trials in a discrete trial format, naturalistic communication training strategies can be used to enhance the generalization to the natural environment. These strategies include the mand model (Rogers-Warren & Warren, 1980), time delay (Halle, Marshall, & Spradlin, 1979), incidental teaching (Hart & Risley, 1975), and providing opportunities for social control (Dyer, 1989; Peck, 1985). Basically, these strategies involve having the teacher arrange the environment between the individual and the caregiver to promote appropriate communication. If the response is not made spontaneously, the environment may be manipulated by withholding preferred items, assistance, or activities until an appropriate communicative response is made by the individual. If the individual does not make a communicative response, the teacher provides the cue for communication. After the individual communicates appropriately, the teacher provides the desired activity or item.

In the *mand-model* procedure, the teacher presents a question or instruction related to the focus of interest (e.g., "What do you want?"). If the individual responds correctly, the teacher provides access to the material or activity and a verbal elaboration of the individual's statement. If the individual responds incorrectly, the teacher models the correct response. After the individual responds correctly to the model, the teacher represents the mand.

A correct response to the mand is followed by access to the material or activity, praise, and verbal elaboration.

In the *time-delay* procedure, the teacher does not immediately provide a mand or give the individual access to the preferred item or activity. Instead, the teacher waits for at least 5 seconds, often with an expectant look and a salient positioning of materials. If the individual responds within the 5-second period, the teacher complies with the request. If the individual doesn't respond or is unintelligible or gives an incorrect response, the teacher presents a second time delay or goes directly to the mand-model procedure.

Because the time delay often involves the salient positioning of stimuli in the initial stages to evoke the communicative response, these stimuli need to be faded to a more natural position. Therefore, the teacher gradually moves the stimulus materials back to their natural location over successive trials. An example of how this can be done was illustrated by Dyer, Callahan, Kovacs, and Chiappe (1991). Specifically, at the beginning of intervention, the teacher is provided with a list of four levels of stimulus condition, ranging from highly salient presentation of the preferred item to having the preferred item placed in a more natural location. These levels are as follows: (1) eye level; (1a) midway between eyes and chest; (2) chest level; (2a) midway between chest and side; (3) off to the side, above the table; (3a) off to the side, just above the table; and (4) off to the side, on the table. The teacher begins the intervention by presenting the reinforcer at Level 1. If the individual requests the preferred item at that level, the next trial is presented at Level 2. The teacher thus progresses from Level 1 to Level 4 over successive trials. If the individual does not spontaneously request the preferred item at a particular level for three consecutive trials, the item is moved back to the substep (e.g., from Level 2 to Level 1a). After one spontaneous request at the substep, the teacher returns to the next step. Each session begins on the last level where the individual requested correctly in the previous session.

In the *incidental-teaching* procedure, the teacher waits until the individual makes a communicative initiation and then prompts an elaborated response by using the time-delay or mand-model procedures. For example, if the individual points to a preferred object, the teacher might withhold the object and say, "Tell me what you want." After the individual says, "I want the cookie," the teacher provides the desired object.

10. *Apply systematic consequences for aberrant behavior throughout the program in functional communication training.* While conducting functional communication training, it is important to deliver systematic consequences for aberrant behavior (Wacker et al., 1990). Two recommended guidelines to follow when selecting the treatments are as follows. The first is to select behavior-modification procedures of documented effectiveness to reduce these

behaviors (Bellack & Hersen, 1985) and to use the treatment procedures that are least restrictive first. These procedures, in order of restrictiveness, are as follows: (1) extinction, (2) time-out, (3) contingent loss of reinforcement, (4) contingent exercise, (5) overcorrection, (6) positive practice, and (7) physical restraint. These procedures are considered temporary reduction strategies and are rapidly faded after the problem behavior is reduced. The second guideline is to establish a "functional match" between the aberrant behavior to be reduced and the treatment procedure (Durand, Crimmins, Caufield, & Taylor, 1989; Wacker et al., 1990). For example, if the functional analysis reveals that the individual engages in aberrant behavior to escape the demands of a difficult task, then time-out would not be an effective treatment, because it would serve to reinforce the aberrant behavior. In this situation, a more effective treatment procedure would be one that would prevent escape, such as positive practice. Conversely, the aberrant behavior may function to gain attention for the individual, such as when an individual engages in aggression every time the teacher attempts to give his or her attention to another student. In this case, extinction or time-out may be the most appropriate treatment choice.

Along these lines, it is very important to prevent the inadvertent reinforcement of aberrant behavior while conducting functional communication training, as in prompting the appropriate communicative response immediately after the individual displays aberrant behavior. For example, if the individual bolted from the work area, a teacher might say, "You need to ask for a break if you want to leave," and then allow the individual to leave the work area after the appropriate request was made. The danger of this approach is that the teacher may strengthen the aberrant behavior by teaching a response chain in which the individual first emits the aberrant behavior and is then prompted to engage in appropriate behavior, which is followed by reinforcement. Consequently, the individual learns to make all requests by first engaging in aberrant behavior.

Specific Training Programs

Aberrant Behavior Occurring When the Individual Desires the Attention of Another Person

One way to teach the skill of getting attention appropriately is first to give the individual an easy task, such as a puzzle, a short vocational activity, or a domestic chore. Ask the individual to get your attention when she or he is finished. If the individual is nonverbal, tapping your arm or raising her or his hand may be an appropriate attention-getting strategy. If the individual is verbal, you might instruct her or him to say "Excuse me" (Cipani, 1991b).

If the individual appropriately elicits attention after task completion, give your attention immediately and reinforce the appropriate response with verbal praise (e.g., "Nice getting my attention. What do you want?"). If the individual does not elicit attention spontaneously, use prompt-fading techniques to elicit the response. For example, the teacher can first look at the individual expectantly and, if there is no response, say, "What do you do to get my attention?" This question can be followed by a more intrusive model, gestural, or physical prompt.

After the individual learns to get attention after completing a task, train the appropriate response when the individual is not presented with a task. In this context, the teacher sets up the environment so that the individual has no task while the teacher attends to other things. If the student does not attempt to gain attention within 15 seconds, the teacher implements a system of least-intrusive prompts. Because it is impossible to provide immediate attention every time it is requested, the teacher can systematically train the individual to wait (Garling & Dyer, 1992). To do this, the teacher begins by immediately acknowledging that the individual has appropriately elicited attention and then provides an instruction to wait (e.g., "I'll be right with you"). First, the teacher waits a brief amount of time (3 to 5 seconds) and then provides the individual with attention after he or she has waited quietly. After the individual has learned to wait quietly for 3 to 5 seconds, the teacher gradually increases the amount of time by 5 seconds until the individual can wait up to a minute before attention is provided.

After the individual consistently elicits attention spontaneously in these structured situations, it is important to ensure that this appropriate attention-getting strategy will be exhibited in other situations. For example, if a parent is talking on the telephone and the individual starts screaming to gain the parent's attention, the parent might first ignore the screaming (i.e., put the behavior on extinction). After the individual has quieted down for about 10 seconds, the parent might implement the mand-model procedure to prompt the appropriate response by saying, "What do you need to do to get my attention?" and, if the individual does not make the appropriate response, to provide him or her with a model ("Say 'Excuse me' ").

Aberrant Behavior Occurring When the Individual Is Having Difficulty with a Task

Set up a situation in which the individual must request help to complete a task. It is important that the task presented not have a history of being aversive to the individual. Instead, the task should be a preferred one, so that the individual will be motivated to complete it. Such a task may involve a tape recorder with a favorite tape that is not working or a bottle of juice that will not open. If the individual spontaneously requests help, provide verbal praise and assistance. If the individual appears to be having trouble with the task (before occurrence of aberrant behavior) and has not requested help, prompt the correct response using a system of least-intrusive prompts.

After the individual learns to request help in these structured, massed-trial situations, prompt the appropriate requesting strategy in other contexts throughout the day. For example, the individual might be struggling with a zipper on her or his jacket. Given this natural opportunity to prompt the response, the parent might implement a time-delay procedure by looking at the individual expectantly for 5 seconds. If the individual does not make a request after this time, the parent might follow with a mand-model procedure by saying, "What do you want to ask me?" The parent would then provide assistance after the individual asks for help.

Aberrant Behavior Occurring When the Individual Is Presented with a Nonpreferred Activity or Food

Present the individual with an item or task that is mildly nonpreferred. It is usually not a good idea to teach the initial protest response with a non-preferred item that has a history of being extremely aversive, because the individual may engage in severe aberrant behavior that will compete with the appropriate communicative behavior you are trying to teach. The first time the mildly aversive item is presented, employ a graduated-guidance prompting procedure to ensure that the response will be made without error. For example, if the desired communicative response is to hand the nonpreferred item back, the teacher can provide a full physical prompt immediately after presenting the item by placing his or her hand over the individual's hand, picking up the object, and placing it near the teacher. After the object is removed, the individual should be provided with a preferred activity for approximately 30 seconds. After 30 seconds, re-present the nonpreferred item, thus providing another opportunity to protest. Over successive trials, fade the prompt in the following sequence: (1) gradually remove your hands, (2) gesture to the individual to hand you the item, (3) verbally prompt the individual to return the item, and (4) look at the individual expectantly.

After the individual learns to consistently protest the nonpreferred activity, and the activity is removed after every protest response, the teacher can teach the individual that there are times when a task needs to be done regardless of whether the individual wants to do it or not. This can be easily accomplished by systematically fading the reinforcement schedule. One way is by honoring only every other appropriate protesting response by removing the item and, during the other times, instructing the individual to complete the task by saying, "Good telling me no, but I want you to do this activity now, and when you are finished, you can take a break and earn (your favorite activity)." The teacher can continue to fade the reinforcement schedule in this way until the individual is being reinforced for approximately every fourth appropriate protest response. In some situations, we have found that, at first, the individual does not tolerate having only every other response reinforced. In these situations, the teacher may have the individual do the task only after every fourth protest response at first and then may fade the schedule.

Another way to fade the reinforcement schedule is to gradually increase the amount of time that the individual has to engage in the nonpreferred activity until it is removed. For example, the teacher might say, "Nice telling me no, but I want you to do this task for just a second," and then remove the task after the individual does it appropriately for 3 to 5 seconds. The teacher can then, over successive training sessions, systematically increase the amount of time that the individual has to engage in the task after giving the appropriate protesting response.

After the individual can protest in the presence of mildly nonpreferred tasks, the teacher can then introduce activities that have a history of being very aversive and can prompt the appropriate protest response under these circumstances. It is also important to ensure that the response will be exhibited across other relevant contexts outside the massed-trial training situation. For example, if a child is given a dish of nonpreferred spinach and says, "I don't want this," the parent might say, "That's nice telling me no, but I'd like you to try one small piece, and then you can eat something else."

Aberrant Behavior Occurring When the Individual Wants a Break from an Activity

During a structured situation, give the individual a long, involved task. Tell the individual that she or he may ask for a break whenever she or he wants. Observe the individual for any indication of boredom or frustration with the task. If the individual spontaneously requests a break during this time, push the task aside, and provide the opportunity to engage in a preferred activity for approximately 30 seconds. After 30 seconds, the individual should return to the task, thus having another opportunity to request a break. After the individual learns to request a break at a high rate, the teacher begins to gradually decrease the number of times that the request for a break is honored by saying, "That's nice asking for a break, but I want you to finish what you are doing."

When this structured training is completed, and the individual is reinforced for approximately every fourth request, appropriate requests for a break can be prompted in other contexts. For example, if the individual is required to do a lengthy domestic chore and begins to look tired, the teacher can provide a mand such as "Do you want to ask me something?" If the individual then requests a break, the teacher might say, "OK, why don't you watch TV for a few minutes and then come back to finish up your work."

Aberrant Behavior Occurring When the Individual Wants an Item or Activity

When teaching the individual to request items appropriately, it is important to be sure that the item is in fact a preferred item. Therefore, it is recommended that a preference assessment be conducted (Dyer, 1987). Ways to determine items to be selected for the assessment are to (1) ask the individual (if appropriate); (2) ask familiar caregivers what the individual likes; (3) watch the individual to see what he or she likes to do for long periods of time without being prompted; (4) identify the type of sensory feedback the individual gains from self-stimulatory behavior; and (5) provide appropriate toys or activities that offer similar feedback (Rincover, Cook, Peoples, & Packard, 1979; Snell, 1983). To conduct a preference assessment, first show the individual how the item can be manipulated if he or she does not already know how, and then give it to him or her. An item or activity can then be defined as preferred if the individual demonstrates at least three of the following behaviors: (1) manipulating the item for more than 15 seconds without prompting; (2) resisting when the teacher attempts to take the item; (3) reaching for the object within 3 seconds when the item is taken and placed about 1 foot away; and (4) exhibiting positive affect while manipulating object. It is important to note that preferences change over time. That is, the same item that is preferred on one day may not be preferred the next day (Dyer, 1989). Therefore, it may be necessary to conduct a preference assessment before each structured training session to be sure that the items to be requested are preferred at that particular time.

When conducting training, set up the preferred items within reach at a table (make sure that the individual knows the labels for the items). Tell the individual that if he or she wants something, he or she should ask for it. If the individual requests an item spontaneously, provide it immediately. If the individual does not ask for it, prompt the correct response by holding up the item and using the time-delay strategy (Halle et al., 1979), and fade the time delay over successive trials (Dyer, Callahan, Kovacs, & Chiappe, 1991). Over successive sessions, it is also important to fade the items even farther away in the environment, such as into a cupboard in the kitchen, or on top of a shelf in the classroom (Cipani, 1991a).

At this point, training should occur across activities in the individual's daily routine. For example, if the individual is at the dinner table and is looking at the mashed potatoes as if he or she wants them, the parent might use a time-delay procedure, holding up the potatoes and looking expectantly at the individual.

Aberrant Behavior Occurring When the Individual Is Misunderstood

Individuals with severe behavior disorders may often be misunderstood. This can occur if their speech is unintelligible to unfamiliar people, or if they use sign language (Rotholz et al., 1989). If this happens consistently, the individual can be taught to use a repair/revision strategy with a communication board (Dyer, 1990). In this training, the teacher first teaches the individual to identify icons on a communication board of items that she or he typically requests. After this prerequisite skill is learned, structured training can begin.

In the training context, set up a situation in which the individual must request an object or food item. Have the individual's communication board readily available on the table. After the individual makes the request, give a quizzical look, or say, "I don't understand," "What?" or "Huh?" If the individual does not repair or revise the request by pointing to the correct picture on the communication board, implement a system of least-intrusive prompts.

Some individuals who use sign language as their primary mode of communication are unable to complete the prerequisite skill of identifying icons on the communication board. In this case, adapt the program by taking pictures of the individual producing each of his or her signs and then putting a written label of the sign on each picture. All of these pictures can then be placed in a communication book, and when the individual is misunderstood, he or she is instructed simply to give the listener the book. On the cover of the book is an explanation that says something like "Hi, my name is John. If you don't understand me when I speak in sign language, you can look in this book to find out what my signs mean." The listener then has to look in the book to find the picture of the individual making the particular sign.

After the individual learns how to give the book to the listener during these structured training situations, begin to alter the training by moving the communication board to a location that is within sight but not within reach of the individual. The individual will learn to look for the board when he or she is misunderstood. It is recommended that the individual be trained, by stimulus-fading techniques, to eventually be able to look for the board when it is out of sight but in a familiar location (Dyer et al., 1990).

After conducting structured training in a massed-trial format, it is important to start to prompt the individual to use the repair/revision strategy throughout the day when she or he makes requests. For example, the individual might verbalize "Ja," at which point the teacher says, "What?" If the individual says "Ja" again, the teacher might prompt the use of the board by looking at the individual expectantly (time delay) and, if she or he doesn't respond, by saying, "Use your communication board" (mand-model procedure).

Case Example of Functional Communication Training with Michael

Michael was a 10-year-old boy with a severe developmental delay who lived in a foster home. During the day, he went to a special-education classroom. In that context, he had learned the sign for the word *eat* but did not have any further success learning sign language or learning to use a communication board. During the past year, he had evidenced a marked regression in his behavior. Of particular concern was his aggressive behavior: biting, hitting, pinching, and kicking. Behavior control medication had been prescribed with only minimal effects. During the day, he spent most of his time in a restraint chair; if he was out of the chair and became aggressive, he was restrained on the floor by adults. Because of these problems, Michael's teachers and foster parent felt they could no longer manage him. He was admitted to a 24-hour residential and educational facility on the condition that he have one-to-one staffing to control his aggressive outbursts.

When Michael was admitted to the May Institute, a functional analysis was conducted to determine the possible motivation(s) of his aggressive behavior. The assessment revealed that the behavior appeared to have multiple functions. For example, he was usually aggressive when he was presented with nonpreferred tasks. He was also aggressive in other contexts: (1) when he wanted a specific item, but the staff member could not figure out what it was; (2) when he had to go to the toilet; and (3) when he was required to wait for a preferred item. Staff speculated that the physical contact that resulted from restraint contingent on aggressive episodes might be reinforcing.

When Michael's initial program was developed, it was decided that he would be taught to communicate with gestures, as previous efforts to teach him speech, sign language, or the use of a communication board had been unsuccessful. While his initial program in functional communication training for the first year was developed by a speech pathologist, the communicative skills were taught by Michael's teachers in his school and home settings. Specifically, each of the programs were included as objectives in Michael's individualized education plan, and short-term objectives delineating teaching procedures for each objective were provided to the teachers by the speech pathologist. The teachers collected daily data to reflect Michael's progress in each program, and the speech pathologist monitored the success of the program by making regular visits to his classroom and house, and then evaluating the data.

The first skills to be taught were (1) pointing to indicate what he wanted; (2) handing back nonpreferred items to indicate protest; (3) patting his abdomen to signal a request for the toilet; and (4) eliciting attention by raising his hand or tapping a teacher's arm, and then waiting for reinforcement.

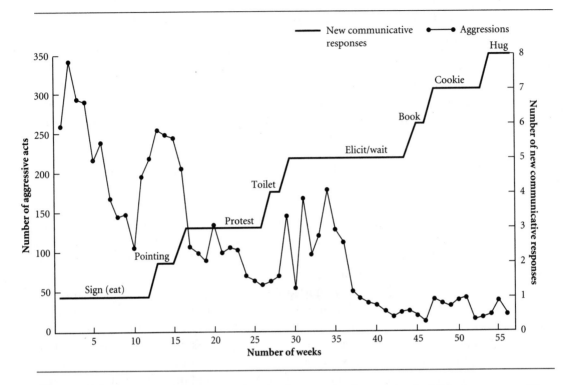

Figure 6-1 *The results of a program in functional communication training for Michael over a year. The data reflect the number of aggressions per week and new, appropriate communicative responses he learned.*

After Michael had learned these basic skills by using gestural communication, specific signs representing highly preferred items were targeted.

In addition to receiving instruction on how to communicate with gestures and sign language, Michael received systematic consequences for his aggressive behavior. The initial treatment was an activities time-out procedure, which involved placing Michael in a chair in the corner after each occurrence of aggressive behavior. The treatment proved to be ineffective because Michael would repeatedly attempt to leave the chair and attack his teachers by pulling their hair, scratching them, or biting them. These episodes often led naturally to Michael's being restrained to prevent further injury to the teachers. Because of these problems, the treatment for aggression was changed to an environmental time-out procedure, which involved placing Michael in a small room away from the group until he had been quiet for a brief period of time.

Figure 6-1 shows the results of this year-long treatment program. As Michael acquired new communicative behaviors, the frequency and quality of his aggressions changed. Initially, most of his aggressions resulted in bruising or breaking skin. Later in treatment, most of his aggressions consisted of light hits in the teacher's direction. At the end of the first year, Michael was still in residential treatment. However, his one-to-one staffing was terminated, as well as his behavior control medication. It is anticipated that he will return to a foster home within the next two years.

REFERENCES

Accreditation Council on Services for People with Developmental Disabilities. (1990). *Standards and interpretation guidelines for services for people with developmental disabilities.* Landover, MD: Author.

Anderson, S. R., & Schwartz, I. S. (1986). Transitional programming. In F. J. Fuoco & W. P. Christian (Eds.), *Behavior analysis and therapy in residential programs.* New York: Van Nostrand Reinhold.

Baer, D. M., Wolf, M. M., & Risley, T. R. (1968). Some current dimensions of applied behavior analysis. *Journal of Applied Behavior Analysis, 1,* 91–97.

Barlow, D. H., & Hersen, M. (1984). *Single case experimental designs.* New York: Pergamon Press.

Bellack, A. S., & Hersen, M. (1985). *Dictionary of behavior therapy techniques.* New York: Pergamon Press.

Bijou, S. W., Peterson, R. F., & Ault, M. H. (1968). A method to integrate descriptive and experimental field studies at the level of data and empirical concepts. *Journal of Applied Behavior Analysis, 1,* 175–191

Bird, F., Dores, P. A., Moniz, D., & Robinson, J. (1989). Reducing severe aggressive and self-injurious behaviors with functional communication training: Direct, collateral, and generalized results. *American Journal of Mental Retardation, 94,* 37–48.

Carr, E. G. (1982). Sign language. In R. L. Koegel, A. Rincover, & A. L. Egel (Eds.), *Educating and understanding autistic children* (pp. 142–157). San Diego: College Hill Press.

Carr, E. G. (1988). Functional equivalence as a mechanism of response generalization. In R. Horner, R. L. Koegel, & O. Dunlap (Eds.), *Generalization and maintenance: Life-style changes in applied settings* (pp. 194–219). Baltimore: Paul E. Brookes.

Carr, E. G., & Durand, V. M. (1985). Reducing behavior problems through functional communication training. *Journal of Applied Behavior Analysis, 18,* 111–126.

Carr, E. G., Robinson, S., Taylor, J. C., & Carlson, J. L. (1990). *Positive approaches to the treatment of severe behavior problems in persons with developmental disabilities: A review and analysis of reinforcement and stimulus-based procedures.* (Monograph No. 4). Seattle: Association for Persons with Severe Handicaps.

Cipani, E. (1991a). Developing functional sign language capability in nonvocal children. In E. Cipani (Ed.), *A guide to developing language comprehension in preschool children with severe and moderate handicaps* (pp. 94–110). Springfield, IL: Charles C Thomas.

Cipani, E. (1991b). "Excuse me, I'll have": Teaching appropriate attention getting behavior to young children with severe handicaps. *Mental Retardation, 28,* 29–33.

Dunlap, G., Kern-Dunlap, L. K., Clarke, S., & Robbins, F. R. (1991). Functional assessment, curricular revision, and severe behavior problems. *Journal of Applied Behavior Analysis, 24,* 387–397.

Dunlap, G., Koegel, R. L., Johnson, J., & O'Neill, R. E. (1987). Maintaining performance of autistic clients in community settings with delayed contingencies. *Journal of Applied Behavior Analysis, 20,* 185–191.

Durand, V. M. (1990). *Severe behavior problems: A functional communication approach.* New York: Guilford Press.

Durand, V. M., & Carr, E. G. (1987). Social influences on "self-stimulatory" behavior: Analysis and treatment application. *Journal of Applied Behavior Analysis, 20,* 119–132.

Durand, V. M., & Crimmins, D. B. (1987). Assessment and treatment of psychotic speech in an autistic child. *Journal of Autism and Developmental Disorders, 17,* 17–28.

Durand, V. M., & Crimmins, D. B. (1988). Identifying the variables maintaining self-injurious behavior. *Journal of Autism and Developmental Disorders, 18,* 99–117.

Durand, V. M., Crimmins, D. B., Caufield, M., & Taylor, J. (1989). Reinforcer assessment: 1. Using problem behavior to select reinforcers. *Journal of the Association for Persons with Severe Handicaps, 14, 113–126.*

Dyer, K. (1987). The competition of autistic stereotyped behavior with usual and specially assessed reinforcers. *Research in Developmental Disabilities, 8,* 607–626.

Dyer, K. (1989). The effects of preference on spontaneous verbal requests in individuals with autism. *Journal of the Association for Persons with Severe Handicaps, 14,* 184–189.

Dyer, K. (1990, May). *Teaching repair/revision strategies to students with autism and other severe handicaps.* Paper presented at the 16th Annual Convention of the Association for Behavior Analysis, Nashville.

Dyer, K., Callahan, D., Kovacs, R., & Chiappe, L. (1991, May). *Fading the time delay: A procedure to transfer control of spontaneous speech to natural stimuli for autistic children.* Paper presented at the 17th Annual Convention of the Association for Behavior Analysis, Atlanta.

Dyer, K., Dunlap, G., & Winterling, V. (1990). Effects of choice making on the serious problem behaviors of students with severe handicaps. *Journal of Applied Behavior Analysis, 23,* 515–524.

Dyer, K., & Kohland, K. (1991). Communication training at the May Center's Integrated Preschool: Assessment, structured teaching, and naturalistic generalization strategies. In E. Cipani (Ed.), *A guide for developing language competence in preschool children with severe and moderate handicaps* (pp. 162–200). Springfield, IL: Charles C Thomas.

Dyer, K., Santarcangelo, S., & Luce, S. C. (1987). Developmental influences in teaching language forms to individuals with developmental disabilities. *Journal of Speech and Hearing Disorders, 52,* 335–347.

Dyer, K., Williams, L., & Luce, S. C. (1991). Training teachers to use naturalistic communication strategies in classrooms for students with autism and other severe handicaps. *Language, Speech, and Hearing Services in Schools, 22,* 313–321.

Garlington, S., & Dyer, K. (1991). *Reducing problem behavior in students with severe behavior disorders with "Delay of Gratification" training.* Paper presented at the Annual Convention of the Association of Behavior Analysis, San Francisco.

Hall, T., Camp, C., & Dyer, K. (1987, October). *The training of a communicative response in the reduction of food stealing.* Paper presented at the Annual Conference of the Berkshire Association of Behavior Analysis and Therapy, Amherst, MA.

Halle, J. W., Marshall, A. M., & Spradlin, J. E. (1979). Time delay: A technique to increase language use and facilitate generalization in retarded children. *Journal of Applied Behavior Analysis, 12,* 431–439.

Hart, B., & Risley, T. R. (1975). Incidental teaching of language in the preschool. *Journal of Applied Behavior Analysis, 8,* 411–420.

Hunt, P., Alwell, M., & Goetz, L. (1988). Acquisition of conversational skills and the reduction of inappropriate social interaction behaviors. *Journal of the Association for Persons with Severe Handicaps, 13,* 20–27.

Iwata, B. A., Dorsey, M. F., Slifer, K. J., Bauman, K. E., & Richman, G. S. (1982). Toward a functional analysis of self-injury. *Analysis and Intervention in Developmental Disabilities, 2,* 3–20.

Iwata, B. A., Pace, G. M., Cowdery, G. E., Kalsher, M. J., & Cataldo, M. F. (1990). Experimental analysis and extinction of self-injurious escape behavior. *Journal of Applied Behavior Analysis, 23,* 11–27.

Koegel, R. L., Dunlap, G., & Dyer, K. (1980). Intertrial interval duration and learning in autistic children. *Journal of Applied Behavior Analysis, 20,* 91–99.

Koegel, R. L., & Rincover, A. (1977). Some research on the difference between generalization and maintenance in extra-therapy settings. *Journal of Applied Behavior Analysis, 10,* 1–16.

Koegel, R. L., & Schreibman, L. (1982). *How to teach autistic and other severely handicapped children.* Lawrence, KS: H & H Enterprises.

O'Neill, R. E., Horner, R. H., Albin, R. W., Storey, K., & Sprague, J. R. (1990). *Functional analysis of problem behavior: A practical assessment guide.* Sycamore, IL: Sycamore Press.

Peck, C. A. (1985). Increasing opportunities for social control by children with autism and severe handicaps: Effects on student behavior and perceived classroom climate. *Journal of the Association for Persons with Severe Handicaps, 10,* 183–199.

Peck, C. A., Killen, C. C., & Baumgart, D. (1989). Increasing implementation of special education instruction in mainstream schools: Direct and generalized effects of nondirective consultation. *Journal of Applied Behavior Analysis, 22,* 197–210.

Peck, C. A., & Schuler, A. L. (1987). Assessment of social communicative behavior for students with autism and severe handicaps: The importance of asking the right question. In T. L. Layton (Ed.), *Language and treatment of autistic and developmentally disordered children* (pp. 35–62). Springfield, IL: Charles C Thomas.

Reichle, J., & Yoder, D. (1985). Communication board use in severely handicapped learners. *Language, Speech, and Hearing Services in Schools, 16,* 146–157.

Rincover, A., Cook, R., Peoples, A., & Packard, D. (1979). Using sensory extinction and sensory reinforcement principles for programming multiple adaptive behavior change. *Journal of Applied Behavior Analysis, 12,* 221–233.

Rincover, A., & Koegel, R. L. (1975). Setting generality and stimulus control in autistic children. *Journal of Applied Behavior Analysis, 8,* 235–246.

Rogers-Warren, A., & Warren, S. (1980). Mands for verbalization: Facilitating the display of newly trained language in children. *Behavior Modification, 4,* 361–382.

Rotholz, D. A., Berkowitz, S. F., & Burberry, J. (1989). Functionality of two modes of communication in the community by students with developmental disabilities: A comparison of signing and communication books. *Journal of the Association for Persons with Severe Handicaps, 14,* 216–226.

Shane, H., & Bashir, A. (1980). Election criteria for the adoption of an augmentative communication system: Preliminary considerations. *Journal of Speech and Hearing Disorders, 45,* 408–414.

Snell, M. E. (1983). Implementing and monitoring the IEP: Intervention strategies. In M. E. Snell (Ed.), *Systematic instruction of the moderately and severely handicapped* (2nd ed.). Columbus, OH: Merrill.

Steege, M. W., Wacker, D. P., Berg, W. K., Cigrand, K. C., & Cooper, J. L. (1989). The use of behavioral assessment to prescribe and evaluate treatments for severely handicapped children. *Journal of Applied Behavior Analysis, 22,* 459–467.

Touchette, P. E., MacDonald, R. F., & Langer, S. N. (1985). A scatter plot for identifying stimulus control of problem behavior. *Journal of Applied Behavior Analysis, 18,* 39–48.

Wacker, D. P., Steege, M. W., Northup, J., Sasso, G., Berg, W., Reimers, T., Cooper, L., Cigrand, K., & Donn, L. (1990). A component analysis of functional communication training across three topographies of severe behavior problems. *Journal of Applied Behavior Analysis, 23,* 417–430.

Chapter
7

Use of Behavior-Modifying Drugs

CYNTHIA R. ELLIS, YADHU N. SINGH,
AND NIRBHAY N. SINGH

INTRODUCTION

Although behavioral therapies are typically the mainstay of treatment for behavior problems in individuals with developmental disabilities, psychotropic medications are also commonly used in the management of severe problem behaviors in this population. The use of these medications is particularly common in individuals who exhibit violent, explosive behavior or engage in life-threatening behaviors (Aman & Singh, 1988). Aggression, agitation, property destruction, and stereotypy are other behaviors that may prompt the use of medication in individuals with developmental disabilities. Historically, psychotropic medications have been used at very high doses to achieve a sedative effect and, thus, to provide behavioral control. However, recent legislation and litigation (Singh, Guernsey, & Ellis, 1992) and increasing concern over the impairment that these medications cause in learning, cognitive performance, and adaptive behavior (Aman & Singh, 1980) have resulted in a more judicious use of psychotropic medications in this population.

Given the large number of individuals with developmental disabilities who receive psychotropic medication, it is important for clinicians and therapists who work with this population to have some basic knowledge of medications and their effects on behavior. If clinicians and therapists are knowledgeable about the effects and side effects of various medications, they can be relied on to monitor the client and provide feedback to the prescribing physician. Studies have shown that informed feedback greatly enhances treatment-related decisions (Sprague & Gadow, 1976). Indeed, recent models of the assessment, diagnosis, and treatment of behavioral and psychiatric disorders rely heavily on informed feedback from parents, clinicians, teachers, and therapists to enhance clinical decision making in multidisciplinary teams (Singh, Parmelee, Sood, & Katz, 1993; Singh, Sood, Sonenklar, & Ellis, 1991). Because there are few methodologically sound studies examining the efficacy of medication in treating behavior problems in individuals with developmental disabilities, medication prescription is frequently based more on clinical judgment than on robust scientific findings. However, good theoretical rationales are available for using psychopharmacological treatments for some behaviors, such as self-injury. In general, it is important to remember that medication, like any other treatment, should be used to improve the individual's general functioning and quality of life rather than strictly to reduce an undesirable behavior (Singh, 1995).

In this chapter, we use the term *psychotropic drug* to refer to any pharmacological agent that is prescribed for the explicit purpose of bringing about behavioral, cognitive, or emotional changes in the individual. The term *psychoactive drug* is used in a more general sense, to refer to any agent that may have these effects, regardless of the doctor's intent when prescribing this type of drug. *Behavioral effects* refers to the effects of medication on the target problem behavior, such as aggression, disruption, and self-injury. Elsewhere, we presented an overview of medication management with reference to children with severe disabilities (Singh, Ellis, & Singh, 1994). For this chapter, we have updated and broadened the basis of that overview to include basic principles of psychopharmacology; the indications for and the effects on behavior and side effects of the most frequently used medications; and the role of interdisciplinary team members in delivering and monitoring the effects of drugs in individuals with developmental disabilities.

PREVALENCE AND PATTERNS OF DRUG USE

Individuals with developmental disabilities are probably the most medicated group in our society. Surveys of psychotropic drug usage in institutions for individuals with developmental disabilities range from a low of 19% to a high of 86%, and most studies report rates between about 30% and 50%. Medication that is used to control epileptic seizures ranges from a low of 24% to a high of 56%, although typically it is between 25% and 45%. In general, the use of psychotropic and antiepileptic medication ranges from 50% to 70%, some individuals being prescribed both types concurrently.

In community-based surveys, the reported use of psychotropic medication with children who have developmental disabilities ranges from 2% to 7%, and for adults, the range is 14% to 36%. The use of medication to control epileptic seizures is between 12% and 31% for children, and between 18% and 24% for adults. The combined prevalence of the use of psychotropic and antiepileptic medication in the community is between 19% and 33% for children and between 36% and 48% for adults.

Various factors influence psychotropic drug use by individuals with developmental disabilities (Singh, Ellis, & Wechsler, in press). Increasing dosages have been found to correlate highly with increasing age and decreasing intellectual impairment. There is a strong relationship between the type of residential facility and the use of medication, with more medication being prescribed in larger facilities and in facilities with very restrictive environments. Further, there is a strong positive correlation between the number and severity of the individual's behavioral and psychiatric problems and the use of medication (Aman & Singh, 1988). For example, individuals who exhibit aggression, hyperactivity, self-injury, screaming, or anxiety are more likely to receive drug treatment than those with milder and less disruptive problems (e.g., noncompliance).

GENERAL MEDICATION PRINCIPLES

Drugs can be classified according to their chemical structure, their mechanism of action, their behavioral effects, or their therapeutic usage. The most common classification system is by therapeutic usage, and the drugs that are prescribed for the treatment of given clinical diagnoses are grouped together. Drug groups that are commonly used in individuals with developmental disabilities include antipsychotics, stimulants, antidepressants, antimanics, and anxiolytics. Further, some drug groups may be used for a number of different purposes. For example, selected antiepileptics, such as carbamazepine (Tegretol), are sometimes used for their antiepileptic as well as for their psychotropic properties. Table 7-1 presents a list of psychotropic and psychoactive drugs by class, generic name, and trade name.

Role of Medication

There is occasionally some confusion among therapists and teachers about the role of medication in the behavior management and learning of individuals with developmental disabilities. Medication is typically used as one component of a broad therapeutic approach to help individuals control their behavior and learn alternative but acceptable forms of behavior (Singh, Ellis, & Jackson, 1996). Medication does *not* teach any new skills; it merely acts as a setting event for the occurrence of appropriate behavior when maladaptive behaviors are reduced. That is, when problem behaviors are reduced, the environment is more conducive to teaching appropriate social and academic skills. For psychiatric problems, such as anxiety or depression, medication provides symptomatic relief, allowing the individual to function more fully at school and at home. Furthermore, it must be remembered that, although medication may relieve the individual's symptoms of psychiatric illness, it does not remove vulnerability to its recurrence because the environmental and constitutional stresses that gave rise to the illness are not affected by medication.

Clinical Decision Making

An interdisciplinary case committee is typically viewed as the best authority in clinical decision making involving all treatment modalities, including drug treatments (see Singh et al., 1993). The members of this committee should include parents, teachers and school personnel, therapists, physicians, nurses, and all others who are involved in the day-to-day activities of the individuals on medication. When compared to the traditional medical model of

TABLE 7-1

Psychoactive and Psychotropic Drugs by Class

Drug Class/Subclass	Generic Name	Trade Name
A. Antipsychotics		
Phenothiazines		
	chlorpromazine	Thorazine
	fluphenazine	Prolixin, Modecate
	mesoridazine	Serentil
	perphenazine	Trilafon
	thioridazine	Mellaril
	trifluoperazine	Stelazine
Thioxanthenes		
	chlorprothixene	Taractan
	thiothixene	Navane
Butyrophenones		
	haloperidol	Haldol
	pipamperon	Dipiperon
Rauwolfia alkaloids		
	reserpine	Rauloydin, Reserpoid, Sandril
Other antipsychotics		
	clozapine	Clozaril
	loxapine	Loxitane
	risperidone	Risperdal
B. Antidepressants		
Tricyclics		
	amitriptyline	Elavil, Amitril, Endep
	clomipramine	Anafranil
	desipramine	Norpramin, Pertofrane
	doxepin	Sinequan, Adapin
	imipramine	Tofranil
	nortriptyline	Pamelor
Monoamine oxidase inhibitors		
	isocarboxazid	Marplan
	phenelzine	Nardil
	tranylcypromine	Parnate
Selective serotonin reuptake inhibitors		
	fluoxetine	Prozac
	fluvoxamine	Luvox
	paroxetine	Paxil
	sertraline	Zoloft

(continued)

TABLE 7-1

Psychoactive and Psychotropic Drugs by Class   (*continued*)

Drug Class/Subclass	Generic Name	Trade Name
Other antidepressants		
	bupropion	Wellbutrin
	trazodone	Desyrel
	venlafaxine	Effexor
C. Antimanics		
	lithium carbonate	Eskalith, Lithane, Lithobid
D. Anxiolytics		
Benzodiazepines		
	alprazolam	Xanax
	chlordiazepoxide	Librium
	diazepam	Valium
	lorazepam	Ativan
	oxazepam	Serax
	prazepam	Verstran
	temazepam	Restoril
	triazolam	Halcion
Antihistamines		
	diphenhydramine	Benadryl
	hydroxyzine	Atarax
	promethazine	Phenergan
Atypical anxiolytics		
	buspirone	BuSpar
E. Stimulants		
	amphetamine sulfate	Benzedrine
	dextroamphetamine	Dexedrine
	methamphetamine	Desoxyn
	methylphenidate	Ritalin
	pemoline	Cylert
F. Antiepileptics		
	carbamazepine	Tegretol
	clonazepam	Klonopin
	diazepam	Valium
	ethosuximide	Zarontin
	felbamate	Felbatol
	gabapentin	Neurontin

TABLE 7-1

Psychoactive and Psychotropic Drugs by Class   (*continued*)

Drug Class/Subclass	Generic Name	Trade Name
F. Antiepileptics		
	phenobarbital	Luminal, Gardenal
	phenytoin	Dilantin
	primidone	Mysoline
	sodium valproate	Depakene, Depakote, Epilim
	sulthiame	Ospolot
G. Others		
Beta-blockers		
	propranolol	Inderal
Alpha-2 blockers (nonspecific)		
	clonidine	Catapres
Alpha-2A blockers (selective)		
	guanfacine	Tenex
Opioid antagonists		
	naloxone	Narcan
	naltrexone	Trexan
Sympathomimetic amines		
	fenfluramine	Pondimin, Ponderax
Anticholinergics		
	benztropine	Cogentin
	biperiden	Akineton
	ethopropazine	Parsidol
	procyclidine	Kemadrin
	trihexyphenidyl	Artane

physician-based treatment decisions, an interdisciplinary team decision-making model results in far fewer individuals being placed on medication (Bisconer, Zhang, & Sine, 1995; Briggs, 1989; Findholt & Emmett, 1990). However, many members of such interdisciplinary committees have little training, either formal or informal, in medication principles and management (Epstein, Singh, Leubke, & Stout, 1991; Singh, Ellis, Donatelli, et al., 1996; Singh, Epstein, Leubke, & Singh, 1990). Therefore, guidelines have been developed to assist nonmedical interdisciplinary team members in making a meaningful contribution to the medication decision-making process. Box 7-1

> ## Box 7-1
>
> ### GUIDELINES FOR TEACHERS AND THERAPISTS ABOUT MEDICATION MANAGEMENT
>
> 1. Learn about the commonly used therapeutic drugs, their indications and contra-indications, and their possible side effects.
> 2. Become better informed about the effects that various drugs may have on the behavior and learning of individuals with developmental disabilities.
> 3. Familiarize yourself with and closely follow your school or agency policy regarding the administration of prescribed drugs. (Schools and agencies lacking such a policy should develop one in order to legally protect personnel who must administer medication.)
> 4. Actively engage in communication with the physician and the interdisciplinary committee regarding each individual's medication.
> 5. Collect data on target behaviors before, during, and after drug treatment. It is also useful to collect data on other behaviors that may change as a consequence of taking medication (e.g., learning).
> 6. Collect data on the anticipated side effects of the drugs. A prior knowledge of the side effects of different drugs will help.
> 7. Discuss the anticipated effects of the drug and its possible side effects with the individual.
> 8. Discuss the anticipated effects of the drug and its possible side effects with the parent. Also explain to the parent why it is essential that the individual take his or her medication as prescribed by the physician.
> 9. Continue to provide the best educational training or occupational program possible, and provide related services where indicated. Remember that drugs do not teach new skills; teachers do.
>
> Adapted and extended from M. H. Epstein and E. Olinger (1987). Use of medication in school programs for behaviorally disordered pupils. *Behavioral Disorders, 12,* 138–145.

presents guidelines, adapted from Epstein and Olinger (1987), that the members of an interdisciplinary treatment team can use to facilitate their contribution to medication-related decisions and their participation in the implementation of a medication treatment plan.

A trial of medication is typically recommended for the treatment of a problem behavior when behavioral interventions have been unsuccessful or when there is no apparent motivation for the behavior and it is presumed to be of organic origin. Before beginning a psychotropic medication, it must be determined that the behavior is not due to a medical condition (e.g., otitis media or migraine headache) or environmental and psychosocial factors (e.g., living conditions, peer taunting, or abuse). In general, the selection of a particular drug is based on a comprehensive assessment and diagnosis of the problem behaviors. Before the selection and institution of treatment with a specific medication, the risks and benefits of each of the possible medication choices must be considered.

Once medication treatment is initiated, an ongoing evaluation of the drug response using repeated assessment measures, such as rating scales and behavioral observations, and monitoring of the side effects is necessary to determine the effects of the treatment. Standard medication management (see Table 7-2) includes dosage titration at periodic intervals based on the data obtained by the ongoing monitoring process. In most cases, if a positive response to medication occurs, it will be evident within a dose range that is specific to each medication. Dosing is usually initiated with a low dose and is titrated to higher doses based on the clinical effects and the emergence of side effects. Because of the large variation in body size and metabolic maturity among children and adolescents, many drug doses for children and adolescents must be based on weight, whereas there are often standard drug doses for adults. It is extremely important that all therapists and clinicians who work with an individual on medication be involved in monitoring the effects of the medication in the setting in which they interact with that individual. While no single assessment instrument can be used for all disorders and with all individuals, the Aberrant Behavior Checklist (Aman & Singh, 1986, 1994) is the only instrument designed specifically to evaluate the effects of psychotropic drugs in children and adults with mental retardation. This rating scale covers the primary problem behaviors for which antipsychotics and other drugs are usually prescribed, as well as a range of other behaviors that may show medication-related changes. In addition, a number of assessment instruments have been designed to record the side effects of medication in general, as well as instruments designed for specific side effects or medications. Finally, a reassessment of the need for continued medication should be undertaken at least once every 30 to 90 days to prevent unnecessarily prolonged treatment. In the rare case in which an individual is on medication for more than a year, it is important that a drug holiday (i.e., a period of time off the medication) be instituted every year to determine the continued need for the medication.

EFFECTS OF DRUGS ON BEHAVIOR AND LEARNING

Antipsychotics

Antipsychotics, the drugs most frequently used with persons who have developmental disabilities, include four major classes of compounds: phenothiazines (e.g., thioridazine and chlorpromazine), butyrophenones (e.g., haloperidol), thioxanthenes (e.g., thiothixene), and Rauwolfia alkaloids (e.g., reserpine). Of these, the phenothiazines and butyrophenones are of prime

TABLE 7-2

Recommended Doses for the Various Classes of Psychotropic Drugs

Drug	Average Daily Dose		
	Children	Adolescents	Adults
A. Antipsychotics			
chlorpromazine (>6 mos of age)[a]	30–200 mg (2.5–6 mg/kg/day)	40–400 mg (3–6 mg/kg/day)	100–800 mg (max dose 2000 mg/day)
thioridazine (>2 yrs of age)[a]	75–200 mg (0.5–3 mg/kg/day)	10–200+ mg	150–800 mg (max dose 800 mg/day)
trifluoperazine (>6 yrs of age)[a]	1–15 mg	1–20 mg	15–40 mg
thiothixene (>12 yrs of age)[a]	2–10 mg	5–30 mg	20–60 mg
haloperidol (>3 yrs of age)[a]	0.5–4 mg (0.05–0.15 mg/kg/day)	2–16 mg	2–16+ mg
reserpine	0.02–0.25 mg	0.1–1.0 mg	0.1–1.0 mg
clozapine (>16 yrs of age)[a]		50–200 mg (3–5 mg/kg/day)	300–450 mg (max dose 900 mg/day)
loxapine (>16 yrs of age)[a]	5–50 mg	20–100 mg	60–250 mg
B. Antidepressants			
amitriptyline (>12 yrs of age)[a]	30–100 mg (1–5 mg/kg/day)	50–100 mg (1–5 mg/kg/day)	75–300 mg
bupropion (>18 yrs of age)[a]	25–150 mg	75–300 mg (3–6 mg/kg/day)	200–450 mg
clomipramine (>10 yrs of age)[a]	25–100 mg	50–150 mg (2–3 mg/kg/day)	100–250 mg
desipramine (>12 yrs of age)[a]	10–150 mg (1–5 mg/kg/day)	50–150 mg (1–5 mg/kg/day)	100–200 mg
fluoxetine (>18 yrs of age)[a]	5–20 mg	10–60 mg (0.5–1 mg/kg/day)	20–80 mg
imipramine (>6 yrs of age)[a]	10–150 mg (1–5 mg/kg/day)	50–200 mg (1–5 mg/kg/day)	75–200 mg
nortriptyline (>12 yrs of age)[a]	10–100 mg	50–100 mg (1–3 mg/kg/day)	75–200 mg
phenelzine (>16 yrs of age)[a]		15–45 mg (0.5–1 mg/kg/day)	45–90 mg
sertraline (not in children)[a]	25–100 mg	50–200 mg (1.5–3 mg/kg/day)	50–200 mg

TABLE 7-2

Recommended Doses for the Various Classes of Psychotropic Drugs (*continued*)

Drug	Average Daily Dose		
	Children	*Adolescents*	*Adults*
C. Antimanics			
lithium carbonate[b] (>12 yrs of age)[a]	300–900 mg	900–1200 mg (10–30 mg/kg/day)	900–1200 mg
D. Anxiolytics			
alprazolam (>18 yrs of age)[a]	0.25–2 mg	0.75–5 mg (0.02–0.06 mg/kg/day)	1–8 mg
chlordiazepoxide (>6 yrs of age)[a]	10–30 mg	20–60 mg	20–100 mg
diazepam (>6 mos of age)[a]	1–10 mg	2–20 mg (max 0.8 mg/kg/day)	4–40 mg
lorazepam (>12 yrs of age)[a]	0.25–3 mg	0.05–6 mg (0.04–0.09 mg/kg/day)	1–10 mg
diphenhydramine	25–200 mg	50–300 mg (1–5 mg/kg/day)	50–400 mg
hydroxyzine	25–100 mg	40–150 mg (2 mg/kg/day)	75–400 mg
buspirone (>18 yrs of age)[a]	2.5–15 mg	5–30 mg (0.2–0.6 mg/kg/day)	15–60 mg
E. Stimulants			
dextroamphetamine (>3 yrs of age)[a]	2.5–15 mg (0.15–0.5 mg/kg/dose)	5–40 mg (0.15–0.5 mg/kg/dose)	10–40 mg (0.15–0.5 mg/kg/dose)
methylphenidate (>6 yrs of age)[a]	2.5–30 mg (0.3–1 mg/kg/dose)	10–60 mg (0.3–1 mg/kg/dose)	20–60 mg (0.3–1 mg/kg/dose)
pemoline (>6 yrs of age)[a]	18.75–75 mg (1–3 mg/kg/day)	37.5–112.5 mg (1–3 mg/kg/day)	37.5–112.5 mg (1–3 mg/kg/day)
F. Antiepileptics			
carbamazepine[b] (>6 yrs of age)[a]	200–800 mg (5–20 mg/kg/day)	400–1000 mg (10–30 mg/kg/day; max dose 1000 mg/day)	600-1200 mg (max dose 1200 mg/day)
ethosuximide[b]	250–800 mg (20–30 mg/kg/day)	500–1500 mg (20–40 mg/kg/day)	750–1500 mg (max dose 1500 mg/day)

(*continued*)

TABLE 7-2

Recommended Doses for the Various Classes of Psychotropic Drugs   (continued)

Drug	Average Daily Dose		
	Children	Adolescents	Adults
F. Antiepileptics			
phenobarbital[b]	<250 mg (4–8 mg/kg/day)	75–250 mg (1–3 mg/kg/day)	150–250 mg
phenytoin[b]	<300 mg (7.5–9 mg/kg/day)	300-500 mg (6–7 mg/kg/day)	300–400 mg
primidone	150–750 mg	750–1500 mg	750–2000 mg
sodium valproate[b]	250–1000 mg	500–2000 mg	500–2500 mg (15–60 mg/kg/day)
G. Others			
propranolol	5–80 mg	20–140 mg (max 2 mg/kg/day)	80–480 mg
clonidine (not in children)[a]	0.25–0.3 mg (3–6 μg/kg/day)	0.3–0.4 mg (3–6 μg/kg/day)	0.3–0.5 mg
naltrexone (>18 yrs of age)[a]	10–50 mg (0.5–1.5 mg/kg/day)	40–120 mg (1–2 mg/kg/day)	50–150 mg (1–2 mg/kg/day)
fenfluramine (>12 yrs of age)[a]	30–60 mg	40–100 mg (1–2 mg/kg/day)	60–120 mg
benztropine (>3 yrs of age)[a]	0.5–4 mg	0.5–6 mg (43–86 μg/kg/day)	2–6 mg

[a]Recommended U.S. Food and Drug Administration guidelines.
[b]Dosage titrated by serum levels.

importance because they are the most widely used in individuals with developmental disabilities.

Effects on Behavior

The antipsychotics are most frequently prescribed for individuals who are aggressive, destructive, self-injurious, hyperactive, and antisocial in an attempt to control these behaviors (see Table 7-3). However, our knowledge of the behavioral effects of these drugs is rather limited because there are so few well-controlled studies from which we can draw firm conclusions. Some of the early studies with chlorpromazine (Thorazine) indicated that the drug was effective in reducing a number of problem behaviors, such as self-injury and stereotypy, in persons with developmental disabilities (Aman & Singh, 1988).

TABLE 7-3

Psychiatric and Behavioral Indications and Side Effects of Various Classes of Drugs

A. Antipsychotics

Indications: Psychotic states; schizophrenia (exacerbations and maintenance); mania (in conjunction with lithium); behavior disorders with severe agitation, aggressivity, and self-injury; and dyskinetic movement disorders (e.g., Tourette's disorder and juvenile Huntington's disease)

Side effects: Anticholinergic effects, including dry mouth, constipation, blurred vision, and urinary retention (most common with low-potency phenothiazines); extrapyramidal reactions, including acute dystonia, akathisia, and tremor (particularly with high-potency phenothiazines); neuroleptic malignant syndrome; tardive dyskinesia (lower risk with clozapine); other central nervous system effects, including sedation, fatigue, cognitive blunting, psychotic symptoms, confusion, and excitement; orthostatic hypotension and cardiac conduction abnormalities; endocrine disturbances (e.g., menstrual irregularities and weight gain); gastrointestinal distress; skin photosensitivity; granulocytopenia and agranulocytosis (clozapine); and allergic reactions

B. Antidepressants

Indications: Enuresis; attention-deficit/hyperactivity disorder; major depressive disorder; and anxiety disorders (including school phobia, separation anxiety disorder, panic disorder, and obsessive-compulsive disorder)

Side effects: *Tricyclics:* Anticholinergic effects, including dry mouth, constipation, blurred vision, and urinary retention; cardiac conduction slowing (treatment requires EKG monitoring), mild increases and/or irregularity in pulse rate, and mild decreases or increases in blood pressure; confusion or the induction of psychosis; seizures; rash; and endocrine abnormalities
Monoamine oxidase inhibitors: Mild decreases or increases in blood pressure; drowsiness; weight gain; insomnia; and hypertensive crisis with nonadherance to dietary restrictions (necessary to eliminate high tyramine foods from diet) or with certain drugs
Selective serotonin reuptake inhibitors: Irritability; gastrointestinal distress; headaches; and insomnia
Other antidepressants: Irritability (bupropion, venlafaxine); insomnia (bupropion, venlafaxine); drug-induced seizures (bupropion, with high doses); changes in blood pressure (trazodone, venlafaxine); priapism (trazodone); sedation and sleepiness (trazodone, venlafaxine); gastrointestinal distress (venlafaxine); and headache (venlafaxine)

C. Antimanics

Indications: Manic episodes of bipolar disorder; unipolar depression/adjunct treatment in major depressive disorder; and behavior disorders with extreme aggression

Side effects: Kidney abnormalities leading to increased urination and thirst; gastrointestinal distress; fine hand tremor, weakness, and ataxia; possible thyroid abnormalities (with long-term use), weight gain, and electrolyte imbalances; sedation, confusion, slurred speech, irritability, headache, and subtle cogwheel rigidity; skin abnormalities; orthostatic hypotension and pulse rate irregularities; and allergic reactions

(continued)

TABLE 7-3

Psychiatric and Behavioral Indications and Side Effects of Various Classes of Drugs   (*continued*)

D. Anxiolytics

Indications: Anxiety disorders; seizure control; night terrors; sleepwalking; insomnia and acute management of severe agitation; adjunct treatment in mania and refractory psychosis; and Tourette's disorder

Side effects: Headache, sedation, and decreased cognitive performance; behavioral disinhibition, including overexcitement, hyperactivity, increased aggressivity, and irritability; gastrointestinal distress; central nervous system disinhibition resulting in hallucinations, psychotic-like behavior, and depression; physical and psychological dependence (particularly with long-acting benzodiazepines); rebound or withdrawal reactions (particularly with short-acting benzodiazepines); blood abnormalities; anticholinergic effects, including dry mouth, constipation, and blurred vision (antihistamines); and allergic reactions

E. Stimulants

Indications: Attention-deficit/hyperactivity disorder (including those with mental retardation, fragile X syndrome, Tourette's disorder, head trauma, pervasive developmental disorder, or other comorbid disorders); narcolepsy; and adjunctive treatment in refractory depression

Side effects: Decreased appetite; weight loss; abdominal pain; headache, insomnia, irritability, sadness and depression, and mild increases in pulse rate and blood pressure; possible temporary suppression of growth (with long-term use); choreoathetosis (pemoline) and, rarely, tic disorders; and elevated liver function tests (pemoline)

F. Antiepileptics

Indications: Seizure control; bipolar disorder; adjunct treatment in major depressive disorder; and severe behavior problems (e.g., aggression and self-injury)

Side effects: Sedation, weakness, dizziness, disturbances of coordination and vision, hallucinations, confusion, abnormal movements, nystagmus, slurred speech, and depression; blood abnormalities; gastrointestinal distress; skin rashes, alterations in pigmentation, and photosensitivity reactions; increased or decreased blood pressure and congestive heart failure; abnormalities of liver functions (sodium valproate, carbamazepine—rare); genitourinary tract dysfunction; coarsening of facial features, enlargement of the lips, gingival hyperplasia, and excessive hair growth (phenytoin); and bone marrow suppression (carbamazepine, sodium valproate)

G. Others
Propranolol

Indications: Behavior disorders with severe aggression, self-injury, or agitation; Tourette's disorder; and akathisia

Side effects: Decreased heart rate, peripheral circulation, and blood pressure; fatigue, weakness, insomnia, nightmares, dizziness, hallucinations, and mild symptoms of depression; shortness of breath and wheezing (especially in patients with asthma); gastrointestinal distress; and rebound hypertension on abrupt withdrawal

TABLE 7-3

Psychiatric and Behavioral Indications and Side Effects of Various Classes of Drugs   (*continued*)

Clonidine

Indications: Attention-deficit/hyperactivity disorder; Tourette's disorder; behavior disorders with severe aggression, self-injury, or agitation; adjunct treatment of schizophrenia and mania; and possible use in anxiety disorders

Side effects: Sedation; decrease in blood pressure; rebound hypertension; dry mouth; confusion (with high doses); and depression

Guanfacine

Indications: Attention-deficit/hyperactivity disorder and Tourette's disorder

Side effects: Sedation (less than with clonidine); decrease in blood pressure (less than with clonidine); rebound hypertension; dry mouth; confusion (with high doses); and depression

Opioid antagonists

Indications: Self-injury and reversal of narcotic depression

Side effects: Drowsiness; dizziness, dry mouth, sweating; nausea, abdominal pain; and loss of energy

Fenfluramine

Indications: Management of obesity and possible use in the control of some behavior problems in pervasive developmental disorder

Side effects: Anorexia, weight loss; drowsiness, dizziness, confusion, headache, and incoordination; mood alterations, anxiety, insomnia, weakness, agitation, and slurred speech; gastrointestinal distress; increased or decreased blood pressure and palpitations; skin rashes; dry mouth; eye irritation; and muscle aches

Anticholinergics

Indications: Treatment of extrapyramidal reactions (dystonia, rigidity, tremor, and akathisia); sleep disorders; and agitation

Side effects: Sedation; cognitive impairment; and anticholinergic effects, including dry mouth, constipation, and blurred vision

Unfortunately, these studies were methodologically flawed in several respects, and their conclusions regarding the efficacy of chlorpromazine on problem behaviors are open to criticism. Indeed, more recent and better-controlled studies suggest that chlorpromazine may actually have a detrimental effect on some appropriate behaviors in some persons (Schroeder, 1988). Other studies have found that, while problem behaviors (e.g., stereotypy) are suppressed, some appropriate behaviors (e.g., conditioning tasks) are worsened (Aman & Singh, 1988). Unless valid and reliable data are available to show otherwise, clinicians should refrain from using this drug.

Thioridazine (Mellaril) is a popular drug used to treat problem behavior in individuals with developmental disabilities. Although many of the published studies are methodologically inadequate (Aman & Singh, 1980), the studies that meet the scientific standards of rigor suggest that thioridazine decreases hyperactivity, aggression, and stereotypy in persons with developmental disabilities. There have been at least five recent studies of this drug, and all have shown positive results. In addition, one study showed that a low dose of thioridazine was as effective as a higher dose in controlling stereotypy (Singh & Aman, 1981). In general, there is fairly good evidence that thioridazine is more effective than chlorpromazine in controlling the problem behaviors of persons with developmental disabilities.

Haloperidol (Haldol) is often used because it is much less sedating than thioridazine or chlorpromazine. It is typically used to suppress hyperactivity, aggression, hostility, and implusivity in persons with developmental disabilities. However, there are very few well-controlled studies attesting to the efficacy of this drug with this population (Aman & Singh, 1991).

Other antipsychotics, such as fluphenazine (Prolixin), mesoridazine (Serentil), trifluoperazine (Stelazine), thiothixene (Navane), and loxapine (Loxitane), are used in institutional settings to control problem behaviors in individuals with mental retardation, but clinicians and therapists should be aware that there are few scientific data attesting to their efficacy and that most of these drugs have not been approved by the U.S. Food and Drug Administration (FDA) for use in this population. Further, the same caution applies to the newer antipsychotics, such as clozapine (Clozaril) and risperidone (Risperdal).

Effects on Learning

The majority of the studies on the effects of antipsychotics have been concerned with the reduction of problem behaviors in persons with developmental disabilities rather than with their effects on learning and performance. Those that have investigated the effects on learning and performance have used either IQ or achievement tests to assess drug effects on learning. Although there are a few studies suggesting that low doses of antipsychotics may actually facilitate learning and performance in some persons with developmental disabilities, probably by suppressing incompatible behaviors, concern remains that cognitive and academic performance may be seriously impaired by antipsychotic use, particularly in children with mental retardation (Aman, 1984). Thus, it is important that physicians, therapists, teachers, direct-care staff, and parents monitor the individual's adaptive, social, and academic behaviors during dosage adjustment, as well as during maintenance medication, to see if any of these behaviors are adversely affected. At all times, the goal should be to use the lowest dosage possible to treat the problem behavior without affecting the learning potential of the individual.

Side Effects

Antipsychotics tend to produce side effects that range from mild to severe. The more common and milder side effects are dry mouth, constipation, difficulty with urination, blurred vision, weight gain, and an increased sensitivity of the skin to the effects of sunlight. Antipsychotics may also cause an increase in heart rate as well as a lowering of the blood pressure. Certain abnormal muscle and movement disorders have also resulted from antipsychotic usage, including acute dystonic reactions (muscle spasms, usually of the face and neck); tardive dyskinesia (involuntary movements of the face, mouth, tongue, trunk, or extremities, which usually appear after prolonged usage or immediately following discontinuation of the medication); and Parkinsonian symptoms (such as muscle rigidity, hand tremor, and a masklike visual appearance). Clinicians must be aware that the individual's alertness may decrease because of the nonspecific sedative nature of most antipsychotic medications.

While all of these side effects are important and must be monitored, clinicians should be particularly sensitive to (1) akathisia, because it is often mistaken for behavioral problems such as agitation and aggression; (2) tardive dyskinesia, because individuals with mental retardation are often prescribed antipsychotics for long periods without the benefit of periodic drug holidays; and (3) those side effects that are not easily observed because many individuals with mental retardation cannot verbally tell their parents or therapists about these side effects. Further, it is important to monitor systematically for the possible emergence of tardive dyskinesia due to exposure to neuroleptic medication. At present, the best instrument for this purpose is the Dyskinesia Identification System: Condensed User Scale (Sprague, Kalachnik, & White, 1985), a scale devised specifically for measuring tardive dyskinesia in individuals with developmental disabilities. When tardive dyskinesia is suspected, a referral to a neurologist is in order.

Antidepressants

Historically, the antidepressants have not been used very much for persons with developmental disabilities. However, despite a lack of scientific evidence to support their use, antidepressants are now increasingly being used to manage problem behaviors in this population. The monoamine oxidase inhibitors (MAOIs), which are rarely used with children and adolescents, do not appear to have much effect on the problem behaviors of persons with developmental disabilities. The role of tricyclic antidepressants in controlling problem behaviors is not very clear because few studies on its effects are available. In the two most recent and well-controlled studies, it was reported that imipramine (Tofranil) increased food consumption, decreased screaming and crying, and stabilized sleep patterns in one study (Field, Aman, White, & Vaithianathan, 1986) and significantly increased irritability, lethargy/social withdrawal, and hyperactivity in the other study (Aman, White, Vaithianathan, & Teehan, 1986). There is some evidence that second-generation antidepressants (e.g., fluoxetine) may be beneficial in the treatment of self-injury in some individuals with mental retardation (Ricketts, Goza, et al., 1993). However, the paucity of research evidence attesting to the efficacy of antidepressants in treating behavior problems in this population should elicit a cautious approach to their use.

As with children in the general population, the antidepressants are probably most commonly prescribed for the treatment of enuresis in persons with developmental disabilities. However, the response of persons with developmental disabilities to the antidepressants is typically associated with a less favorable outcome than in their nondisabled peers, and enuresis has not appeared to respond well to antidepressants (Aman & Singh, 1988).

Effects on Learning

We do not know what effects antidepressants have on the learning, cognition, and adaptive behavior of persons with developmental disabilities.

Side Effects

The antidepressants have several side effects similar to those reported for the antipsychotics, including dry mouth, constipation, difficulty with urination, and blurred vision. Tricyclics may also cause a decrease in blood pressure, a rapid heart rate, and, occasionally, more serious changes in heart function. Because of the serious nature of the potential changes in cardiac conduction associated with the use of certain tricyclic antidepressants (particularly desipramine in children), appropriate EKG monitoring is mandatory. The newer, selective serotonin reuptake inhibitors (e.g., fluoxetine, sertraline, paroxetine, and fluvoxamine) have less adverse anticholinergic, sedative, and cardiovascular effects than the tricyclic antidepressants.

Antimanics

Lithium carbonate is the only important antimanic drug that is used for individuals with developmental disabilities. It appears to be the drug of choice for treating bipolar disorder and is also used in the treatment of recurrent unipolar depression in this population (Chandler, Gualtieri, & Fahs, 1988). Individuals diagnosed as having bipolar disorder typically exhibit one or more manic episodes (elevated or irritable mood) alternating with major depressive episodes. The few well-controlled studies that are available indicate that lithium may have a modest but clinically significant effect on affective symptoms (i.e., manic and depressive episodes). In addition, several case reports and a small number of studies of individuals with developmental disabilities have found lithium to increase "adaptability" and to reduce aggression, motor activity, restlessness, excitability, and self-injury. Lithium also appears to be useful in treating those individuals who have nonspecific behavior disorders and a strong family history of bipolar disorder, severe behavior disorders that are cyclic in nature, and uncontrolled, explosive aggressive behavior (Chandler et al., 1988).

Effects on Learning

As with the antidepressants, we do not know what effects antimanic drugs have on the learning, cognition, and adaptive behavior of persons with developmental disabilities. What little is known about the effects of lithium on these functions has been extrapolated from studies of nondisabled persons.

Side Effects

The most serious side effect of lithium carbonate is the potential for a central nervous system confusional state, including sluggishness, tremor, ataxia, coma, and seizures (which, in rare cases, have resulted in death).

Anxiolytics

The anxiolytics, or antianxiety drugs, such as diazepam (Valium) and chlordiazepoxide (Librium), are used fairly extensively in persons with developmental disabilities. In addition to the treatment of anxiety, these drugs are also used as hypnotics or anticonvulsants (e.g., diazepam) or for their psychotropic effects in controlling such behaviors as hyperactivity, agitation, aggression, and disruption. There are no empirical studies evaluating the effects of anxiolytics on anxiety in persons with developmental disabilities. The two best-controlled studies evaluated their effects on acting-out and hyperactive behaviors and showed that anxiolytics significantly worsened these behaviors in persons with developmental disabilities (LaVeck & Buckley, 1961; Walters, Singh, & Beale, 1977). Buspirone (BuSpar), a relatively new serotonergic anxiolytic, has been used in the management of behavior problems in children and adults with developmental disabilities, and the available case studies suggest that it may be effective in only some individuals (Ricketts et al., 1994).

Clearly, we need more data on the efficacy of the anxiolytics in this population, but, in the meantime, a cautious approach to their use is advised.

Effects on Learning

No empirical data are available on the effects that these drugs may have on the learning or cognition of persons with developmental disabilities.

Side Effects

Over the short term, the most frequent side effects involve the sedative actions of the drugs; other short-term effects include headaches, nausea, skin rashes, and impaired sexual performance. Even at low doses, the anxiolytics may induce aggressiveness and irritability. At higher doses, there may be an increase in activity, psychotic-like behavior, and suicidal actions. The long-term side effects include a continuation of some of the short-term effects, along with the potential for physical and psychological dependence with the benzodiazepines.

Stimulants

The stimulants, such as methylphenidate (Ritalin), dextroamphetamine (Dexedrine), and pemoline (Cylert), are the drugs of choice for treating attention-deficit/hyperactivity disorder in children. However, they are not widely used in persons with developmental disabilities. The early, usually uncontrolled studies of the effects of stimulants on persons with developmental disabilities showed that they had few positive effects on a variety of problem behaviors. More recent studies, particularly those of persons who have mild to moderate levels of disability, have shown a modest but statistically significant improvement in hyperactivity and other behavior problems with the use of stimulant drugs (e.g., Varley & Trupin, 1982). However, studies show that the stimulants do not improve the hyperactive behavior of persons with more severe developmental disabilities (Aman & Singh, 1982). What we can conclude from the results of the better-controlled studies is that the effects of stimulants on hyperactivity, lack of attention, and impulsivity decrease as the functional level of the person decreases (Aman, in press).

In one of the few studies reporting the effect of stimulants on a behavior other than those associated with hyperactivity in children with developmental disabilities, the frequency of pica decreased in three adolescents with profound mental retardation while on methylphenidate, possibly because of the diminished dopaminergic neurotransmission associated with the drug (Singh, Ellis, Crews, & Singh, 1994).

Effects on Learning

The cognitive effects of the stimulant drugs have not been well studied in persons with developmental disabilities. The general findings from the few studies available suggest that it may worsen intellectual performance, as measured on the Wechsler Adult Intelligence Scale (see Aman & Singh, 1991).

Side Effects

Insomnia, decreased appetite, weight loss, abdominal pain, and headaches are the most frequently reported side effects of the stimulant drugs. Less common side effects are drowsiness, sadness, increased talkativeness, and dizziness. Furthermore, there is a possible temporary suppression of growth with the chronic administration of methylphenidate. Studies of children with developmental disabilities have shown that those with mental retardation have a higher rate of adverse effects (e.g., tics and social withdrawal) from stimulants than children in the general population (Handen, Feldman, Gosling, Breaux, & McAuliffe, 1991).

Antiepileptics

The management of a seizure disorder is the most common indication for prescribing an antiepileptic for an individual with a developmental disability. Up to 20% of individuals with mental retardation and 50% of those with mental retardation and cerebral palsy have a seizure disorder. The antiepileptics are used to manage a variety of convulsive disorders, collectively known as epilepsy. A typical episode of epilepsy involves the disturbance or loss of consciousness, abnormal and excessive EEG discharge, convulsions or repetitive body movements in a characteristic pattern, and an increase in autonomic activity. Although there are over a dozen distinguishable forms of epilepsy, the three most common forms are generalized tonic-clonic (grand mal), generalized absence (petit mal), and complex partial focal (psychomotor) epilepsy. The primary mode of treatment for epilepsy is drug treatment, and such treatment is usually very effective (Stores, 1988). In addition, even when prescribed for the control of epilepsy, a number of antiepileptic drugs appear to have effects on problem behaviors and cognition.

Psychotropic Effects of the Antiepileptics

Antiepileptics are also thought to have useful psychotropic properties and may be prescribed specifically for the control of problem behaviors. The primary psychiatric use of antiepileptics in individuals with developmental disabilities is for affective disorders, such as mania, bipolar disorder, or schizoaffective disorder, particularly if these disturbances have been resistant to traditional treatment. Early studies strongly suggested that phenytoin (Dilantin) may have some behavioral effects on individuals with developmental disabilities, but these claims have not been validated in well-controlled investigations (see Aman & Singh, 1991). Carbamazepine (Tegretol), valproic acid (Depakene, Depakote), and, to a much lesser extent, clonazepam (Klonopin) are currently being used for this purpose. Although some clinicians advocate the use of antiepileptic medications for their psychotropic effects, this is truly a case where clinical enthusiasm is far in excess of the scientific evidence supporting its purported effects.

Unintended Behavioral Effects

As noted above, antiepileptics are usually prescribed for the management of seizure disorders. There is some concern that the long-term administration of these drugs may cause untoward behavioral, cognitive, or motoric effects. At high drug concentrations, the long-term administration of phenobarbital (Luminal), phenytoin (Dilantin), and primidone (Mysoline) is associated with psychomotor deterioration. Deterioration of learning following the administration of antiepileptics has been noted on tests of intelligence, specialized tests of learning and cognitive style, neuropsychological tests, retrospective clinical judgments, and rating scales (Gay, 1984). Although some studies have actually indicated an improvement on some of these measures, if one judges the research as a whole, the studies show a consistent pattern of worsening performance following medication (Trimble & Corbett, 1980).

Phenobarbital has been noted to elicit hyperactivity and aggression in persons with developmental disabilities, particularly children (Schain, 1979). Primidone has also been noted to elicit hyperactivity in children. However, there is little evidence in the literature to suggest that carbamazepine (Tegretol) causes a deterioration in psychomotor functions. Indeed, the opposite is true, and some studies report cognitive enhancement with this drug. Similar effects have been noted with some other antiepileptics, such as ethosuximide (Zarontin). Minimal adverse effects have been noted with other drugs, such as valproic acid (Depakene).

Toxic or Side Effects

At high doses, the antiepileptics occasionally have toxic effects that may become confused with the developmental disability of the individual. These include mental confusion, disturbances of coordination and vision, lethargy, and slurred speech. Especially with the drug phenytoin, these and other adverse effects resulting in behavioral abnormalities, reduction in IQ, and other neurological symptoms may seem to represent a progressive deterioration in the individual's neurological status. Blood abnormalities, gastrointestinal distress, and skin rashes are additional potential adverse reactions.

Novel Agents

A number of novel psychoactive agents are being used with persons with developmental disabilities. The rationale for their use has been the discovery of biochemical abnormalities associated with cognitive, behavioral, or motor problems that may be amenable to treatment with specific drugs.

Fenfluramine

Elevated levels of the neurotransmitter serotonin, a chemical active in the brain, has been hypothesized as a causal factor in certain behavioral, cognitive, and motor problems in persons with developmental disabilities. For example, about 30% of persons with autism have been reported to have elevated serotonin levels. It has been suggested that a powerful serotonin antagonist drug, such as fenfluramine (Pondimin), may be useful in treating their problem behaviors by decreasing serotonin activity to within the normal range.

Early studies, particularly those by Ritvo and his colleagues (see Ritvo et al., 1986), reported enhancement of IQ with fenfluramine, but this finding has not been replicated in subsequent studies. Although the data are mixed, there is a consistent pattern of results that show enhanced social relatedness, a reduction in stereotypical and overactive behavior, and an improved attention span in children with autism (Aman & Kern, 1989). Only further research will establish how well individuals with developmental disabilities respond to this drug.

Naloxone and Naltrexone

Recently, a number of studies have reported that opioid antagonists (naloxone, naltrexone) may provide an effective treatment for self-injury in some individuals with mental retardation. A dysfunction of the endogenous opioid system may be the etiological factor in some cases of self-injury, thus providing a good rationale for the use of these medications (Harris, 1992). Although it is limited, current research does suggest that opioid antagonists may be effective in controlling the self-injury of some individuals with developmental disabilities (Ricketts, Ellis, Singh, & Singh, 1993). Clinicians wishing to use opioid antagonists should note that, although this drug has shown some reduction of self-injury in some cases, the changes have been small and not quite as dramatic as one might expect from the theoretical rationale. Indeed, the reduction in self-injury may in fact be a result of the sedative side effect of the drug and may have little to do with a dysfunction of the endogenous opioid system in these children.

Propranolol

Propranolol (Inderal) has been found to control violent, explosive, and aggressive behaviors in some individuals with developmental disabilities (Singh & Winton, 1989). However, the basis of our knowledge of the effects of this drug on the behavior of persons with developmental disabilities comes from several case reports and uncontrolled studies. Despite the lack of scientific evidence of efficacy, there is intense interest in this drug because it promises control over a range of serious problem behaviors that often prove intractable to both behavioral and psychopharmacological treatment.

Minerals, Diets, and Vitamins

Therapists and parents should be aware that various minerals, diets, and vitamins have been purported to have some beneficial effect on the behavior of persons with disabilities. At one time or another, a number of different treatments have been proposed, including glutamic acid, several vitamins, pituitary extract, sicca cell, and thyroid therapies. Based on the extant research literature, we can state with considerable confidence that none of these substances have a major effect on the behavior of persons with developmental disabilities (Singh, Ellis, Mattila, Mulick, & Poling, 1995).

Some mention should be made of the Feingold diet, although it is typically used with nondisabled hyperactive children. Only about 5% of hyperactive children benefit from this diet (Singh, 1987), but the enthusiasm of some physicians and parents for it has not diminished since it was first introduced. Studies of persons who are mentally retarded show little effect of the diet on their behavior. Given the lack of empirical verification, the Feingold diet does not present a viable alternative to other, proven treatments.

CONCLUSION

Medication is frequently used as one component in the prevention and treatment of severe and refractory problem behaviors in individuals with developmental disabilities. Although clinicians are now much more cognizant of both the beneficial and the detrimental effects that medications can have on these individuals, there is only a small scientific literature supporting their use. In general, however, the theoretical rationales, indications, and management principles that drive drug therapy in the general population are consistent with medication use in individuals with developmental disabilities. It is critical that pharmacotherapy in individuals with developmental disabilities be fully integrated with all other treatment modalities in order to maximize both behavioral control and an improvement in the individual's quality of life. Thus, although the physician is directly responsible for prescribing the medication, it is important that an interdisciplinary team, including members of a variety of different disciplines, as well as parents, participate in the development, administration, and monitoring of the drug treatment. To be able to make a meaningful contribution to drug-related treatment decisions, it is useful for these team members to be familiar with the various drug classes; their indications, intended effects, and side effects; and the appropriate medication-monitoring procedures.

REFERENCES

Aman, M. G. (1984). Drugs and learning in mentally retarded persons. In G. D. Burrows & J. S. Werry (Eds.), *Advances in human psychopharmacology* (Vol. 3, pp. 121–163). Greenwich, CT: JAI Press.

Aman, M. G. (in press). Stimulant drugs in the developmental disabilities revisited. *Journal of Developmental and Physical Disabilities.*

Aman, M. G., & Kern, R. A. (1989). Review of fenfluramine in the treatment of the developmental disabilities. *Journal of the American Academy of Child and Adolescent Psychiatry, 28,* 549–565.

Aman, M. G., & Singh, N. N. (1980). The usefulness of thioridazine for treating childhood disorders: Fact or folklore? *American Journal of Mental Deficiency, 84,* 331–338.

Aman, M. G., & Singh, N. N. (1982). Methylphenidate in severely retarded residents and the clinical significance of stereotypic behavior. *Applied Research in Mental Retardation, 3,* 1–14.

Aman, M. G., & Singh, N. N. (1986). *Aberrant Behavior Checklist and manual.* New York: Slosson Educational.

Aman, M. G., & Singh, N. N. (1988). *Psychopharmacology of the developmental disabilities.* New York: Springer-Verlag.

Aman, M. G., & Singh, N. N. (1991). Psychopharmacological intervention. In J. L. Matson & J. A. Mulick (Eds.), *Handbook of mental retardation* (2nd ed., pp. 347–372). New York: Pergamon Press.

Aman, M. G., & Singh, N. N. (1994). *The Aberrant Behavior Checklist: Community manual.* New York: Slosson Educational.

Aman, M. G., White, A. J., Vaithianathan, D., & Teehan, C. J. (1986). Preliminary study of imipramine in profoundly retarded residents. *Journal of Autism and Developmental Disorders, 16,* 263–273.

Bisconer, S. W., Zhang, X., & Sine, L. F. (1995). Impact of a psychotropic medication and physical restraint review process on adults with mental retardation, psychiatric diagnoses, and challenging behaviors. *Journal of Developmental and Physical Disabilities, 7,* 123–135.

Briggs, R. (1989). Monitoring and evaluating psychotropic drug use for persons with mental retardation: A follow-up report. *American Journal of Mental Retardation, 93,* 633–639.

Chandler, M., Gualtieri, C. T., & Fahs, J. J. (1988). Other psychotropic drugs. In M. G. Aman & N. N. Singh (Eds.), *Psychopharmacology of the developmental disabilities* (pp. 119–145). New York: Springer-Verlag.

Ellis, C. R., Singh, N. N., & Jackson, E. V. (1996). Problem behaviors in children with developmental disabilities. In D. X. Parmelee (Ed.), *Child and adolescent psychiatry* (pp. 263–275). St. Louis: C. V. Mosby.

Epstein, M. H., & Olinger, E. (1987). Use of medication in school programs for behaviorally disordered pupils. *Behavioral Disorders, 12,* 138–145.

Epstein, M. H., Singh, N. N., Leubke J., & Stout, C. (1991). Psychopharmacological intervention: II. Teacher perceptions of psychotropic medication for learning disabled students. *Journal of Learning Disabilities, 24,* 477–483.

Field, C. J., Aman, M. G., White, A. J., & Vaithianathan, C. (1986). A single-subject study of imipramine in a mentally retarded woman with depressive symptoms. *Journal of Mental Deficiency Research, 30,* 191–198.

Findholt, N. E., & Emmett, C. G. (1990). Impact of interdisciplinary team review on psychotropic drug use with persons who have mental retardation. *Mental Retardation, 25,* 41–46.

Gay, P. E. (1984). Effects of antiepileptic drugs and seizure type on operant responding in mentally retarded persons. *Epilepsia, 25,* 377–386.

Handen, B. L., Feldman, H., Gosling, A., Breaux, A., & McAuliffe, S. (1991). Adverse side effects of Ritalin among mentally retarded children with ADHD. *Journal of the American Academy of Child and Adolescent Psychiatry, 30,* 241–245.

Harris, J. C. (1992). Neurobiological factors in self-injurious behavior. In J. K. Luiselli, J. L. Matson, & N. N. Singh (Eds.), *Self-injurious behavior: Analysis, assessment, and treatment* (pp. 59–92). New York: Springer-Verlag.

LaVeck, G. D., & Buckley, P. (1961). The use of psychopharmacologic agents in retarded children with behavior disorders. *Journal of Chronic Diseases, 13,* 174–183.

Ricketts, R. W., Ellis, C. R., Singh, Y. N., & Singh, N. N. (1993). Opioid antagonists: II. Clinical effects in the treatment of self-injury in individuals with developmental disabilities. *Journal of Developmental and Physical Disabilities, 5,* 17–28.

Ricketts, R. W., Goza, A. B., Ellis, C. R., Singh, Y. N., Chambers, S., Singh, N. N., & Cooke, J. C. (1994). Clinical effects of buspirone on intractable self-injury in adults with mental retardation. *Journal of the American Academy of Child and Adolescent Psychiatry, 33,* 270–276.

Ricketts, R. W., Goza, A. B., Ellis, C. R., Singh, Y. N., Singh, N. N., & Cooke, J. C. (1993). Fluoxetine treatment of severe self-injury in young adults with mental retardation. *Journal of the American Academy of Child and Adolescent Psychiatry, 32,* 865–869.

Ritvo, E. R., Freeman, B. J., Yuwiler, A., Geller, E., Schroth, P., & Yokota, A. (1986). Fenfluramine treatment of autism: UCLA collaborative study of 81 patients at nine medical centers. *Psychopharmacology Bulletin, 22,* 133–147.

Schain, R. J. (1979). Problems with the use of conventional anticonvulsant drugs in mentally retarded individuals. *Brain and Development, 1,* 77–82.

Schroeder, S. R. (1988). Neuroleptic medications for persons with developmental disabilities. In M. G. Aman & N. N. Singh (Eds.), *Psychopharmacology of the developmental disabilities* (pp. 82–100). New York: Springer-Verlag.

Singh, N. N. (1987). Diet and childhood behavior disorders. In J. Birkbeck (Ed.), *Are we really what we eat?* (pp. 35–45). Auckland, New Zealand: Dairy Advisory Bureau.

Singh, N. N. (1995). Moving beyond institutional care for individuals with developmental disabilities. *Journal of Child and Family Studies, 4,* 129–145.

Singh, N. N., & Aman, M. G. (1981). Effects of thioridazine dosage on the behavior of severely mentally retarded persons. *American Journal of Mental Deficiency, 85,* 580–587.

Singh, N. N., Ellis, C. R., Crews, W. D., & Singh, Y. N. (1994). Does diminished dopaminergic neurotransmission increase pica? *Journal of Child and Adolescent Psychopharmacology, 4,* 93–99.

Singh, N. N., Ellis, C. R., Donatelli, L., Williams, D. E., Ricketts, R. W., Goza, A. B., Perlman, N., Everly, D. E., Best, A. M., & Singh, Y. N. (1996). Professionals' perceptions of psychotropic medication for individuals with mental retardation in residential facilities in Texas. *Journal of Intellectual Disability Research, 40,* 1–7.

Singh, N. N., Ellis, C. R., Mattila, M. J., Mulick, J. A., & Poling, A. (1995, June). *Vitamin, mineral, and dietary treatments for individuals with developmental disabilities.* Paper presented at the Nisonger-The ARC International Consensus Conference on Psychopharmacology, Columbus, OH.

Singh, N. N., Ellis, C. R., & Singh, Y. N. (1994). Medication management. In E. Cipani & F. Spooner (Eds.), *Curricular and instructional approaches for persons with severe handicaps* (pp. 404–423). Boston: Allyn & Bacon.

Singh, N. N., Ellis, C. R., & Wechsler, H. A. (in press). Psychopharmacoepidemiology in mental retardation. *Journal of Child and Adolescent Psychopharmacology.*

Singh, N. N., Epstein, M. H., Leubke, J., & Singh Y. N. (1990). Psychopharmacological intervention: I. Teacher perceptions of psychotropic medication for seriously emotionally disturbed students. *Journal of Special Education, 24,* 283–295.

Singh, N. N., Guernsey, T. F., & Ellis, C. R. (1992). Drug therapy for persons with developmental disabilities: Legislation and litigation. *Clinical Psychology Review, 12,* 665–679.

Singh, N. N., Parmelee, D. X., Sood, A. A., & Katz, R. C. (1993). Collaboration of disciplines. In J. L. Matson (Ed.), *Handbook of hyperactivity in children* (pp. 305–322). Boston: Allyn & Bacon.

Singh, N. N., Sood, A., Sonenklar, N., & Ellis, C. R. (1991). Assessment and diagnosis of mental illness in persons with mental retardation: Methods and measures. *Behavior Modification, 15,* 419–443.

Singh, N. N., & Winton, A. S. W. (1989). Behavioral pharmacology. In J. K. Luiselli (Ed.), *Behavioral medicine and developmental disabilities* (pp. 152–179). New York: Springer-Verlag.

Sprague, R. L., & Gadow, K. D. (1976). The role of the teacher in drug treatment. *School Review, 85,* 109–140.

Sprague, R. L., Kalachnik, J. E., & White, D. M. (1985). *Dyskinesia Identification System: Condensed User Scale (DISCUS).* Champaign, IL: Institute for Child Behavior and Development, University of Illinois at Urbana-Champaign.

Stores, G. (1988). Antiepileptic drugs. In M. G. Aman & N. N. Singh (Eds.), *Psychopharmacology of the developmental disabilities* (pp. 101–118). New York: Springer-Verlag.

Trimble, M. R., & Corbett, J. A. (1980). Behavioral and cognitive disturbances in epileptic children. *Irish Medical Journal, 73,* 21–28.

Varley, C. K., & Trupin, E. W. (1982). Double-blind administration of methylphenidate to mentally retarded children with attention deficit disorder: A preliminary study. *American Journal of Mental Deficiency, 86,* 560–566.

Walters, A., Singh, N. N., & Beale, I. L. (1977). Effects of lorazepam on hyperactivity in retarded children. *New Zealand Medical Journal, 86,* 473–475.

PART
2

M E T H O D S

Chapter
8

Self-Injury

David Wacker, John Northup,
and Laura K. Lambert

INTRODUCTION

Treatment approaches for self-injurious behavior are well established in the literature; multiple techniques have been described, criticized, and evaluated. In many cases, the merits of one treatment versus a no-treatment baseline are presented in the literature, whereas in other cases, one technique is compared to another. Comparisons across treatments are frequently not meaningful because the treatments address different functions of the target behavior. Over the last several years, it has become increasingly clear that treatments should be matched to the function (the maintaining condition) of self-injury (Iwata, Dorsey, Slifer, Bauman, & Richman, 1982). We provide several case examples of how treatments for self-injurious behavior can be derived from functional analysis procedures, describe how treatments can be matched to the function of behavior, and discuss why the function of behavior is more important than its form or appearance.

PREVALENCE

Among the estimated 4 million people in the United States with developmental disabilities, approximately 160,000 engage in significant destructive behavior (National Institutes of Health, 1989). Destructive behavior is generally categorized as self-injurious behavior (SIB) or aggressive behavior. Common examples of SIB include face slapping, hand biting, and headbanging. Regardless of its form, SIB involves repeated motoric movements that, because of their frequency, duration, or intensity, may result in tissue damage or the potential for tissue damage.

The prevalence of SIB is generally correlated with developmental level and is usually accompanied by other maladaptive behavior. Self-injury has also been observed to be cyclical, in that it occurs and recurs throughout an individual's life span. Finally, it is often associated with various syndromes (e.g., Lesch-Nyhan) and impoverished environments.

BEHAVIORAL ASSESSMENT AND ANALYSIS

Mace (1990) described a comprehensive approach to the assessment of SIB that includes the following phases: (1) a descriptive assessment in the natural environment (e.g., the setting in which the SIB is occurring); (2) a formulation of hypotheses regarding the function of SIB; (3) a functional analysis of maintaining events; and (4) single-case evaluation of the effectiveness of treatment. Each of these phases of assessment is based on direct observation.

We prefer the use of direct observation, even brief direct assessments (Northup et al., 1991), to psychometric or indirect measures (e.g., surveys) because the purpose of assessment is to prescribe treatment (Hayes, Nelson, & Jarrett, 1987). Thus, although a checklist or survey may provide information on the specific characteristics of the target behavior and on environmental situations that are correlated with the occurrence of the behavior, it is only through direct observation that changes in behavior can be shown to occur because of changes in the environment.

As mentioned previously, a large number of treatments currently exist for SIB. The problem occurs when one attempts to select the "best" treatment for any given individual. This problem is associated with assessment. We need assessment approaches that are useful in helping us to identify treatments that work or, at least, procedures that make sense given the function of the target behavior (Wacker, Northup, & Cooper, 1991). For the selection of the best possible treatments, assessments must be based on directly observing changes in students' behavior in response to various environmental conditions (Iwata et al., 1982).

Descriptive Assessment and Formulating Hypotheses

The major purpose of a descriptive assessment is to identify whether changes in behavior occur because of naturally occurring changes in environmental conditions (antecedent and consequent) (Bijou, Petersen, & Ault, 1968). For example, in a typical classroom, the types of tasks, the demands made of students, the presence of the teacher and peers, and the amount of noise all vary throughout the day. These environmental events both precede (antecedents) and follow (consequences) student behavior. When maladaptive behavior such as SIB occurs, the descriptive assessment is used to identify those environmental conditions that are correlated with its occurrence.

Perhaps the best way to conduct a descriptive assessment is to use what Bijou et al. (1968) called an ABC (antecedent-behavior-consequence) assessment. This procedure is so termed because each occurrence of the target behavior (in this case, SIB) is recorded along with the environmental events that preceded (antecedent) and followed (consequences) the behavior. From a consistent record of the antecedents and consequences corresponding to SIB, hypotheses about which environmental events are maintaining (causing) SIB can be determined. As shown in the case example provided in Box 8-1, an ABC assessment can be useful for generating or partially confirming hypotheses

Box 8-1

CASE EXAMPLE OF AN ABC PROCEDURE WITH BEN

Ben was a 7-year-old boy with severe mental retardation who engaged in frequent hand biting. The behavior occurred throughout each day, and his teacher thought that he engaged in the behavior because he was frustrated (i.e., to escape demands). To better assess the behavior, she conducted an ABC assessment. Before the assessment, the teacher defined events in the classroom that were likely, on a typical day, both to precede and to follow Ben's SIB. These events were then divided into antecedents and consequences. Antecedents were divided into high and low demands, and consequences were divided into ignoring or verbal redirection ("hands down"). She also had a final category of "alone," a situation that typically occurred when Ben was waiting for instruction or was given a toy or activity but was left alone. The average number of occurrences of SIB on the first three days were recorded as follows:

Antecedent	Consequence	Average Daily Occurrence of SIB
High demand	Redirection (attention)	78
Low demand	Redirection	85
High demand	Ignored	12
Low demand	Ignored	15
Alone	Ignored	3

As shown by these results, SIB occurred most frequently when it was followed by attention (in this case, verbal redirection) and thus was not related to the demands of the task. Based on these results, the teacher changed her hypothesis about Ben's SIB; it appeared to be attention-motivated.

about why SIB occurs. In this case, the initial hypothesis was apparently incorrect, as the results suggested that SIB was related more to attention than to demands.

An ABC assessment is usually conducted under natural conditions. Each occurrence of the target behavior is recorded as it occurs, and the antecedent and consequent events associated with its occurrence are also recorded. Sometimes, as in the case example shown in Box 8-1, the results are clear; that is, the environmental events associated with SIB seem clear. However, it should also be noted that ABC assessments may be very complex, and that no clear patterns of behavior may emerge even after several days of assessment. This problem occurs because it is often difficult to separate or differentiate all of the possible events preceding and following behavior. For example, the presence or absence of demands, staff instructions, peers, particular activities, and so on, may all serve as antecedents to behavior. Determining which one, or which combination, is most often associated with SIB can be a confusing and difficult task!

We have found that the best way to conduct an ABC assessment is the method highlighted in Box 8-1. First, determine the activities and events in the natural environment that typically precede and follow the behavior; then group these activities or events into categories, such as high and low demands. Next, observe the behavior as it naturally occurs, keeping track of each time it occurs as well as recording the events that precede and follow the behavior. It may help to record behavior in an event-recording table, as shown in Box 8-1.

A successful descriptive assessment, as displayed in Box 8-1, provides us with the environmental conditions that correlate with SIB. In this case, teacher attention was correlated most often with the occurrence of SIB. This correlation between teacher attention and SIB suggests a functional relationship: SIB occurs to receive teacher attention. However, the correlation is only suggestive; we still do not know if SIB is attention seeking. For example, the student might be escaping tasks more often when receiving verbal redirection than when ignored. In that case, SIB may be occurring to escape working on tasks rather than to receive attention. The results, while suggestive that attention is controlling behavior, are nevertheless only correlational. Thus, we do not know what function the behavior is serving. That is why we believe that a functional analysis must always be conducted, even after a relatively clear pattern of behavior emerges within a descriptive assessment.

Functional Analysis

Functional analysis is a method of behavior assessment that is used to identify the function, or purpose, of behavior (Iwata et al., 1982). In the example in Box 8-1, a functional analysis would be used to directly assess Ben's SIB occurred primarily as a means of escaping demands (whether high or low) or of obtaining attention (positive or negative) from the teacher. Both explanations are plausible; determining which one is correct will be critical as a treatment is developed. It is also clear that further descriptive assessment will not clarify this situation.

Functional analysis, as discussed here, is based on the work of Carr and Durand (1985) and Iwata et al. (1982) and is conducted before the initiation of treatment. Indeed, its purpose is to prescribe a treatment that will match the function of a given behavior. Functional analysis techniques require that we change our view of behavior from only observing what is occurring to determining why it is occurring; that is, our focus changes from the specific form or appearance of behavior to its function. For example, two apparently distinct behaviors (e.g., screaming and hand biting) may occur for the same

<table>
<tr><td rowspan="2">**Box 8-2**</td><td>CASE EXAMPLE OF A FUNCTIONAL ANALYSIS WITH BEN FOLLOWING AN ABC ASSESSMENT</td></tr>
</table>

CASE EXAMPLE OF A FUNCTIONAL ANALYSIS WITH BEN FOLLOWING AN ABC ASSESSMENT

Ben's teacher decided to conduct a modified functional analysis of his SIB after obtaining the results in Box 8-1. She hypothesized that Ben engaged in SIB to gain her attention but also thought that he might be using SIB to escape task demands temporarily while being verbally redirected. To answer the question of whether his hand biting served an attention or escape function, she set up two 15-minute analog conditions that she conducted twice a day for five days. In the first condition, attention, she set tasks (e.g., sorting silverware) on Ben's lap tray and directed him to complete the task as usual in the classroom. When he engaged in SIB, she directed him to put his hands down and "scolded" him for 10 to 15 seconds (e.g., "Don't do that; you'll hurt yourself"). Thus, each time he attempted to bite himself, he received attention in the form of verbal redirection. In the second condition, escape, she presented the same tasks, but in this condition, she turned away from him for about 15 seconds (nonexclusionary time-out) each time he bit himself. Thus, in the escape condition, he avoided the task for 15 seconds after each occurrence of SIB but received no attention for SIB. The average number of hand bites per session was 12 during the attention condition and 4 during the escape condition.

These results confirmed her hypothesis that Ben engaged in SIB to gain her attention. Because the function of Ben's hand biting was to receive attention, a logical treatment would involve removing teacher attention each time Ben bit his hand. Therefore, the results provided one approach to treatment: brief, nonexclusionary time-out. In fact, this approach was already working, as no occurrence of SIB was observed in the escape condition during the final two days of assessment. This effect very likely resulted from the teacher's removing her attention after each occurrence of SIB during the escape condition. The average occurrences of SIB were as follows:

	Monday	*Tuesday*	*Wednesday*	*Thursday*	*Friday*
Attention	12	6	8	14	20
Escape	3	8	4	0	0

reason (to gain attention) or for distinct reasons. The point is that, in the selection of effective treatments, the function of behavior is more important than its appearance.

Functional Analysis Using Analog Conditions

In most cases, a functional analysis is conducted within a series of counterbalanced, tightly controlled analog conditions. The analogs are constructed both to closely resemble (or duplicate) natural conditions *and* to provide greater clarity regarding the functions of the occurrence of behavior. The specific analog conditions selected are based on the hypotheses about the behavior generated from the descriptive assessment. The critical difference between descriptive assessment and functional analysis using analog conditions is that, in a descriptive assessment, antecedents and consequences are recorded as they naturally occur, yet these events are directly manipulated in an analog assessment. This direct manipulation of antecedent and consequent events allows for a more systematic, and thus a more predictive, approach to determining a behavior's function. An example of this approach is provided in Box 8-2 and was used with the same boy, Ben, described in Box 8-1.

As shown in Box 8-2, the results were very convincing that Ben's SIB served an attention function. By separating the results into daily averages, we can also see that SIB increased across days during the attention condition but decreased during the escape condition. Trends in behavior over time are often at least as important as overall averages in behavior. That is why we often graph the results rather than rely on tabled data.

The above example shows how a functional analysis can be used both to confirm a hypothesis about why SIB is occurring and to help in the selection of the intervention that best matches the function a behavior serves. In other cases, the functional analysis is used because hypotheses are not possible following a descriptive assessment (e.g., no clear patterns emerged). On numerous occasions, we have been unsure of why the behavior was occurring. Investigators have isolated four basic classes of conditions that serve to maintain (reinforce) SIB (Carr & Durand, 1985; Iwata et al., 1982): (1) social attention, which, as shown, often occurs in the from of social disapproval or verbal redirection; (2) escape from or avoidance of tasks or physical contact; (3) tangible, meaning that the client is attempting to gain a preferred item or access to a preferred activity; and (4) automatic, which refers to an intrinsic motivation (i.e., something about the behavior itself is reinforcing). These four classes of maintaining conditions, and some of their variations, are provided in Table 8-1. A case example of how analogs were used to assess each function is provided in Box 8-3.

Two aspects of the results in Box 8-3 are important. First, the assessment was conducted within an experimental design (in this case, an alternating-treatments design). A functional analysis is always conducted within an experimental design and is most often conducted within an alternating-treatments design. An alternating-treatments design is usually preferred because the various hypothesized functions of SIB can be alternated in a random or counterbalanced order and can thus rule out the confounding variables that may be present during a descriptive assessment. Assessment continues until a clear pattern emerges.

TABLE 8-1

Maintaining Conditions Assessed in a Functional Analysis

Possible Maintaining Conditions	Description	Types
Attention	Student's behavior serves to gain social attention (positive reinforcement)	Social disapproval Verbal redirection Comfort Discussion Physical contact
Escape	Client's behavior serves to escape or avoid undesired or aversive situations (negative reinforcement)	Tasks Physical contact Peers or staff Noise
Tangible	Client's behavior serves to gain desired activities or items (positive reinforcement)	Toys Activities Edibles
Automatic	Client's behavior is itself reinforcing for intrinsic or unknown reasons	

Second, as shown in the case example, functional analyses can be used in the absence of descriptive assessment or hypotheses about why SIB is occurring. Descriptive assessments provide useful information about possible functions, or about the specific controlling events (e.g., the types of demands or attention) that serve to maintain SIB in the natural environment. However, because a descriptive assessment yields only correlational relationships between behavior and function, a functional analysis is needed before more definitive conclusions can be reached.

The four conditions used in Box 8-3 each provide information about possible maintaining events. Depending on the magnitude and trends in the results, the maintaining condition might be attention, escape, tangible, or automatic. An automatic function is often a "default" option; it occurs when no trend is apparent (i.e., when there is no differentiation across conditions). In addition, when the function appears to be automatic, we typically conduct an alone condition, where the student is left alone with nothing to do. If SIB occurs at similar levels across each of the conditions in Box 8-3, as well as during the "alone" condition, we usually consider the function automatic.

It should be noted that the same behavior may serve different functions and that different forms of SIB may serve different functions. For example, Wacker et al. (1990) reported that, for one child, SIB served both an

Box 8-3

CASE EXAMPLE OF THE USE OF FUNCTIONAL ANALYSIS WITH BILL, USING ANALOG CONDITIONS

Bill was admitted to a hospital inpatient unit because of severe self-injury in multiple forms. He was 6 years old and profoundly mentally retarded. Bill's teachers and parents believed that self-injury occurred for an automatic function; he was thought to engage in self-injury because of physical discomfort. The inpatient team conducted a functional analysis that consisted of the following conditions: (1) attention, in which he was told to "stop" after each occurrence but was otherwise ignored; (2) escape, in which he was allowed to escape a self-care task (toothbrushing) for 15 sec after each occurrence; (3) tangible, in which he was given a preferred toy for 15 sec after each occurrence ("Stop that; here, play with this"); and (4) toy play, in which he was given toys and staff attention when not engaged in SIB and SIB was ignored. The toy play condition was designed to approximate an enriched, stimulating environment in which SIB is unlikely to occur. This condition was included as a control for other conditions. Each session continued for 15 minutes and was conducted twice per day. Each occurrence of self-injury was recorded by a 6-second, partial-interval recording system. The results for the first week are shown in Figure 8-1. Clearly, self-injury rarely occurred in any condition other than escape. Thus, it appears reasonable to conclude that Bill's SIB occurred to escape demands.

Figure 8-1

An example of the use of a functional analysis to identify escape-motivated self-injury

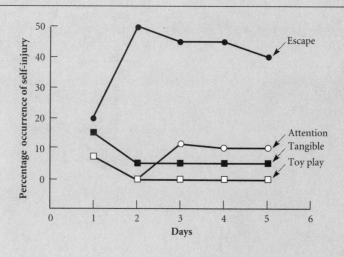

escape and a tangible function. Similarly, two topographies of behavior (e.g., aggression and stereotypy) may each serve a different function (e.g., escape and automatic). Nevertheless, if conducted carefully, functional analyses can separate behaviors by function, which should be useful in selecting treatments.

<table>
<tr><td>Box 8-4</td><td>CASE EXAMPLE OF A BRIEF FUNCTIONAL ANALYSIS CONDUCTED IN AN OUTPATIENT CLINIC</td></tr>
</table>

Phil was referred for an outpatient assessment of severe self-injury, which consisted of headbanging and hand biting. He was 31 years old and diagnosed as autistic. No reason for his behavior was provided in his records; it was simply noted that he engaged in SIB randomly throughout each day. The outclinic assessment consisted of a brief functional analysis (Wacker & Steege, 1993), which is a modified version of the extended assessment described by Iwata et al. (1982). A brief assessment was necessary because, as for all psychological evaluations, only 90 minutes was available for assessment in the outclinic setting. To partially compensate for the limited time available, each condition lasted for only 10 minutes, and only one data point was available per condition. The assessment was divided into three phases: (1) an initial assessment, which assessed various maintaining conditions (in this case, escape and attention); (2) replication, in which the results of the initial assessment were partially replicated, the conditions producing the highest and lowest levels of SIB being repeated; and (3) contingency reversal, in which the conditions maintaining SIB (in this case, escape) were provided contingently for an appropriate response (signing "please") and were withheld for SIB. Observations were recorded with a 6-second, partial-interval system. The results are shown in Figure 8-2.

As shown, the analyses revealed that self-injury occurred only during the escape condition, and this initial result was replicated within a multielement design. During the contingency reversal, Phil quickly learned to sign "please" to gain about 30 seconds of a break, and once he learned to sign, his frequency of self-injury decreased substantially.

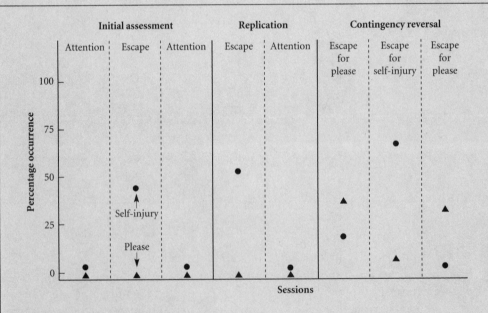

Figure 8-2   *An example of the use of a brief functional analysis to identify escape-motivated self-injury and manding "please"*

Brief Functional Analyses

In most cases, a functional analysis is conducted over several sessions or days. These extended functional analyses permit an inspection of stability over time and are the preferred method of assessment. In some cases, however, the pragmatics of the situation or the acceptability of the assessment necessitates the use of brief versions of the analysis. An example of a brief functional analysis is provided in Box 8-4 and is based on a study completed by Northup et al. (1991).

Three aspects of the results in Box 8-4 are important to note. First, the clarity of the results makes it possible to conduct a modified functional analysis even under the severe restrictions of an outclinic. Derby et al. (1992) recently reported that definitive patterns of behavior such as those shown in Box 8-4 occur about 50% of the time based on a sample of over 80 outclinic evaluations. Second, like the results of the functional analyses described previously, the results prescribe a specific treatment (in this case, mand training, which involved training an appropriate alternative response, the "please" sign). A third unique feature of the analysis shown in Box 8-4 is the contingency reversal, in which the reinforcer maintaining SIB was also shown to maintain an appropriate response (signing "please"). In this case, the contingency reversal demonstrated that escape (negative reinforcement) was a general reinforcer and was not unique to SIB.

Summary

A number of variations of functional analysis procedures are available; we have provided only a few in this chapter. A functional analysis requires that direct observation of maintaining events must be conducted within an experimental design. The benefit of a functional analysis is that the results may lead directly to treatment. Once the general class (positive, negative, or automatic) of reinforcement for SIB is identified, treatments can be selected that match those conditions and that are acceptable to the client and the care providers.

TREATMENT APPROACHES

As discussed previously, a successful functional analysis may also be the initiation of treatment. This is obvious when a procedure such as the contingency reversal described in Box 8-4 is provided, but it also occurs in cases such as in Box 8-2 when two competing hypotheses are evaluated. In most cases, how-

Box 8-5

CASE EXAMPLE OF AN ANTECEDENT APPROACH TO TREATING SIB

Two team teachers who instructed the same student had very different results when interacting with the same student. The 16-year-old student, Stan, was severely mentally retarded and blind. When Terry instructed him to complete a task, he was compliant, and his behavior was very appropriate. When Sara attempted to interact with him on the same task, he was often upset and noncompliant and frequently engaged in SIB and aggressive behavior. This discrepancy was confusing because both teachers used the same prompt sequence (least to most) and used praise as the major reward for compliance.

A brief functional analysis conducted with both teachers indicated that SIB served an escape function with both teachers. However, in the classroom setting, only Sara had difficulty. A descriptive (ABC) assessment was then repeated with, initially, no consistent pattern of differences noted between the teachers. The focus then shifted to the types of instructions provided by the teachers, and only one major difference was evident. Terry always phrased directives as questions, whereas Sara used declarative statements. To test the hypothesis that questions were better than declaratives, the teachers switched their way of phrasing instructions. Almost immediately, Stan became more compliant with Sara and less compliant with Terry. Both teachers began to use questions, and few behavior problems occurred.

When these results were discussed with Stan's mother, she indicated that she always phrased requests as questions, with good results. It seemed possible, therefore, that Stan had somehow learned that questions were a discriminative stimulus for receiving praise for compliance.

ever, a treatment plan is formulated after the results of the functional analysis are clear. The key to successful treatment is to provide the same reinforcer that maintains SIB for an appropriate, alternative response, and to withhold reinforcement for SIB. Alternatively, the tasks or activities associated with SIB may be eliminated or altered.

Antecedent Strategies

Few antecedent strategies (often termed *stimulus-based treatments*) have been developed for use with SIB. Of those that are available, most involve a change in the tasks, situations, directions, or people associated with SIB. Berg, Wacker, and Northup (1991), for example, showed that changes in how a direction is presented to a client may have a major impact on client compliance and SIB. The case example in Box 8-5 shows that even subtle differences in how tasks are presented may be associated with very different results. In the case of Stan, how requests were phrased resulted in very different responses.

An advantage of identifying an antecedent event that results in SIB is also obvious in Box 8-5. When the antecedent is changed, acceptable behavior

> ## Box 8-6
>
> ### CASE EXAMPLE OF STIMULUS FADING IN THE TREATMENT OF SELF-INJURY
>
> Rhonda was 7 years old and engaged in severe headbanging on hard surfaces, such as her desk as school. Her SIB was sufficiently severe that she was physically restrained in her chair whenever she was at her desk. The initial approach at school was to remove the desk, so that she sat in her chair with restraints. Her restraints were gradually faded until she sat alone without restraints. A card table was introduced next but was placed about 2 feet in front of her. The table was gradually positioned in front of her, and the desk was then placed next to the table. Over several weeks, the desk replaced the card table, and Rhonda was able to sit at her desk without restraints and without engaging in SIB.

often occurs almost immediately. This change may very often be the treatment of choice. In other cases, a fading plan may be attempted, in which the antecedent that is associated with SIB is initially removed and then gradually reintroduced. This approach is summarized in Box 8-6.

The example in Box 8-6 was probably successful for two major reasons. First, the desk was a discriminative stimulus for headbanging, and once it was removed, the headbanging stopped. Second, the introduction of the card table was a novel stimulus in that the client had no history of headbanging with this stimulus. Fortunately, the card table was distinct enough from her desk so that it did not occasion headbanging. When the card table was gradually replaced with the desk, the headbanging remained absent.

A final antecedent approach to be discussed here was described by Dunlap et al. (1991). Dunlap et al. conducted a combined functional analysis and a descriptive assessment. The functional analysis revealed that escape is a major factor in aberrant behavior. The descriptive assessment revealed that attempts to escape occur more often in some tasks than in others (e.g., tasks requiring fine-motor rather than gross-motor behavior). The treatment consisted of reducing both the number of fine-motor tasks required and the amount of time spent in any activity involving fine-motor skills.

Response-Contingent Strategies

A large number of consequence procedures currently exist for treating SIB. These procedures, in general, can be divided into two categories: (1) accelerative approaches that use reinforcement to shape alternative behavior and (2) decelerative approaches that are used to decrease the probability of SIB.

TABLE 8-2

Common Treatments Based on Positive and Negative Reinforcement

Treatment	Description	Presumed Function
Differential reinforcement of appropriate behavior (DRA)	Social attention, praise, or a tangible item is presented for a specific, preselected appropriate behavior, and inappropriate behavior is ignored.	Attention or tangible
Differential reinforcement of other behavior (DRO)	Inappropriate behavior is ignored, and attention, praise, or tangibles are provided for any behaviors other than inappropriate ones after a fixed period of time has elapsed.	Attention or tangible
Functional communication training (FCT)	The client is taught an alternative mand to request reinforcement (e.g., to sign "please" for attention).	Attention, tangible, or escape
Preferred activities or Premack principle	Highly preferred activities are provided contingent on appropriate behavior. In some cases, these preferred activities may involve high-frequency behaviors, even stereotypy.	Tangible and escape (and attention if provided during preferred activity)
Negative reinforcement	Brief breaks are made contingent on appropriate behavior (DRA), after a certain amount of time has elapsed (DRO), or when the client requests a break appropriately (FCT).	Escape

Procedures Based on Reinforcement

Given the results of a successful functional analysis, it is often possible to match a treatment to the functions of SIB. In most cases, this means that the same reinforcer that maintains SIB is now used contingently to shape an alternative, replacement response (Carr, 1988). In Table 8-2, some common treatments based on reinforcement are provided. In most cases, a consequence for SIB is needed, in addition to reinforcement contingent on a selected alternative, even if this means that SIB is ignored (extinction). The use of consequent events for SIB (reductive techniques) may facilitate the speed with which SIB is decreased to zero occurrence and may be needed to keep SIB at zero occurrence (Wacker et al., 1990). Some common reductive techniques that are often paired with reinforcement treatments are provided in Table 8-3. The

TABLE 8-3

Common Reductive Techniques That Are Paired with Reinforcement

Treatment	Description	Function
Extinction	SIB is ignored or otherwise prevented from resulting in reinforcement. For SIB that is maintained by positive reinforcement, each occurrence is ignored. For SIB that serves an escape function, the task or demand is continued. SIB that serves an automatic function is prevented. In all cases, SIB can be blocked to prevent injury.	Attention, tangible, escape, or automatic
Time-out	The client is removed (exclusionary) from attention, or attention is stopped (nonexclusionary; staff turns away) for brief periods of time. Similarly, if the client has access to a preferred item or activity, either the client or the task or activity is removed.	Attention or tangible
Guided compliance	When SIB occurs in response to a demand (usually to comply with a directive), continued physical guidance is used to complete or continue the task.	Escape

use of reductive techniques may serve at least three purposes: (1) removing reinforcement for SIB, (2) providing a mildly aversive or punishing contingency for SIB, and (3) disrupting ongoing response chains that include or result in SIB.

To illustrate these techniques, we have provided three case examples in Boxes 8-7, 8-8, and 8-9. In Box 8-7, we provide an example in which SIB is maintained by attention. In Box 8-8, SIB is maintained by escape, and in Box 8-9, it is automatic. In all the examples, we used functional communication training as the reinforcement procedure, combined with time-out, guided compliance, and extinction, respectively.

These case examples show how treatment packages can be matched to functional analysis results showing the maintaining of conditions for SIB. In the first two cases, an erroneous hypothesis about the reason for SIB led to a treatment that may have inadvertently made the SIB worse. Following the functional analysis, a better treatment package was implemented with good success.

In some cases, SIB occurs for more than one reason. In these situations, different treatments have to be implemented, given the probable reason for

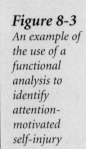

Box 8-7

CASE EXAMPLE OF FUNCTIONAL COMMUNICATION TRAINING PLUS TIME-OUT FOR SIB MAINTAINED BY ATTENTION

Sally was 5 years old, profoundly mentally retarded, nonambulatory, and engaged in severe hand biting. Her teacher and parents believed that the function was automatic; that is, that it occurred for some intrinsic reason. The current treatment approach was for her teacher to soothe her by rubbing her back. However, the results of a functional analysis (shown in Figure 8-3) clearly indicated that hand biting was used by Sally to gain attention. Given these results, functional communication training was incorporated to provide Sally with a more appropriate means of gaining attention. In addition, any instances of hand biting resulted in nonexclusionary time-out. Sally was trained to press a microswitch that activated a tape player. On the tape player was the prerecorded message, "Please come here." When she pressed the switch, the teacher attended to her for about 30 seconds. When she bit her hand, however, the teacher turned away from her. After about three weeks of treatment, Sally learned to press the switch independently, and after another five weeks, no occurrences of self-injury occurred.

Figure 8-3

An example of the use of a functional analysis to identify attention-motivated self-injury

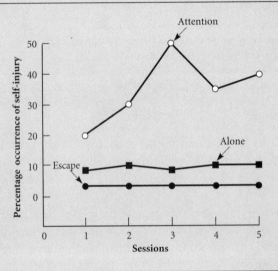

SIB within a particular context. The case example in Box 8-10 shows one example of how this can be accomplished, again by the use of functional communication training as a primary treatment component.

Thus far, we have provided examples of functional communication training (FCT). With FCT, the initial goals are to achieve independent signing and substantial decreases in SIB. Trying to achieve this goal can be quite disruptive to both task completion and staff. One response to this potential problem is to build in delays gradually before the reinforcer is delivered *after* the initial goal

Box 8-8	**CASE EXAMPLE OF FUNCTIONAL COMMUNICATION TRAINING PLUS GUIDED COMPLIANCE FOR ESCAPE-MOTIVATED SIB**

Laura was 28 years old and engaged in a variety of problem behaviors, most notably screaming and hand biting. She was profoundly mentally retarded and nonambulatory. Given the group home staff's assumption that hand biting was automatic, their strategy for dealing with Laura's SIB was to place her in a "quiet room," where she could calm down, for up to 30 minutes. A brief functional analysis, however, suggested that her behavior was escape-motivated. Given the results of the brief functional analysis, the treatment plan included two components: teaching her to sign "please" to receive brief breaks from tasks, and hand-over-hand physical guidance from staff. Thus, when she screamed or bit her hand, she was physically guided to complete more of the task. With physical prompting to sign about once every 5 minutes plus guided compliance, her self-injury decreased to zero occurrence in a few weeks. It took almost a year for her to begin signing independently, but after learning the "please" sign, she learned two more signs ("drink" and "chips") during the next month. Three years after treatment began, she used about 12 signs independently, and no occurrences of self-injury occurred after about one year.

Box 8-9	**CASE EXAMPLE OF FUNCTIONAL COMMUNICATION TRAINING PLUS EXTINCTION FOR SIB MAINTAINED BY AUTOMATIC REINFORCEMENT**

Bill was 4 years old and profoundly mentally retarded, and he engaged in almost constant hand mouthing. An extended (seven-day) functional analysis conducted on an inpatient unit revealed no patterns in hand mouthing across conditions. Instead, he had his hands placed in his mouth over 80% of the time. The only time Bill was not observed (even infrequently) to engage in hand mouthing was when loud music was playing and when he wore gloves. Based on these observations, Bill was taught to request music via a pretaped message (he used a large pressure switch to play the message "Let's listen to music" on a tape recorder), and he was provided with gloves. Given both the gloves (extinction) and the music, his hand mouthing never occurred. With only the gloves, he bit the gloves in an apparent attempt to remove them. With only the music, he still mouthed his hands about 30% of the time.

of independent signing and decreased SIB is achieved. Thus, if the behavior is maintained by escape, the break is delayed by a few seconds or after the next step in the task analysis is completed. Steege et al. (1990), for example, was able to increase task compliance gradually until the child was able to complete the entire task before manding for a break. A similar approach can be used with behavior maintained by attention.

Box 8-10	CASE EXAMPLE OF MULTIPLE TREATMENTS USED WITH SIB THAT OCCURRED FOR BOTH ATTENTION AND ESCAPE IN DIFFERENT CONTEXTS

Betty was 7 years old and had been diagnosed as being moderately to severely mentally retarded. She had both hearing and visual impairments that were becoming more pronounced because of a degenerative neurological disorder. Betty displayed a number of topographies of SIB, but the most severe was banging her head on hard surfaces. A brief functional analysis showed that SIB served both escape and attention functions but never occurred during alone times. In addition, a descriptive assessment showed that the controlling events for escape-motivated behavior were requests to perform nonpreferred tasks or physical contact with nonpreferred staff. With preferred staff, however, she engaged in SIB only when ignored, so that, with certain staff, Betty's SIB was clearly attention-motivated. Given these results, on demanding tasks or with non-preferred staff, Betty was taught to sign "no" and was given a 30-second break. With preferred staff, she was taught to sign "please" and received immediate attention for about 30 seconds. Extinction was used for SIB. She learned to sign almost immediately, but improvement in SIB was initially slow. It took almost three months for noticeable reductions in SIB to occur, even though signing was frequent. After about nine months, SIB decreased to almost zero. Three years after treatment, she had learned about 30 signs and said one or two mands ("no"), and no occurrences of SIB had been noted in over a year.

An alternative approach is to use differential reinforcement (DRA or DRO) during task completion. In many cases, we use both DRA and DRO initially during training and then gradually fade out the DRO component. As shown in Box 8-11, one potential benefit of a DRA/DRO treatment approach over FCT is that the client is working on the task at the very beginning of treatment. However, as noted by Horner and Day (1991), one frequent advantage of FCT over DRA/DRO is that manding is very efficient and may therefore result in quicker effects. The decision about which treatment to use is probably one of personal preference.

CONCLUSION

The success of treatment depends on the accuracy with which we can assess the function of SIB. Descriptive assessments provide information on the most probable times or activities during which SIB occurs, the specific events that precipitate its occurrence, and the possible consequent events. Functional

<table>
<tr><td>

Box
8-11

</td><td>

CASE EXAMPLE OF DRA AND DRO WITH ESCAPE-MOTIVATED SIB

Ron was 29 years old, had been diagnosed as autistic, and engaged in severe head slapping. A functional analysis confirmed the workshop staff's hypothesis that the behavior was escape-motivated. One task that Ron was learning was to sort clothes into cold- and hot-water loads in a laundry room. The initial treatment involved DRA, in which he was given brief breaks (about 1 minute) after each item was sorted. SIB was ignored. The result was a substantial reduction in SIB, but after three months, multiple instances still continued every day. Thus, a DRO component was added, in which he received an additional break of a shorter duration (about 15 seconds) after every minute of task completion without SIB. This approach successfully reduced SIB to zero occurrence after one week. After no occurrences of SIB were reported for one month, the DRO component was gradually faded each week, so that a break was then provided after 2 minutes, 3 minutes, and so on. Once the DRO component was removed, the DRA component was also faded, so that the break was provided after two items, three items, and so on. The DRA component was eventually maintained after five items, as further fading resulted in a return of SIB.

</td></tr>
</table>

analyses are used to confirm, at least partially, those hypotheses and to prescribe the general class of treatment, given the class of maintaining events (positive, negative, or automatic reinforcement). In selecting treatments, the key is both to reinforce an alternative response and to remove all reinforcement for continued SIB.

References

Berg, W., Wacker, D., & Northup, J. (1991, May). *Training the use of an approach and escape communicative response simultaneously for the treatment of self-injury.* Paper presented at the annual convention of the Association for Behavior Analysis, Atlanta.

Bijou, S. W., Petersen, R. F., & Ault, M. F. (1968). A method to integrate descriptive and experimental field studies at the level of data and empirical concepts. *Journal of Applied Behavior Analysis, 1,* 175–191.

Carr, E. G. (1988). Functional equivalence as a mechanism of response generalization. In R. Homer, R. Koegel, & G. Dunlap (Eds.), *Generalization and maintenance: Life style changes in applied settings* (pp. 194–219). Baltimore: Brookes.

Carr, E. G., & Durand, V. M. (1985). Reducing behavior problems through functional communication training. *Journal of Applied Behavior Analysis, 18,* 111–126.

Derby, K. M., Wacker, D., Sasso, G., Steege, M., Northup, J., Cigrand, K., & Asmus, J. (1992). A three-year evaluation of the use of brief functional analysis techniques to assess maladaptive behavior in an outclinic setting: A summary of 79 cases. *Journal of Applied Behavior Analysis, 25,* 713–721.

Dunlap, G., Kern-Dunlap, L., Clarke, M., & Robbins, F. (1991). Functional assessment, curricular revision, and severe behavior problems. *Journal of Applied Behavior Analysis, 24,* 387–397.

Hayes, S. C., Nelson, R. O., & Jarret, R. B. (1987). The treatment utility of assessment: A functional approach to evaluating assessment quality. *American Psychologist, 42,* 963–974.

Horner, R. H., & Day, M. H. (1991). The effects of response efficiency on functionally equivalent, competing behaviors. *Journal of Applied Behavior Analysis, 24,* 719–732.

Iwata, B. A., Dorsey, M. F., Slifer, K. J., Bauman, K. E., & Richman, C. S. (1982). Toward a functional analysis of self-injury. *Analysis and Intervention in Developmental Disabilities, 2,* 3–20.

Mace, F. C. (1990). Functional analysis and treatment of aberrant behavior. *Research and Analysis in Developmental Disabilities, 18,* 45–68.

National Institutes of Health. (1989). *Consensus development conference on treatment of destructive behaviors in persons with developmental disabilities.* Washington, DC: Author.

Northup, J., Wacker, D., Sasso, C., Steege, M., Cigrand, K., Cook, J., & DeRaad, A. (1991). A brief functional analysis of aggressive and alternative behavior in an outclinic setting. *Journal of Applied Behavior Analysis, 24,* 509–522.

Steege, M., Wacker, D., Cigrand, K., Novak, C., Reimers, T., Sasso, C., & DeRaad, A. (1990). Use of negative reinforcement in the treatment of self-injurious behavior. *Journal of Applied Behavior Analysis, 23,* 459–467.

Wacker, D., Northup, N., & Cooper, L. (1991). Behavioral assessment. In D. Greydanus & M. Wolraich (Eds.), *Behavioral pediatrics.* New York: Springer-Verlag.

Wacker, D., & Steege, M. (1993). Providing outclinic services: Evaluating treatment and social validity. In S. Axelrod & R. Van Houten (Eds.), *Behavior analysis and treatment* (pp. 297–319). New York: Plenum Press.

Wacker, D., Steege, M., Northup, J., Reimers, T., Berg, W., & Sasso, C. (1990). Use of functional analysis and acceptability measures to assess and treat severe behavior problems: An outpatient clinic model. In A. C. Repp & N. N. Singh (Eds.), *Perspectives on the use of nonaversive and aversive interventions for persons with developmental disabilities* (pp. 349–359). Sycamore, IL: Sycamore.

Chapter
9

Stereotypy

JOHANNES ROJAHN, DAVID HAMMER,
AND TRACY L. KROEGER

INTRODUCTION

Many people with mental retardation have socially conspicuous, repetitive behaviors. Among the more typical forms are body rocking, hand clapping, hand postures, repeated vocal noises, and ritualistic manipulations of objects. These behaviors, often called *stereotyped behaviors,* or *stereotypies,* are voluntary (i.e., the person is able to control them), and in their appearance, they resemble to some extent the behavior of infants. Stereotypies typically have fixed movement patterns involving the same body parts. Each individual appears to have a unique set of movements.

Many biological and environmental factors contribute to the development of stereotyped behavior. Clinically, the most useful explanations are based on operant conditioning theory. For instance, we know that stereotyped behavior in some persons is maintained by positive reinforcement. Reinforcers may be social (e.g., the behavior attracts attention from other persons) or sensory. Stereotyped behavior maintained by sensory reinforcement is also known as *self-stimulation.* Other stereotyped behaviors may be reinforced by terminating or delaying an aversive condition (i.e., negative reinforcement or escape/avoidance conditioning). For instance, a person may body-rock more frequently in the day program than at night at home, because the day program is associated with demanding and unpleasant tasks, and because body rocking often leads to a reduction of those demands. Both positive and negative reinforcement hypotheses of stereotyped behavior are the basis of clinically and educationally useful forms of treatment.

PREVALENCE

Estimates of stereotyped behavior prevalence vary from 5 to 35%, which equals 50 to 350 in every 1,000 people with mental retardation. These large discrepancies are caused by methodological differences in those estimates.

Preparation of this manuscript was supported in part by grants from the U.S. Department of Health and Human Services, Administration on Developmental Disabilities (Grant #07DD0270/16), and the Bureau of Maternal and Child Health and Resources Development, Division of Maternal and Child Health (Grant MCJ#922), awarded to the Nisonger Center for Mental Retardation and Developmental Disabilities at the Ohio State University. The authors would like to thank Wallis Harsch for careful readings and tremendously helpful editorial suggestions.

Estimates vary drastically depending on the way stereotyped behaviors are defined, and depending on the surveyed population. We know for a fact, however, that there is an inverse relationship between stereotyped behavior and the level of mental retardation; it is much more common among people with low cognitive abilities and low levels of adaptive behavior than in people with a mild mental disability. Prevalence peaks around late childhood and early adolescence and then gradually drops off. Stereotypical behavior is much more prevalent in restrictive and segregated public residential facilities than in less restrictive ones located in the community.

BEHAVIORAL ASSESSMENT AND ANALYSIS

Behavioral analysis is conducted to identify the mechanisms that maintain the target behavior, to assist in choosing an appropriate type of intervention, and to evaluate the effectiveness of the intervention. Chapter 8 includes a comprehensive discussion of behavioral assessment and analysis of self-injury that largely applies to stereotyped behavior as well. The reader is therefore referred to this chapter for more information on the topic.

TREATMENT APPROACHES

It is legitimate to ask why stereotypies should be treated in the first place, since these are relatively harmless behaviors. The usual reasons given are that stereotyped behaviors interfere with learning, are incompatible with adaptive functioning, may develop into self-injurious behavior, and are stigmatizing and therefore make it more difficult for the person to be integrated into the community.

There are several different forms of treatment for stereotyped behavior, but the most successful one is behavior modification (applied behavior analysis). The two basic strategies of behavior modification are (1) to reduce the behavior directly through manipulation of the behavior's consequences, and (2) to increase appropriate behavior and thereby indirectly reduce stereotypies. We will first describe some indirect methods because they are usually more benign and therefore less controversial among parents or guardians, advocates, service providers, and professionals.

Box 9-1

ENVIRONMENTAL MODIFICATION WITH SCATTER PLOT ASSESSMENT

Shawna was an 18-year-old female with autism attending classes for teenagers with multiple disabilities in a public school system. She was referred for psychological evaluation concerning frequent episodes of stereotyped behavior in the form of holding her ear and making high-pitched sounds repeatedly. This behavior was of concern because it interfered with her instruction and caused considerable distraction in the classroom. Interviews with the classroom staff yielded no indication of possible controlling motivational factors. Thus, a so-called scatter-plot data-collection system was employed. The school day was divided into 15-minute time periods on a single sheet of paper representing a month-long period. Teachers and aides were asked to make a slash through any 15-minute period in which the stereotypical sounds were heard. After three weeks, a pattern emerged that showed that approximately 80% of the subject's stereotypical sounds occurred during three specific 15-minute segments of the school day. When staff were asked about the typical school day during those times, a common feature became evident: group activities with low individual structure and high noise levels. It was recommended that the teacher first try to include Shawna in these activities by using smaller groups for shorter time periods, and then slowly increasing first the time and then the group size. This strategy succeeded in reducing the stereotyped behavior by 60% to 70% and in improving Shawna's participation in the activities.

Indirect Strategies

Environmental Modification

Environmental modifications are systematic changes in the environment of the person in order to decrease stereotyped behavior. Stereotyped behavior is known to vary with situational characteristics such as the noise level in a room, the size of the group relative to the available space, the kinds of demands placed on the person, or the availability of attractive toys. Touchette, MacDonald, and Langer (1985) demonstrated how such environmental characteristics that are related to stereotyped behavior in a functional way can first be detected and then modified. First, they found through systematic observation and monitoring that a problem behavior in a certain client seemed to be triggered by certain scheduled activities. The behavior was apparently escape-motivated. The intervention consisted of a simple rescheduling of activities, which led to the elimination of the target behaviors (see Box 9-1 for a more detailed clinical example).

Another way to use environmental change to reduce escape-motivated stereotyped behavior is to change certain aversive aspects of the situation. Gaylord-Ross, Weeks, and Lipner (1980) provided an example in the literature. They showed the effectiveness in reducing stereotyped behavior of mak-

Box 9-2

REDUCTION OF AVERSIVE TASK PROPERTIES

Community mobility in the form of using public transportation was a key factor in Henry's program to acquire supported employment. Unfortunately, this 20-year-old man with autisticlike features had trouble with using public transportation. Shortly after entering the bus, he began to body-rock, flap his hands, and make a loud humming noise. His misbehavior made him quite visible to the public and resulted in a number of embarrassing and potentially dangerous instances. As a consequence, it diminished his ability to gain independent mobility, which was a prerequisite for getting to his job-training site. During an investigation of this behavior, the functional analysis interview with his foster parents indicated that this behavior pattern was frequent in situations that Henry disliked and that he liked to get away from. One of the situations that made Henry feel most uncomfortable was closeness to strangers. In order to test this hypothesis, Henry's bus-riding schedule was altered to periods of the day when only a few passengers were on the bus. As a result, Henry's stereotyped behavior on the bus decreased rapidly, so that he was able to begin his supported work training without incident.

ing changes to reduce some aversive characteristics of a particular task that was associated with that behavior. The clients had previously been allowed to escape from that task by exhibiting stereotyped behavior; their escape led to a worsening of the behavior (see Box 9-2 for another example).

Although changing the environment alone is not always powerful enough to obtain clinically satisfactory breakthroughs, it may at least play an important role in a more comprehensive treatment plan. The clinician is well advised to carefully explore environmental conditions for a possible relationship to the target behavior and to try to adjust them accordingly, if appropriate or possible, before other, more invasive forms of intervention are considered.

Training Adaptive Behavior

Systematically adding to or expanding a person's adaptive behavior is another useful way of reducing stereotyped behavior. For instance, teaching meaningful interaction with the environment, such as playing skills, may lead to reductions in stereotyped behavior, particularly if the person seems to engage in stereotypies for self-stimulation and the lack of other things to do. A more focused version of adaptive behavior training is functional communication training (FCT), which is particularly called for when the target behavior is either escape-motivated or maintained by positive social reinforcement. Communication skills enable the client either to escape an unwanted situation

---

Box 9-3

FUNCTIONAL COMMUNICATION EQUIVALENCE

Danny was an 18-year-old male with severe mental retardation who resided at home with his parents and his younger sister. For six hours each day, Danny attended a state-funded program for those with severe delays. Although wheelchair-bound, he was quite mobile and relied on a repertoire of ten signs for purposes of functional communication. While generally compliant and good-natured at home, Danny had particular difficulty in the classroom. The noise level in such close quarters was especially upsetting to him and would consistently result in vigorous body rocking and yelling. Often this behavior became so disturbing that Danny's mother would simply allow him to stay at home. In an attempt to provide Danny with an adaptive alternative to express his displeasure, classroom staff made a joint effort to teach Danny to sign "ear." Contingent on this response, a pair of earmuffs was placed on Danny's head, successfully attenuating the noise and enabling Danny to stay in class without body rocking. Each morning, the classroom aide would respond to the first instance of body rocking by manually guiding Danny's fingers to sign "ear." Following the sign for "ear," earmuffs were placed on Danny's head. The prompts were gradually faded from the signing process. Within five days of training, Danny was successfully using the sign for "earmuff," and his body rocking had been reduced by over 95% in the classroom.

---

or to attract attention by more appropriate and acceptable forms of communication. For example, Durand and Carr (1987) were able to "replace" inappropriate body rocking and hand flapping with socially acceptable signing for assistance. Box 9-3 shows a clinical example of how such a functional-equivalence communication training is implemented.

Differential Reinforcement

Another group of relatively noninvasive, indirect interventions for stereotyped behavior are differential reinforcement procedures. The most widely used procedures are differential reinforcement of other behavior (DRO) and differential reinforcement of incompatible behavior (DRI). With DRO, a reinforcer is given after a certain period of time in which the target behavior has not occurred. The length of the time may vary from half a minute to over an hour, depending on several different factors, such as the child's level of functioning and how frequently the behavior occurs. The intervals chosen are shorter in the beginning and gradually increase. Box 9-4 briefly describes a practical example of a DRO procedure.

Although the case scenario in Box 9-4 shows a successful treatment outcome, it must be pointed out that DRO may not be powerful enough as a treatment procedure by itself. However, DRO can play a very useful role as part of a comprehensive behavior management plan.

> ### *Box 9-4*
>
> ### DIFFERENTIAL REINFORCEMENT OF OTHER BEHAVIORS (DRO)
>
> Fifteen years old at the time and diagnosed with severe mental retardation, Dave had some receptive, but virtually no expressive, language. Only inconsistently did he follow simple commands. In addition, he engaged in high rates of mouthing objects. Observations and interviews with the parents and teachers indicated that he received much social attention for this behavior because of the concern that he would swallow something harmful. A treatment plan was developed to reduce this inappropriate behavior through a schedule of differential reinforcement. The target behavior was defined as contact of the oral region with an inedible object. During the 30-minute treatment sessions, Dave was rewarded with physical affection and verbal praise if he did not exhibit any mouthing behavior during a particular DRO interval. Initially, data were collected to determine a baseline rate per minute for mouthing. The mean response rate per minute determined the length of the DRO interval. The mean rate was three responses per minute during baseline; therefore, the DRO interval was one-third of a minute, or 20 seconds. Later, when mouthing had decreased during treatment by 50%, the DRO interval was increased by 50% to 30 seconds. Over a two-month treatment period, mouthing decreased to 16% of its original rate. At 6- and 12-month follow-ups, mouthing was still maintained at acceptable rates (20% and 25%, respectively, of baseline rates).

DRI is similar to DRO, but it has one important additional stipulation. Besides not performing a stereotyped behavior during an interval, the child must also exhibit a specific behavior in order to obtain a reinforcer; this behavior must be incompatible with the stereotyped behavior. To be incompatible with the stereotyped behavior, a behavior must be physically impossible to perform at the same time as the stereotyped behavior.

Behavioral Momentum

As we all know from our own experience, it is not realistic to expect that all things in life will be pleasant. The same is true, of course, for people with mental retardation. Therefore, it is not in their best interest to be protected from all unpleasantness, and there comes a point when they need to learn to perform tasks that are not enjoyable. Behavioral momentum is a treatment procedure for stereotyped behavior that is motivated by the avoidance of unpleasant situations. The idea is to assist a client in performing unpleasant tasks without that person's trying to escape by using stereotyped behavior. This procedure is facilitated by building up a response momentum, in which requests for aversive tasks are imbedded in a series of requests for easy-to-perform, pleasant tasks. Box 9-5 gives an example of the clinical application of a behavioral momentum program.

> ### Box 9-5
>
> ## BEHAVIORAL MOMENTUM
>
> As a resident in a group home, Carolyn, a 35-year-old woman who had been diagnosed in the moderate to severe range of mental retardation, spent most of her free time alone. As Carolyn increasingly withdrew from social contact, compliance became an issue of concern, and the frequency of a previously rare hand-wringing behavior had begun to escalate. Staff observed that whenever demands were made to pick up her clothes and put them into her closet, Carolyn began to engage in hand wringing; the timing suggested that the behavior was escape-motivated. Since both compliance and stereotypical behavior were of interest in this case, a behavioral momentum program was developed that addressed both issues: (1) making it easier for Carolyn to respond to certain demands and (2) thus making it unnecessary to try to avoid those demands by engaging in stereotypies. In order to increase compliance with key tasks (e.g., "Brush your hair," "Wash your hands"), requests for a series of four highly preferred tasks were issued first, one every 10 seconds ("Give me a hug," "Shake my hand," "Clap your hands," "Flip the light switch"). Compliance with these preferred tasks was praised enthusiastically. After ten commands for preferred tasks, a request to pick up her clothes was issued. As days went by, fewer and fewer preferred tasks were necessary (i.e., a shorter momentum had to be built up) for Carolyn to comply with the unpopular task of cleaning up in her room. After four days, the low-preference behavior was preceded by only one preferred-behavior request. Two days later, preferred-behavior requests were unnecessary for her to comply with the low-preference behaviors without engaging in hand wringing.

Reinforcer Displacement

It is a known fact that we learn faster if reinforcers are presented each time a behavior occurs (continuous reinforcement), rather than with inconsistent (intermittent) reinforcement. However, any behavior maintained by intermittent positive reinforcement takes much longer to extinguish when reinforcement is withheld, compared to the same behavior learned through continuous reinforcement. Reinforcer displacement is a procedure that reduces intermittently reinforced undesirable behavior by taking advantage of these behavioral laws. In practice, this procedure is accomplished by first continually reinforcing the target behavior. Second, once the target behavior is firmly controlled by the more powerful continuous reinforcement schedule, reinforcement is ended abruptly.

It must be pointed out, however, that clinical research on reinforcer displacement has been scarce. It is prudent, therefore, not to expect too much from this procedure. Box 9-6 illustrates what a clinical example of a reinforcer displacement procedure would look like.

<table>
<tr><td>

*Box
9-6*

</td><td>

REINFORCER DISPLACEMENT

Joe was a 12-year-old adolescent with profound mental retardation and a severe visual impairment. He had a long history of body rocking, which was defined as four continuous back-and-forth oscillations of the shoulders in a 10-second interval. This behavior had been highly resistant to several intervention attempts in the past and appeared to be maintained by the attention it generated from Joe's instructors and parents. A reinforcer displacement program was designed for Joe to reduce his stereotypical rocking. After taking week-long daily baseline data, intervention began. It consisted of a schedule of continuous reinforcement for body rocking, which meant that each occurrence of body rocking was rewarded with an edible, in this case an M&M. After the third day of the five-day period, it became very apparent that Joe was now rocking to obtain the edible reinforcement. After five days of reinforcement of stereotyped behavior, the reinforcement schedule was abruptly stopped. During the extinction, no instance of body rocking received any reinforcement. This sequence of reinforcement and extinction successfully reduced body rocking by over 95% within one week.

</td></tr>
</table>

Direct Response-Decreasing Strategies

Extinction

If a functional analysis shows that stereotyped behavior is maintained by identified positive reinforcers, and if it turns out that these reinforcers are easily accessible and can be manipulated, then extinction is a feasible treatment. Technically, extinction means reducing a behavior's occurrence rate by withholding the reinforcers. Extinction in clinical practice usually refers to withholding positive social reinforcement (see Box 9-7 for a clinical example). For instance, if a child's repetitive yelling is motivated by attracting her or his parent's attention, giving the attention acts as a reinforcer. Systematically withholding attention would be an example of an extinction procedure.

Behavior maintained by negative reinforcement can also be extinguished. This process is called *avoidance extinction*. The goal of avoidance extinction is to disrupt the relationship between the target behavior and the reinforcement so that the target behavior cannot "produce" the reinforcing condition anymore. For example, when the child makes the connection between body rocking and being permitted to terminate work on an unwanted task, that connection is likely to reinforce body rocking. Consequently, body rocking will begin to increase whenever that task is likely to appear. In an avoidance-extinction procedure, the child would be required to continue to perform the task, and the body rocking would be ignored. Thus, the client slowly learns that, in the future, stereotyped behavior will not help him or her to terminate unpleasant tasks.

EXTINCTION OF SOCIALLY REINFORCED BEHAVIOR

Kelly, a 19-year-old woman with moderate to severe mental retardation, was employed at a workshop. Lately, she had become almost totally unproductive on her assigned task, presumably because of increased rates of table slapping. This high-frequency behavior was judged to be not only significantly disruptive of Kelly's assignments, but also a considerable nuisance to others. Informal observations suggested that Kelly did not receive a great amount of attention at work, except when she slapped the table. Her co-workers started to look at her, laughed, or began to engage in inappropriate behavior themselves. As a consequence, workshop staff approached Kelly and asked her to stop. Occasionally, they tried to hold down her hands in an effort to stop the noise. An extinction program was developed in which staff were instructed not to interfere with Kelly's table slapping, and to ignore her completely for 30 seconds after the behavior had occurred. Between table-slapping episodes, staff were asked to pay as much attention to Kelly as possible and to praise her work behavior. After several weeks of this extinction procedure, Kelly had reduced her table slapping to almost zero.

Compliance Training

Conceptually related to avoidance extinction is compliance training. Compliance training also teaches the child that stereotyped or other undesirable behaviors do not lead to a release from compliance with requests. The trainer makes systematic repeated requests to the client to perform certain tasks. These requests provide the client with an opportunity either to comply or to try to avoid the task by engaging in stereotyped behavior. If a misbehavior occurs, it is ignored. Compliance, on the other hand, is "forced" by prompting and gradual guidance procedures.

Sensory Extinction

Stereotyped behavior is frequently maintained by the very sensation it produces, which presumably has given rise to the term *self-stimulation*. Sensory extinction deals with self-stimulatory stereotyped behavior (i.e., behavior that is maintained by sensory consequences). If the internal reinforcer can be identified, and if there are ways to alter it, then sensory extinction is a treatment option. For instance, in one of the earliest publications on sensory extinction, Rincover (1978) worked with a child who almost incessantly spun his plate. Observations indicated that the behavior was maintained by auditory feedback. Rincover carpeted the tabletop to block out the noise created by the spinning plate, and the behavior quickly receded. With another child, hand flapping was treated with a vibrator that was taped to the back of the hand.

Box 9-8

EXTINCTION OF SENSORIALLY REINFORCED BEHAVIOR

Jimmy was an 11-year-old child diagnosed as having childhood schizophrenia with several autistic characteristics. He had an age equivalent of 3.5 years on the Vineland Social Maturity Scale. The presence of a high rate of repetitive hand movements (specifically, hand clapping) made Jimmy a candidate for a program combining sensory extinction with a DRI procedure. Two classroom aides, in conjunction with the primary classroom instructor, agreed to implement an extinction program through the application of mittens. The purpose was to eliminate the noise of the clapping, which might be the sensory reinforcer that maintained the behavior. On entering the classroom at eight o'clock each morning for two weeks, Jimmy was expected to put on a pair of heavy cotton mittens. Worn throughout the entire day, the mittens were removed only for a 15-minute period during lunch and a 5-minute break during snack time. Otherwise, the mittens remained on Jimmy's hands until 5 minutes before he left for the day. In addition to the sensory extinction procedures, differential reinforcement was given to those behaviors incompatible with hand clapping (folded hands, hands in lap, appropriate work). The combination of DRI and sensory extinction reduced the target behavior by almost 98% at the end of the two-week treatment period. The mittens were later faded by slowly cutting off small parts until only a wristband remained.

Since the behavior decreased, it was assumed that the vibrations masked the proprioceptive stimulation, thus extinguishing the behavior.

Sensory extinction usually requires considerable ingenuity on the therapist's part to engineer devices that can prevent these self-stimulating sensations without blocking freedom of movement, or without limiting other sensory input. Probably because it often requires elaborate technical gadgetry, sensory extinction is less frequently found in clinical practice than the other extinction procedures mentioned above. A technologically simple clinical example of sensory extinction is described in Box 9-8.

Sensory Change

In a variation of sensory extinction, called *sensory change,* the consequences of stereotyped behavior are changed or interfered with, rather than made entirely imperceptible. In one report, for instance, hand-flapping behavior was treated by having the client wear loosely fitted costume-jewelry bracelets on her arms, which would bounce around with her arm movements. Wearing the bracelets led to a decrease in hand flapping, presumably because it changed the sensations the child was accustomed to when she did her hand flapping. It is important to report that it was possible, in that particular case, to successfully fade out the bracelets after treatment.

Box 9-9

RESPONSE INTERRUPTION

Nancy was a 6-year-old girl with moderate mental retardation who was enrolled in a program for children with visual impairments. As is typical of this population, she frequently engaged in self-stimulatory behavior, notably hand flapping. To reduce the frequency of hand flapping, a relatively nonaversive procedure involving response interruption was introduced into Nancy's daily routine. Staff members who maintained contact with Nancy throughout the day were trained in the appropriate response-interruption procedures. Every time she engaged in hand flapping, an instructor delivered a verbal reprimand and guided her hands either to her lap or to the edge of a table, where they were to remain for 2 minutes. In addition, the instructor was careful to limit physical contact to light manual guidance or shadowing. If Nancy moved about or attempted to engage in hand flapping during the last 10 seconds of the 2-minute period, the period was extended until 10 seconds had elapsed without this behavior. Great care was also taken to reinforce any display of appropriate alternative hand movements through a DRO schedule. For each 2-minute period without hand flapping, Nancy received both verbal praise and physical affection. The contingent use of response interruption continued throughout the school day. Within one week, the hand flapping had been reduced to 10% of its original rate.

Response Interruption

Response interruption consists of physically preventing stereotyped behavior. Azrin and Wesolowski (1980) first described this procedure with a client who had rhythmic hand-flapping behavior. They seated him across the table from one therapist, who interacted with him and rewarded simple task completion. A second therapist was positioned behind him. As soon as the client started to flap his hands, the second therapist took the client's hands, gave a verbal reprimand ("No, John, don't flap your hands"), and guided his hands to his lap, where they were to remain for 2 minutes.

It is important for the therapist to remember that the interruption must not lead to a physical struggle with the client, and that it ought to be executed with the least amount of force necessary (graduated manual guidance). Generally speaking, response interruption is not the procedure of choice when the behavior is motivated by social reinforcement, because the intervention may be similar to those reinforcers that maintained the behavior in the first place. For a clinical illustration of response interruption see Box 9-9.

Overcorrection

Overcorrection refers to several different treatments that have been widely used with different forms of problem behaviors. The most important form of overcorrection for the treatment of stereotyped behavior is positive practice over-

<table>
<tr><td>Box
9-10</td><td>OVERCORRECTION</td></tr>
</table>

Bob, a 21-year-old with autism and an estimated IQ below 25, was a resident of a state hospital. Among other self-stimulatory behaviors, he exhibited an unacceptably high rate of body rocking. That behavior, particularly when sitting on a couch that was placed against the wall, had recently become of concern because Bob had been seen occasionally to knock his head against the wall. Therefore, staff was concerned that body rocking might be a precursor of severe headbanging. Rocking behavior was defined as two or more back-and-forth oscillations of the shoulders in a 5-second period while sitting. In an effort to reduce body rocking, staff members first conducted functional analyses and found that the behavior was maintained neither by positive social reinforcement nor by successful avoidance of unwanted tasks. The treatment team therefore agreed that overcorrection supplemented by DRO was warranted. Bob was required to practice maintaining his shoulders firm against the back of a chair for 5 minutes, as in a normal sitting position. The overcorrection procedure was implemented throughout the course of the day by staff members. While encouraged to engage in outward-directed activities, Bob was also required to perform the overcorrection program for each instance of body rocking. Whenever he self-stimulated, a staff member immediately instructed him not to move his shoulders and directed him to another area of the room. Standing behind Bob, the staff member required him to practice the shoulder position for a period of 20 minutes. Throughout the day, each 30-minute period without body rocking was rewarded with social praise and an opportunity to shake hands for 5 seconds, a highly preferred activity for Bob. By the end of one month, body rocking had been reduced by over 90%.

correction. Immediately after the target behavior occurs, the client has to perform a rigorous program of repeated motor movements that may last from several minutes to half an hour. These movements are usually incompatible with the target behavior and are developmentally appropriate. To get the client to perform these strenuous exercises, verbal and graduated physical prompts (with the least amount of force required) are used. One of the more noteworthy features of overcorrection has been its claim of combining a punitive form of intervention with the opportunity to teach new and desirable behavior in the process. Box 9-10 gives an example of a positive-practice overcorrection program. It should be mentioned that overcorrection is a very work-intensive intervention, not only for the client, but for the therapist as well.

Time-Out from Positive Reinforcement

Another frequently used procedure is time-out from positive reinforcement. Technically, it consists of making positive reinforcement unavailable for a specified period beginning immediately after the targeted behavior has

	CONTINGENT IGNORING TIME-OUT
Box 9-11	Debbie was a 30-year-old woman with profound mental retardation and a long history of hand-flapping behavior. This behavior seemed largely attention seeking in nature. Previous attempts had proved ineffective in eliminating the hand-flapping behavior. Recently, however, it had been noted that her hand flapping had changed into a mild form of face slapping. This development was of major concern because of the possibility that it might develop into a serious behavior problem. A behavior management program using contingent ignoring time-out was designed. Integral to the success of the procedure was the establishment of a strong association between a preferred object (S^D) and positive reinforcement. After a baseline period, Debbie was given a bracelet to wear during specified periods of time. During these periods, increased attention was given, while face slapping was ignored. After a week of this heavy reinforcement schedule, the time-out procedure was introduced. Contingent on a face-slapping response, the bracelet was removed. Following 2 minutes without face slapping, the bracelet was returned. Emphasis was placed on providing lavish attention and reinforcement during the two times when the bracelet was worn. This program was followed throughout the day and evening by staff members, regardless of activities. After two weeks, Debbie's face slapping had been reduced to 98% of its original rate.

occurred. One key to successful time-out procedures is a highly rewarding environment (the "time-in"), so that the loss of rewards is quickly noticeable to the client. In clinical practice, withholding reinforcers takes many forms, ranging from very benign procedures to quite intrusive ones. One of the milder forms of time-out is differential ignoring, in which the trainer is instructed to withdraw attention from the client for a short period of time (e.g., 30 seconds) after the target behavior has occurred. When several trainers and clients are present in the same setting, it may be difficult for the therapists to keep up with current time-out status. The client can wear a simple sign, such as a ribbon tied to the arm, to indicate the favored status and eligibility for reward. As soon as stereotyped behavior occurs, the ribbon is removed, signaling to everyone that no rewards should be given (see Box 9-11 for an example of contingent ignoring time-out).

If differential ignoring time-out does not produce the desired results, a variety of gradually more restrictive variations are available. Exclusion time-out, for instance, involves temporary exclusion of the client from ongoing activities. An even more restrictive procedure is the expulsion from ongoing activities and placement in a special area of the room. It may even involve removal from the room and seclusion in a different room. Exclusion, expulsion, and seclusion time-out procedures have not been very important in the treatment of stereotyped behavior, because stereotypies are often self-

> ## *Box 9-12*
>
> ### IMMOBILIZATION
>
> Sarah, a 21-year-old woman with profound mental retardation, was a resident of a privately funded intermediate-care facility for persons with multiple disabilities. She engaged in self-stimulatory head tapping and body rocking. Lately, the stereotypies had become a real problem. The staff members noticed that Sarah's slow progress in developing adaptive functioning skills was a direct result of the competing self-stimulatory behavior. They were also concerned that her head tapping was becoming more intense. In an effort to decrease her inappropriate behaviors, an immobilization procedure was used to address the head tapping, the more disturbing of the two stereotyped behaviors. Each time she tapped her head, a direct-care worker grasped Sarah's forearm and gently but firmly held her arm at her side for 15–20 seconds. Before that, a brief verbal reprimand was delivered ("Sarah, don't tap your head"). In order to emphasize more appropriate, adaptive behavior, a 5-minute DRO contingency was added, which consisted of both verbal praise and a hug, which was particularly reinforcing for Sarah. Over the course of one month, while the immobilization procedure was in effect, direct-care workers recorded the occurrence of both the head tapping and the body rocking. Head tapping decreased rapidly and significantly. A small corresponding decrease was seen in body rocking as well.

stimulatory. Excluding the client would be counterproductive because it would not reduce, but enhance, the opportunity to engage in stereotyped behavior.

Immobilization

The immobilization procedure involves the temporary physical restraint of gross-motor movement contingent on the target behavior. One can only speculate on exactly why this procedure works, but it is probably because of the abrupt interruption of the ongoing behavior and the unpleasant experience of being restrained. As in overcorrection, the therapist must use only minimal force to avoid a struggle with the client. See Box 9-12 for a short clinical example of immobilization. Movement restraint itself is a component in several other treatment procedures as well, such as exclusion time-out and positive practice overcorrection.

Visual and Facial Screening

In facial screening, the therapist temporarily draws a cloth over the client's face when the stereotyped behavior occurs, in an attempt to block the visual input. For practical purposes, the cloth is often attached to the client's neck like a bib. In visual screening, the therapist's palm is used to cover the client's

> ### Box 9-13
>
> ### VISUAL SCREENING
>
> Finger flicking and pill rolling were two stereotypical hand movements of Chris, a 22-year-old woman with severe mental retardation. The highly repetitive nature of these movements was particularly disruptive. In order to help Chris become more independent and proficient in her tasks, several benign behavior programs had been tried, but without success. Finally, the treatment team decided to use a visual screening program in combination with a heavy DRO procedure. Often occurring in conjunction with one another, instances of finger flicking and pill rolling were addressed by a verbal statement ("No finger flicking, Chris") and the shielding of her eyes for 10 seconds. During screening, a staff member stood behind Chris and held one hand in front of her eyes and the other against the back of her head until the behavior ceased or 10 seconds had elapsed. Hugs and pats on the back were given during periods when no stereotypical behavior occurred. After ten days, the stereotypical behavior had almost disappeared. This success had still been maintained at 6-month and 12-month follow-ups.

eyes. In most cases, the back of the client's head must be held during screening to prevent escape. Two salient features of screening techniques are physical restraint and temporary visual restriction. Research has shown that the more essential component of the two is blocking the client's vision. For a clinical example of a visual screening procedure see Box 9-13.

Punishment

Punishment means delivering a stimulus immediately after the target behavior occurs. Punishment must actually decrease the behavior, but it does not have to be noxious or painful. In most cases, of course, punishment is unpleasant for the client. Some behavior analysts have therefore excluded punishment as a treatment option, while others have not. Those who have not excluded this option believe that, in extreme cases of dangerous behavior, punishment, because of its rapid and decisive effect, may be clinically and ethically the most appropriate intervention. However, since stereotyped behavior is not usually a dangerous behavior, it does not warrant such invasive forms of treatment.

PROGRAMMATIC CONSIDERATIONS

Staff Training

It is important to remember that, although some behavior management procedures may appear simple, they are complex in theory and practice. Designing a workable individual behavioral treatment plan and a reliable assessment program requires extensive training and clinical experience. Parents, teachers, or other service providers who help implement behavior treatment programs must also be trained and closely supervised.

The responsible clinician who develops behavioral treatment programs not only should have thoroughly investigated the functional properties of a client's stereotyped behavior but should also be familiar with the relevant literature. It would also be useful for the therapist to be familiar with other aberrant movements, such as medication-induced extrapyramidal symptoms (tardive dyskinesia), or other conditions that involve movement disorders (e.g., Huntington's chorea, Tourette's syndrome, and seizure disorders).

As most of the clinical vignettes in this chapter illustrate, treatment plans must contain some form of reinforcement, regardless of what the rest of the program consists of. And since a stimulus may be reinforcing for one person but not for another, clinicians should be able to select effective reinforcers.

Finally, it is important to develop a plan to maintain and generalize the treatment effects from the treatment environment to the client's everyday life. It is relatively easy to demonstrate the effectiveness of a behavior management program in a highly structured setting. The difficulties arise in efforts to transfer the program and to integrate it into everyday routines. This requires very careful planning and a high degree of cooperation by those who have to implement the procedure.

Service Delivery

An issue in service delivery is selecting effective treatment procedures that are also socially acceptable. Almost 80% of all state agencies for mental retardation and developmental disabilities have adopted the least-to-most-restrictive decision model, which requires demonstrating that less intrusive treatments have been tried without achieving clinically sufficient effects before more intrusive programs can be used. The responsible clinician needs to be aware of state regulations concerning restrictive procedures. States differ in which behavior programs require prior approval and who needs to sign written consent.

In addition to being in accordance with state guidelines, treatment procedures must also be acceptable to the client, the client's parents or guardians, and other significant persons, such as the teachers or the responsible day-program staff. This is not only an ethical issue but also necessary if treatment gains are to be safely transferred to the everyday environment.

And as mentioned before, the issue must be raised whether there is reasonable clinical justification to treat stereotyped behavior in the first place. Stereotyped behavior should not be treated without a sound clinical rationale, because any form of behavioral treatment implicitly curtails a person's freedom of self-determination, and the benefits must be carefully balanced against the drawbacks. The introduction of this chapter included a brief description of why stereotypies are believed to be a problem. Nevertheless, a careful determination needs to be made if these reasons are to be deemed relevant for a particular client.

CONCLUSION

Stereotyped behaviors are harmless but bizarre behaviors and may therefore warrant behavioral intervention. Behavior-management program options range from very benign and indirect procedures, which focus on increasing desirable behaviors, to relatively restrictive ones, which are designed to directly reduce undesirable stereotypies. Given the nature of these behaviors, very restrictive procedures are hardly ever warranted. In any case, the decision about which program is to be used must be made case by case and should be based on a careful analysis of the functional properties of the behavior. It is important to ensure that the clinical staff who develop behavioral programs have the necessary theoretical and practical expertise, and that those who implement the programs are also appropriately trained. Program administrators must be adequately informed about federal and state regulations concerning the approval of certain procedures and written informed consent.

REFERENCES

Azrin, N. H., & Wesolowski, M. D. (1980). A reinforcement plus interruption method of eliminating behavioral stereotypy of profoundly retarded persons. *Behavior Research and Therapy, 18,* 113–119.

Durand, V. M., & Carr, E. G. (1987). Social influences on "self-stimulatory" behavior: Analysis and treatment application. *Journal of Applied Behavior Analysis, 20,* 119–132.

Gaylord-Ross, R. J., Weeks, M., & Lipner, C. (1980). An analysis of antecedent, response, and consequence events in the treatment of self-injurious behavior. *Education and Training of the Mentally Retarded, 15,* 35–42.

Rincover, A. (1978). Sensory extinction: A procedure for eliminating self-stimulatory behavior in developmentally disabled children. *Journal of Abnormal Child Psychology, 6,* 299–310.

Touchette, P. E., MacDonald, R. F., & Langer, S. N. (1985). A scatter plot for identifying stimulus control of problem behavior. *Journal of Applied Behavior Analysis, 18,* 343–351.

Chapter 10

Aggression

JOHNNY L. MATSON AND DEE DUNCAN

INTRODUCTION

Aggression is a common problem in individuals with mental retardation. Aggressive behavior may be a symptom of a psychiatric disorder or a product of faulty learning. For example, aggression is often a symptom of such psychiatric disorders as disruptive behavior disorders, disorders of impulse control, and certain personality disorders (e.g., antisocial personality disorder). In such cases, the treatment is derived from an analysis of the underlying psychiatric disturbance, and the aggressive behavior is the subject of psychopharmacological and psychosocial interventions. If the aggression is the result of faulty learning, a functional analysis provides the basis for behavioral interventions. The focus of this chapter is on this type of aggressive behavior.

We present a multicomponent assessment model and briefly review a number of treatment strategies for aggression that have been successfully used with individuals with mental retardation. Further, for each treatment strategy, we provide an illustrative case from our own research or from the published literature.

PREVALENCE

It has been estimated that about 139,000 of the 6 million persons with mental retardation in the United States engage in aggression and property damage (National Institutes of Health, 1991). Schroeder, Rojahn, and Oldenquist (1991) reviewed three large data sets and calculated that the prevalence of aggressive behavior ranged from 8.9% to 23.4% of cases. Aggression has been reported to be exhibited by 45% of the clients living in institutions, 20% of clients living in community group homes, and 20% of individuals with mental retardation living with their parents (Eyman & Call, 1977). Further, aggression has been found to be the most frequently occurring behavior problem of clients referred to a metropolitan mental-health program serving individuals with mental retardation (Reiss, 1982).

MULTICOMPONENT ASSESSMENT AND TREATMENT MODEL

Gardner and Cole (1990) have proposed a multicomponent model for the assessment and treatment of aggression. Their model includes the assessment of those variables involved in the genesis of aggressive behaviors, as well as those contributing to its maintenance. Their model deemphasizes a unitary approach to suppressing aggression with behavioral procedures. Instead, they propose a three-step process: (1) gathering assessment data relative to the conditions under which aggression is likely to occur; (2) generating hypotheses concerning potential influences; and (3) developing hypothesis-driven treatment procedures (Gardner & Cole, 1987).

Initially, the clinician needs to consider factors (e.g., environmental and client characteristics) that may instigate aggression, contribute to the acquisition of aggressive behavior (e.g., aggressive peer role models), and lead to the persistent recurrence of aggression (e.g., events that strengthen and maintain the behavior). Traditional assessment data on events that decrease aggression, such as the removal of positive events or the presentation of aversive events, are also obtained. The clinician then develops hypotheses about current factors that may contribute to the client's aggression. Given the complex nature of aggression, more than one hypothesis is usually generated. In the final step, the clinician develops a hypothesis-driven treatment protocol that uses one or more behavioral procedures, depending on the current motivation for the aggressive behavior.

TREATMENT STRATEGIES

Antecedent Strategies

It is necessary to determine whether stimuli presented before or concurrently with aberrant behavior serve as discriminative stimuli, as part of a chain of discriminative stimuli, or as setting events (Mace, Lalli, & Lalli, 1991). If a stimulus serves to elicit aggression, its removal typically preempts the occurrence of the behavior. Aggressive behavior that occurs as a result of a chain of escalating behaviors or events can be treated by interrupting the response chain early in the sequence. Setting events refer to the environmental context in which a stimulus-response interaction occurs, and which influences the stimulus-response function. Examples include the physical environment (e.g., crowding), the social context (e.g., the presence of specific staff), or the current physiological condition of the client (e.g., a preseizure aura). The Setting Events Checklist (Gardner, Cole, Davidson, & Karan, 1986) is useful in identifying these global influences on the client's aggressive behavior. When it has been determined that setting events reliably predict the occurrence of aggression, alteration of the setting events is typically the treatment of choice. Treatment strategies that focus on antecedent events have been successful in reducing aggression in individuals with mental retardation (Favell, 1991; Gardner & Cole, 1988). We briefly review some of these strategies.

CASE EXAMPLE OF THE USE OF DRO

The client was an 8-year-old boy with a diagnosis of moderate retardation with congenital rubella, blindness in the left eye, severe speech difficulty, hyperkinesis, and several other organic dysfunctions. Classroom observations showed that he exhibited the following aggressive behaviors: hitting, biting, kicking, pinching others, throwing objects, tearing papers, spitting, and overturning furniture.

Using an ABAB design, staff collected frequency data during baseline and provided him no consequence for engaging in aggressive behaviors. The treatment consisted of setting a kitchen timer for the prescribed DRO interval, resetting the timer if an aggressive behavior occurred and giving a verbal reprimand (saying, "No"), and if no aggressive behavior occurred, the client received a star on his board. Each star could be traded for a puzzle piece, and when the client had earned all of the puzzle pieces, he could take the puzzle to his home cottage. The effects of the DRO and the other treatment procedures were dramatic, and the boy's aggressive behavior was reduced substantially within a few sessions.

Differential Reinforcement

If the clinician is unable to identify any antecedent behaviors or events that predict aggressive behavior, then the clinician may consider using operant reinforcement procedures, such as differential reinforcement of other behaviors (DRO), to reduce the behavior. This is a commonly used procedure: The aggressive individual receives reinforcement for the *absence* of the target behavior during a specified time period. Other reinforcement procedures that may be used are differential reinforcement of appropriate behavior (DRA), differential reinforcement of incompatible behavior (DRI), and differential reinforcement of low rates of behavior (DRL).

The implementation of a DRA, DRI, or DRL procedure follows many of the same guidelines and basic requirements as for the DRO. Further, identifying and operationally defining the target behavior, selecting potent reinforcers, and using valid and reliable data-collection methods and informative visual displays (graphs) of the data trends are also required for interpretation of differential reinforcement procedures. Repp and Dietz (1974) used DRO to reduce a number of aggressive behaviors of a young boy with moderate mental retardation. Box 10-1 describes this case as an illustration of the use of a differential reinforcement procedure for controlling aggression.

Token Reinforcement

Token reinforcement is an intervention based on the delivery of positive reinforcement for specific target behaviors within a token economy system

> ## Box 10-2
>
> ### CASE EXAMPLE OF THE USE OF A TOKEN ECONOMY
>
> Four young adults with mental retardation were placed on a token economy program to increase their desirable behaviors and to reduce their aggressive behaviors. Desirable behaviors included performing routine self-care tasks (i.e., personal tidiness, personal hygiene, punctuality, table manners, and room tidiness). Aggressive behaviors included property destruction and physical or verbal abuse of staff or peers. The token program allowed the clients to earn a maximum of 30 points per day for engaging in the desirable behaviors, but they lost tokens for engaging in aggressive behaviors. The tokens could be exchanged daily for home leave, recreation, or various goods and services within their residential facility.
>
> Frequency data were collected during the baseline and treatment phases, within an ABAB design. During baseline, the four young adults did not receive any consequences for failing to complete desirable behaviors or for engaging in aggressive behavior. During treatment, the token program was implemented. Appropriate behaviors improved during the treatment phase, and the frequency and severity of the aggressive behaviors decreased with time.

(Kazdin, 1985). A token economy involves awarding secondary reinforcers, which may be exchanged for a variety of backup reinforcers, for the performance of desired behaviors. To set up a token economy, the clinician selects a token (e.g., tickets, poker chips, stars, or play money) and a number of rewards or backup reinforcers and then devises the rules that determine how the client can earn the tokens, when they can be spent, and what the "cost" of each backup reinforcer is. As an intervention for aggression, token economies are often paired with other procedures, such as DRO or response cost. The client earns tokens for prosocial behaviors and/or skills acquisition, such as those identified in an individual educational plan (IEP). However, in a DRO procedure, clients would not receive a token if aggression occurs, or in response cost, they would have to "pay" a token if aggression occurs. In Box 10-2, we describe a token economy program for four young adults with aggressive behavior, based on a study by Sanford and Nettelbeck (1982).

Teaching Alternative Skills

Accurate assessment is needed to determine if the client has a skills deficit or a performance deficit (i.e., a failure to implement the requisite skills at the appropriate time). If the client lacks the skill in his or her behavioral repertoire, training may be required to allow the acquisition of the new skill. If the client has the skill but does not use it, or uses it at the wrong time, discrimination training may be indicated.

Box 10-3

CASE EXAMPLE OF THE USE OF SOCIAL SKILLS TRAINING

The clients were four institutionalized women with mental retardation who engaged in frequent arguing and fighting. At times, assistance from hospital security was needed to keep them from hurting other patients. All four clients had been prescribed neuroleptics for their aggressive behavior for an extended period, but there had been no change in their behavior.

A preliminary assessment of their social skills was undertaken to determine the target behaviors for which role-play scenes needed to be developed. In addition, their aggressive behaviors were recorded. Aggression was defined as physically abusing another person. The social skills training consisted of instructions, modeling, role playing, and feedback. The frequency of aggression markedly decreased and remained at near-zero levels throughout treatment.

Social skills. If the assessment process indicates that the client's aggressive behavior is related to inappropriate interactions with others, social skills training may be indicated. Social skills training is used to teach clients to engage in prosocial behaviors as alternatives to aggression. Social skills help the person maximize desirable outcomes in interpersonal relations without infringing on others' rights (Polyson & Kimball, 1993). A typical social-skills training session includes instruction, modeling, behavioral rehearsal, feedback, and homework assignments to practice the new behavior. The topics for the individual or group sessions may be determined through a task analysis that identifies the components of the prosocial behavior and that determines which components the client lacks in his or her behavior repertoire. The basic criterion for selecting target skills is social significance or social validity, generalization being a primary concern during treatment. In Box 10-3, we present an illustrative example of the use of social skills training for four women who had a long history of aggressive behavior.

Self-monitoring. Self-monitoring may be used by higher-functioning clients to track their own behavior and may also serve as a treatment procedure. Self-monitoring involves systematically observing, recording, and evaluating one's own behavior (Beck, 1985). These three steps include discriminating when target behaviors occur, systematically recording the response, and evaluating one's self-observation data. Self-monitoring is used for the pretreatment identification of the antecedents and consequences of the target behavior, an evaluation of treatment effectiveness, and reactivity of self-monitoring as a form of treatment (Bornstein, Hamilton, & Bornstein, 1986). The act of self-monitoring has proved effective in reducing problem behaviors (Agran & Martin,

Box 10-4	CASE EXAMPLE OF THE USE OF SELF-MONITORING

Five children, who were patients in a psychiatric hospital school program for children with mental retardation and behavioral disturbances, were treated for aggressive and disruptive behavior. These behaviors were defined as hitting peers, throwing or banging objects, out-of-seat without permission, talking out of turn, and interfering with the work of peers. The aggressive and disruptive behaviors were initially reduced through a token economy program controlled by the teacher. The token system was then phased out, and in order to maintain the treatment gains, the children received instructions on self-monitoring, self-management, and self-reinforcement. The children's aggressive and disruptive behavior, which had initially been reduced through a teacher-controlled token economy program, was maintained by the children themselves through the self-monitoring of their own behavior.

1987; Bornstein et al., 1986). In Box 10-4, we present an example of the use of self-monitoring, self-management, and self-reinforcement for maintaining treatment gains once the aggressive behavior of five children had been brought under control through a token economy system.

Relaxation training.   For clients who appear to be agitated and whose behavior is likely to escalate into an aggressive episode, relaxation training may be useful in defusing the situation. Relaxation training as a treatment process is a set of specific conditions designed to induce relaxation in an individual presumed to be stressed (Rickard, 1986). It has been used to treat many conditions, including aggression (Hughes & Davis, 1980). General procedures for its implementation vary, and there are not many well-controlled outcome studies. Most therapists develop a personalized approach to their use of relaxation training. In general, the therapist creates a setting that induces relaxation either through listening to a tape or through progressive muscle relaxation by alternating the tension and relaxation of the different muscle groups. If biofeedback equipment is available, the client can be taught to relax by using visual and auditory displays to self-monitor his or her tension level. For example, Hughes and Davis (1980) used biofeedback to treat the aggressive behavior of a man with mental retardation. This study provides the basis of the case example presented in Box 10-5.

Anger management.   Anger management training teaches clients self-control skills that will enable them to handle anger-arousing situations in socially acceptable ways (Benson, 1986). Multimethod assessment procedures are used to identify anger-producing situations. Clients are taught to monitor themselves in order to obtain baseline data on the frequency of aggression and

---

Box 10-5

CASE EXAMPLE OF THE USE OF RELAXATION TRAINING

The client was a 27-year-old man with mental retardation and autisticlike behaviors who had a limited vocabulary but could carry on a conversation. He engaged in a number of aggressive behaviors, including kicking, batting with his head, throwing objects, and verbal assaults.

A biofeedback machine that monitored muscle tension levels and produced an auditory tone was used to teach the man relaxation. The baseline consisted of collecting data on the frequency of his aggression during reading and comprehension sessions. Relaxation training occurred in two steps. The client was taught to lower the pitch of the feedback tone by closing his eyes and attempting to relax. Then, the client was given discrimination training through the intermittent presentation of the biofeedback tone. The client received praise and pennies for successfully lowering the pitch in the two phases. Treatment consisted of collecting data on the frequency of aggression in the reading and comprehension sessions while the client was hooked up to the biofeedback machine and given the instructions to lower the auditory pitch. Relaxation, as taught by use of the biofeedback machine, was successful in reducing the frequency of aggression.

Box 10-6

CASE EXAMPLE OF ANGER MANAGEMENT

The subjects were 54 adult volunteers from 10 different vocational training centers with mild or moderate retardation, and were screened for positive responses to "losing your temper" at work. The subjects were divided into four groups: Group 1 received muscle relaxation training; Group 2 received self-instruction using coping statements during role plays; in Group 3, the subjects were taught problem-solving skills using a four-step method during role plays; Group 4, the anger management group, used all three interventions: relaxation, self-instructions, and problem solving.

Using a between-groups design, statistical analysis indicated no differences between the groups before treatment. The anger management group showed decreases in the measures of aggressive responses in role-play situations, but the differences from the other groups were not statistically significant. This finding would appear to suggest that one or more of the techniques would be useful in reducing aggressive responses, and that persons with mental retardation can benefit from group therapy formats.

---

on the antecedent mood. The treatment includes teaching clients to recognize and identify their emotions, relaxation training, self-instructional training, and training in problem-solving skills. Individual sessions have the general format of instruction, modeling, behavioral rehearsal and role playing, feedback, and homework. Box 10-6 provides a brief overview of a study by Benson, Rice, and Miranti (1986) that evaluated the impact of anger management training on adults with mild or moderate mental retardation.

**Box
10-7**

CASE EXAMPLE OF THE USE OF COMMUNICATION TRAINING

The client was a 14-year-old male with autism who engaged in frequent aggressive and self-injury behaviors that were hampering his academic progress. An assessment indicated that the client was influenced by the tangible consequences that frequently followed the destructive behaviors. Communication training consisted of teaching him to point to pictures of favorite objects and activities. The author cautions that two possible traps will undermine the communication training. First, do not try to make it easier for the client by prompting him verbally (e.g., "Do you want this one?") and continuing to prompt him until you finally happen to say the object of choice. Second, avoid responding to and/or accepting other nonverbal cues that the client may use to indicate his selection. The client must make the desired response before receiving a reinforcer.

Communication training.   Aggressive behavior may function as a means of communicating the client's needs and wants, especially in nonverbal persons with mental retardation (Durand, 1990). Communication training has two components: (1) teaching the client a response that serves the same function as the aggressive behavior and (2) making the aggressive behavior nonfunctional by using response-independent consequences for the aggressive behavior (Durand, 1990). An initial assessment is undertaken to uncover the many possible functions of aggression. For example, if a functional analysis indicates that the aggressive behavior is motivated by escape, a request for an object, a request to obtain sensory stimulation, or a lack of attention, the appropriate intervention would be to teach a socially acceptable alternative response to aggression, whether it be a verbal statement or a sign. For example, Durand (1990) taught a young man with autism and aggression to point to pictures of his favorite objects and activities instead of using aggression as a means of communicating. This case study of communication training for reducing aggression is presented in Box 10-7.

Aversive and Punishment Strategies

When a reduction in aggression is not achieved through reinforcement procedures alone, other techniques may also be implemented. The procedures discussed next involve either the removal of positive reinforcement or the presentation of an aversive stimulus contingent on the occurrence of the aggressive behavior. With respect to the degree and the rapidity of suppression, the following procedures, together with differential reinforcement of alternative positive behaviors, produce the most immediate and complete suppression (Schroeder et al., 1991).

> **Box 10-8**
>
> ### CASE EXAMPLE OF THE USE OF TIME-OUT
>
> The client was a 17-year-old youth with moderate retardation and third-grade reading and writing ability and good expressive and receptive language skills. The client engaged in a high rate of poking other people while engaging in conversation. The behavior had persisted for many years and was found to be highly aversive by everyone who came in contact with the client. In baseline, the client's arm was pushed away during poking behavior as he was verbally requested to stop. In treatment, movement suppression was implemented, which consisted of telling the client to go immediately to the corner while guiding or forcing him into the corner as quickly as possible. The client positioned himself with his chin against the corner, both hands behind his back, and both feet close together touching the wall. Whenever the client moved or made a verbalization, the staff said, "Don't talk" or "Don't move" in a firm, loud voice while pressing the client into the corner by placing one hand against his upper back between the shoulder blades. The length of the time-out was 2 minutes. The result was a reduction in the rate per hour of poking behavior. Contingent restraint was also evaluated in the study but was found to be less effective than the movement suppression procedure.

Time-Out

If the functional assessment indicates that environmental reinforcement may be maintaining the aggressive behavior, time-out from reinforcing effects of the environment may be warranted. Time-out is a procedure in which positive reinforcement is not available for a period of time. Schroeder, Mulick, and Schroeder (1979) discuss the various forms of time-out, including contingent observation (the person is removed from the activity and made to observe other individuals behaving appropriately), nonexclusionary (the person remains in the activity but does not receive edibles or social reinforcers), seclusion (the person is placed in an area or room that is relatively nonreinforcing), and contingent restraint (the placement of the person in a physical restraint such as a chair).

The effectiveness of the time-out procedure depends on the contrast between time-out and time-in. If being personally restrained or taken to time-out provides more than normal attention, the procedure may reinforce aggression. If time-out allows the person to escape from or avoid an unpleasant task, then time-out will reinforce aggression. Further, the length of the time-out does not have to be long to effect a change. For example, White, Nielsen, and Johnson (1972) reported that a 15-minute time-out was as effective as one that was twice as long. In another study, Rolider and Van Houten (1985) used a 2-minute movement suppression time-out to control the aggressive behavior of an adolescent with moderate mental retardation. In Box 10-8, we present this case as an example of the use of time-out in suppressing aggressive behavior.

Overcorrection

When the target behaviors are maintained by escape from tasks and/or involve a disruption of the environment (e.g., overturning furniture or throwing objects), overcorrection may be useful in reducing the aggressive behaviors. Overcorrection is the use of a set of aversive procedures contingent on the client's engaging in maladaptive behavior. These procedures have been used to suppress a wide range of inappropriate behaviors in various populations (Miltenberger & Fuqua, 1981).

Restitution and positive practice are the two techniques typically used when overcorrection is indicated. Restitution involves restoring the disrupted environment to its original condition following a disturbance. For example, if a client trashes the dayroom, he or she must pick up everything that was disrupted and clean all the debris. Positive practice refers to the repeated practice of correct forms of the desired behavior contingent on aggression. Foxx and Azrin (1972) used a restitution procedure to control the aggressive and self-injurious behavior of a young woman with profound mental retardation. In Box 10-9, we describe the use of restitution with this woman as an example of the use of overcorrection in controlling aggressive behavior.

Response Cost

If a functional analysis indicates that the loss of previously acquired reinforcers (e.g., tokens, points, stars, or special privileges) is aversive to the client, response cost may be effective in reducing aggression. In response cost, a person loses an acquired reinforcer contingent on an inappropriate behavior. For example, receiving a traffic ticket for a violation requires paying a fine (i.e., money, which is an acquired reinforcer). The basic principle involved is the removal of a positive reinforcer from the client's environment as a result of engaging in an unwanted behavior. The reinforcer is often a secondary reinforcer, such as a token that the client could have exchanged for a preferred activity, but it may also be the loss of nontangible items, such as acquired privileges (e.g., not being able to stay up later than usual). Response cost is typically used in conjunction with a token economy program, so that the client loses a predetermined number of tokens contingent on engaging in the target behaviors. An example of the use of response cost in a study by Burchard and Barrera (1972) is presented in Box 10-10.

CASE EXAMPLE OF THE USE OF RESTITUTION

The client was a 22-year-old woman with profound retardation who had been institutionalized at age 14 following reports by neighbors that the client had attempted to kill her siblings. The client engaged in biting, tearing off others' clothing, scratching the eyes of other clients, banging their heads, and grabbing the crotch area of female staff. Previously unsuccessful attempts at treatment included shock treatments, chemical restraints (up to 1500 mg of Thorazine), physical restraints, and isolation.

The baseline consisted of verbal instruction each morning not to attack anyone, verbal reprimand, and 15 minutes of seclusionary time-out for each occurrence of the target behavior. The treatment consisted of oral hygiene training contingent on biting behavior: The client's mouth was cleansed for 10 minutes with a toothbrush soaked in an oral antiseptic. If the bite broke the skin of the victim, medical assistance training was implemented: The client washed the bitten area, applied an antiseptic solution, bandaged the area, and nodded her head in agreement as each statement of the hospital incident report was read to her. Social reassurance training was required after each crotch-grabbing and biting episode: The client lightly and continuously stroked the victim's back in assurance that the incident would not be repeated. The combined restitution procedures lasted a minimum of 30 minutes. The result was a decrease to near-zero levels in the mean daily frequency of the target behaviors.

CASE EXAMPLE OF THE USE OF RESPONSE COST

Six adolescents between the ages of 15 and 19 who had mild retardation and a history of antisocial behavior were exposed to either a response cost or a time-out contingent on engaging in target behaviors. Antisocial behaviors were defined as swearing, personal assault, property damage, and "other" unwanted behaviors. When an individual engaged in a target behavior, he was required to give up either 5 or 30 of his tokens, or to take 5 or 30 minutes of time-out. Each child experienced each type of penalty over the course of the program.

Group data indicated that the larger magnitude of response cost (as well as the longer time-out duration) was more effective in suppressing the unwanted behaviors. Further, the baseline condition used both the 5-token and the 5-minute conditions and it is possible that the combination of these two had a greater suppressive effect than either condition separately.

Contingent Exercise

With younger aggressive clients who have reduced activity levels and who do not enjoy exercising, contingent exercise may be useful in reducing aggressive behaviors. This procedure requires the client to engage in a predetermined physical exercise contingent on engaging in the target behaviors. If a clientt

CASE EXAMPLE OF THE USE OF CONTINGENT EXERCISE

The client was a 7-year-old male who engaged in autisticlike behaviors. When school staff reported that the client's frequency of aggressive behavior toward others had increased, hitting was selected as the target behavior. The baseline consisted of no systematic contingencies for aggressive behavior. Contingent exercise consisted of standing up and sitting down on the floor ten times. Initially, graduated guidance was required to prompt the client to perform the exercises. After the behavior was learned, a command from the nearest adult, such as "No hitting. Stand up and sit down ten times," was all that was necessary for compliance. The result was a reduction in the daily frequency range of hitting, and two months of continued monitoring indicated only three episodes of hitting during the entire follow-up period.

engages in kicking, contingent exercise may take the form of forced running, and for hitting, pinching, or slapping, the client may be required to engage in vigorous arm exercises (Cataldo, 1991). The procedure requires considerable staff effort and attention, especially for noncompliant, resistive, or strong clients, and some staff may not be able to implement the procedure accurately and judiciously. Box 10-11 presents a case example of the use of contingent exercise, based on a study by Luce, Delquadri, and Hall (1980).

Facial Screening

Facial screening involves the use of a terry cloth bib to cover the client's face, for a brief time, contingent on the occurrence of the target behavior (Lutzker, 1978). If the functional assessment indicates that the client receives reinforcement from the environment, especially during the implementation of a decelerative treatment procedure, facial screening may be warranted to reduce aggressive behavior. Facial screening uses a soft cloth to cover the client's eyes for a brief time contingent on the target behavior. If a bib is used, it is placed over the head of the client in a manner that allows the client unrestricted breathing. In visual screening, a variation of the facial screening procedure, the therapist uses his or her hand rather than a cloth to cover the individual's eyes. The case example presented in Box 10-12 is derived from a study by Dixon, Helsel, Rojahn, Cipollone, and Lubetsky (1989), who used visual screening to reduce aggression in a young boy with severe mental retardation.

Noxious Odors

If a functional analysis indicates that an aggressive client does not like strong smells, the presentation of a noxious odor contingent on the aggressive

Box 10-12

CASE EXAMPLE OF THE USE OF VISUAL SCREENING

The client was a 6-year-old male with severe mental retardation who was readmitted to an inpatient psychiatric unit serving children and adolescents when his frequency of maladaptive behaviors began to increase. The client had been discharged to his parents' home with a treatment protocol using visual screening, but the frequency of aggression was increasing.

The treatment efficacy was evaluated by a BABCBCB design, in which Phase B consisted of the continuation of the visual screening protocol used in the previous admission; Phase A consisted of the withdrawal of the visual screening to demonstrate control over the behavior; and Phase C was a pairing of the visual screening procedure with a smell aversive (aromatic ammonia) to produce a conditioned aversive and a greater reduction in the target behaviors. The study also evaluated the effectiveness of anticonvulsant medications in reducing aggression, but those results are not discussed here. The visual screening was effective in reducing aggression, but further reductions were obtained when the visual screening was paired with a smell aversive. That is, visual screening alone was effective in reducing the rate of aggression, but contingent aromatic ammonia paired with the visual screening reduced the rate of behavior to near-zero levels.

Box 10-13

CASE EXAMPLE OF THE USE OF AN AVERSIVE SMELL

The client was a 7-year-old boy with mental retardation who engaged in aggressive behavior, defined as hitting, pushing, poking, kicking, butting, bumping, scratching, pinching others, pulling others' hair, spitting, throwing objects, jerking objects, tantrums, and jerking away abruptly when held. Previous unsuccessful attempts to reduce the aggressive behavior included DRO, Dilantin injections, contingent reprimands, contingent 2-second soundings of a handheld buzzer, 5-minute time-outs in a closed room, positive practice overcorrection, contingent brief restraint, contingent arm pinching, and contingent hand slapping.

The baseline consisted of a two-week period when there were no consequences for engaging in aggressive behavior during the training sessions. The treatment consisted of olfactory applications of ammonia spirits contingent on the client's aggressive behavior by holding the vial under his nose until his first inhaled breath. A substantial reduction in aggressive behavior occurred.

behavior may result in a reduction of its rate. This procedure involves using a strong, nontoxic odor that is held under the nose of the client contingent on engagement in the aggressive behavior. For example, Box 10-13 describes a case study by Doke, Wolery, and Sumberg (1983), who used aromatic ammonia to decrease the aggressive behaviors of a young boy with mental retardation.

<table>
<tr>
<td>

Box
10-14

</td>
<td>

Case Example of the Use of a Water Squirt

The client was a 4-year-old nonambulatory, nonverbal male with mental retardation who engaged in aggressive behavior. The target behaviors were defined as biting and gouging others. Previous unsuccessful treatments included DRO, time-out, a modified extinction procedure, and a mild hand slap.

The baseline consisted of a contingent hand slap for engaging in aggressive behavior, the procedure in place at the time of the referral. Staff concerns about the safety of the other children in the classroom required the use of the procedure for baseline. The treatment consisted of placing the water mister in full view of the client; it was also always readily available for staff use. When the client performed a target behavior, a staff member approached him, said "No," and squirted him in the face. A substantial suppression of the daily mean frequency of the target behaviors occurred, and no aggressive behavior was observed at a six-month follow-up.

</td>
</tr>
</table>

Water Mist

If a functional analysis indicates that the client finds water sprayed on his or her face aversive, a squirt of water to the face contingent on an aggressive act may be successful in reducing the behavior. For example, a water squirt was used by Gross, Berler, and Drabman (1982) to reduce aggression in a young aggressive boy with mental retardation (see Box 10-14). A plastic household plant mister was set to deliver a stream of water that was directed at the face of the boy contingent on aggressive behavior. A variation on this procedure is to set the spray bottle to emit a mist rather than a stream of water

Electric Shock

Electric shock is believed to have the most rapid suppression effects on problem behavior (Cataldo, 1991). Several problems are associated with its use. For example, the social acceptability of the procedure by professionals is generally low, the potential for misuse and abuse is high, concern about the legal and ethical guidelines being followed correctly exists, and there is concern about safety. Only after meeting all the prerequisite conditions should electric shock be considered, and conversely, it may be considered a violation of the client's right to effective treatment if this option is not considered when all other appropriate treatment options have failed (Griffith, 1983).

A functional assessment of the variables that may be maintaining aggression is also part of a comprehensive treatment package using brief electric shock. In a review of the basic research on the effectiveness of shock, Cataldo (1991) pointed out that the elimination of any variables that may be main-

> **Box 10-15**
>
> ### CASE EXAMPLE OF THE USE OF ELECTRIC SHOCK
>
> The client was a 20-year-old blind male with mild mental retardation. The client had been engaging in aggression since being institutionalized at age 7. Aggressive episodes were defined as property destruction and pinching, kicking, hitting, and hair pulling during assaultive behavior toward staff. Unsuccessful prior treatments included DRO, DRI, relaxation, contingent exercise, water mist, time-out, medications, overcorrection, ammonia, and contingent restraint.
>
> The baseline conditions included a belt-and-cuff restraint while on the unit and ammonia spirits in school settings. The treatment used an electric shock device made of two shock devices (electrodes), a remote-control device, and a handheld direct stimulator. The client wore an elastic armband around his upper arm, in which the electrodes were imbedded and arranged to stimulate the backside of the arm when activated by the remote device. The armband was frequently destroyed by the client, and the handheld direct stimulator was used the majority of the time. Shock was delivered contingent on the occurrence of each aggressive behavior. During treatment, a gradual decrease in the frequency of aggressive episodes was observed over a 30-day period and remained at near-zero levels for 15 months thereafter. The authors point out that shock was only one component of a comprehensive treatment package. Concurrent procedures included a high density of positive reinforcement to construct a new motivational system; brief, intensive compliance training; transfer of programmatic responsibility to direct-care staff and parents; and a relaxation procedure to interrupt the aggressive response chain. Shock was phased out after 32 months and replaced with decreasing durations of nonexclusionary time-out and a high density of naturally occurring reinforcers.

taining the aggression and the availability of alternative responses are two essential features of the effective and efficient use of electric shock as a procedure for reducing aggression. These features were included in a case study by Foxx, McMorrow, Bittle, and Bechtel (1986), who treated the aggressive behavior of a young man with mild mental retardation (see Box 10-15).

Extinction and Planned Ignoring

Extinction comprises procedures in which positive reinforcement is no longer available for the aggressive behavior (Cataldo, 1991). For aggressive behavior that is reinforced by social attention, extinction requires ignoring the client during an aggressive episode and providing only minimal attention to ensure a safe environment. Planned ignoring means ignoring the client only while the client is engaging in the aggressive behaviors.

For aggression that is maintained by escape from a task, extinction requires that the client continue with the task during the aggressive episode or as soon after it as is feasible. A singular event that typically occurs with the implementation of an extinction procedure is a rapid increase in the target

Box 10-16

CASE EXAMPLE OF THE USE OF EXTINCTION

The client was a 22-year-old institutionalized female with mental retardation who engaged in aggressive behaviors of property destruction and kicking, biting, and hitting others and herself. Unsuccessful treatments included drug routines and time-out.

In an ABA design, Phase A consisted of ignoring the aggressive behaviors and Phase B consisted of providing social attention for aggressive acts, such as "Stop it," "Don't do that ever again," or "How can you behave that way?" while holding the client's wrists. Aggression occurred about four times each in the first 10 sessions, then gradually declined to near-zero levels within 50 sessions. Phase B resulted in a return to the previous rates of aggression by the 40th session. A return to Phase A resulted in near-zero levels after five sessions.

behavior after implementation (i.e., an extinction burst). Clinicians who use extinction as the treatment of choice should alert staff and parents of the impending extinction burst, allowing them to prepare themselves as necessary. In Box 10-16, we present an example of the use of extinction to treat aggression, based on the study by Martin and Foxx (1973).

CONCLUSION

Aggression too often interferes with the programming and training that is available to assist the client in attaining his or her maximum potential. Procedures are needed to reduce aggression to a manageable level so that the client can extract the maximum benefit from the services available and can experience a more productive and personally satisfying life (Gardner & Cole, 1990). Aggression is very costly in terms of the dollars spent to repair damage to residential and vocational environments, to pay for medical services for injuries to clients and/or staff resulting from an aggressive episode, and to pay for the additional staff hours required to provide programming and training for the client. Staff are often reluctant or hesitant to interact with an aggressive client; thus, the learning opportunities for the client are decreased. A possible unwanted side effect of the aggressive behavior may be covert staff resistance or displeasure if they are assigned to the units, cottages, or workstations of aggressive clients.

A considerable amount of research literature has been generated on the assessment and treatment of this problem due to the factors noted above. Studies have focused on punishment and, more recently, on positive approaches. Because of the controversy that surrounds the use of punishment, there has been a great deal of recent research on the development of non-aversive treatment alternatives. While social skills, communication, and self-control strategies have been among the areas where major advances have been made, more controversial techniques cannot be ruled out at this point.

REFERENCES

Agran, M., & Martin, J. E. (1987). Applying a technology of self-control in community environments for individuals who are mentally retarded. In M. Hersen, R. M. Eisler, & P. M. Miller (Eds.), *Progress in behavior modification* (Vol. 21). Newbury Park, CA: Sage.

Beck, S. (1985). Token economy. In A. S. Bellack & M. Hersen (Eds.), *Dictionary of behavior therapy*. New York: Pergamon Press.

Benson, B. (1986). Anger management training. *Psychiatric Aspects of Mental Retardation Reviews, 5,* 51–55.

Benson, B., Rice, C. J., & Miranti, S. V. (1986). Effects of anger management training with mentally retarded adults in group treatment. *Journal of Consulting and Clinical Psychology, 54,* 728–729.

Bornstein, P. H., Hamilton, S. B., & Bornstein, M. T. (1986). Self-monitoring procedures. In A. R. Ciminero, K. S. Calhoun, & H. Adams (Eds.), *Handbook of behavior assessment* (2nd ed.). New York: Wiley.

Burchard, J. D., & Barrera, F. (1972). An analysis of timeout and response cost in a programmed environment. *Journal of Applied Behavior Analysis, 5,* 271–282.

Cataldo, M. F. (1991). The effects of punishment and other behavior reducing procedures on the destructive behaviors of persons with developmental disabilities. In *Consensus development conference on treatment of destructive behaviors in persons with developmental disabilities* (Report No. 91-2410). Washington, DC: National Institutes of Health.

Dixon, M. J., Helsel, W. J., Rojahn, J., Cipollone, R., & Lubetsky, M. J. (1989). Aversive conditioning of visual screening with aromatic ammonia for treating aggressive and disruptive behavior in a developmentally disabled child. *Behavior Modification, 13,* 91–107.

Doke, L., Wolery, M., & Sumberg, C. (1983). Treating chronic aggression: Effects and side effects of response-contingent ammonia spirits. *Behavior Modification, 7,* 531–556.

Durand, V. M. (1990). *Severe behavior problems: A functional communication training approach.* New York: Guilford Press.

Eyman, R. K., & Call, T. (1977). Maladaptive behavior and community placement of mentally retarded persons placed in community and institutional settings. *American Journal of Mental Deficiency, 82,* 137–144.

Favell, J. (1991). Environmental foundations of destructive behavior. In *Consensus development conference on treatment of destructive behaviors in persons with developmental disabilities* (Report No. 91-2410). Washington, DC: National Institutes of Health.

Foxx, R. M., & Azrin, N. H. (1972). Restitution: A method of eliminating aggressive-disruptive behavior of retarded and brain damaged patients. *Behavior Research and Therapy, 10,* 15–27.

Foxx, R. M., McMorrow, M. J., Bittle, R. G., & Bechtel, D. R. (1986). The successful treatment of a dually-diagnosed deaf man's aggression with a program that included contingent electric shock. *Behavior Therapy, 17,* 170–186.

Gardner, W. I., & Cole, C. I. (1987). Managing aggressive behavior: A behavioral diagnostic approach. *Psychiatric Aspects of Mental Retardation Reviews, 6,* 21–25.

Gardner, W. I., & Cole, C. I. (1988). Conduct disorders: Psychological therapies. In J. L. Matson (Ed.), *Handbook of treatment approaches in childhood psychopathology.* New York: Plenum Press.

Gardner, W. I., & Cole, C. I. (1990). Aggression. In J. L. Matson (Ed.), *Handbook of behavior modification with the mentally retarded* (2nd ed.). New York: Plenum Press.

Gardner, W. I., Cole, C. I., Davidson, D. P., & Karan, O. C. (1986). Reducing aggression in individuals with developmental disabilities: An expanded stimulus control, assessment, and intervention model. *Education and Training of the Mentally Retarded, 21,* 3–12.

Griffith, R. G. (1983). The administrative issues: An ethical and legal perspective. In S. Axelrod & J. Apsche (Eds.), *The effects of punishment on human behavior.* New York: Academic Press.

Gross, A. M., Berler, E. S., & Drabman, R. S. (1982). Reduction of aggressive behavior in a retarded boy using a water squirt. *Journal of Behavior Therapy and Experimental Psychiatry, 13,* 95–98.

Hughes, H., & Davis, R. (1980). Treatment of aggressive behavior: The effect of EMG response discrimination biofeedback training. *Journal of Autism and Developmental Disorders, 10,* 193–202.

Kazdin, A. E. (1985). Token economy. In A. S. Bellack & M. Hersen (Eds.), *Dictionary of behavior therapy.* New York: Pergamon Press.

Luce, S. C., Delquadri, J., & Hall, R. V. (1980). Contingent exercise: A mild but powerful procedure for suppressing inappropriate verbal and aggressive behavior. *Journal of Applied Behavior Analysis, 13,* 583–594.

Lutzker, J. R. (1978). Reducing self-injurious behavior by facial screening. *American Journal of Mental Deficiency, 78,* 510–513.

Mace, F. C., Lalli, J. S., & Lalli, E. P. (1991). Functional analysis and treatment of aberrant behavior. *Research in Developmental Disabilities, 12,* 155–180.

Martin, P. L., & Foxx, R. M. (1973). Victim control of the aggression of an institutionalized retardate. *Journal of Behavior Therapy and Experimental Psychiatry, 4,* 161–165.

Miltenberger, R. G., & Fuqua, R. W. (1981). Overcorrection: A review and critical analysis. *The Behavior Analyst, 4,* 123–141.

National Institutes of Health. (1991). *Consensus development conference on treatment of destructive behaviors in persons with developmental disabilities* (Report No. 91-2410). Washington, DC: Author.

Polyson, J., & Kimball, W. (1993). Social skills training with physically aggressive children. In A. J. Finch, Jr., W. M. Nelson III, & E. S. Ott (Eds.), *Cognitive-behavioral procedures with children and adolescents.* Boston: Allyn & Bacon.

Reiss, S. (1982). Psychopathology and mental retardation: Survey of a developmental disabilities health program. *Mental Retardation, 20,* 128–132.

Repp, A. C., & Dietz, S. M. (1974). Reducing aggression and self-injurious behavior of institutionalized retarded children through reinforcement of other behavior. *Journal of Applied Behavior Analysis, 7,* 313–325.

Rickard, H. C. (1986). Relaxation training for mentally retarded persons. *Psychiatric Aspects of Mental Retardation Reviews, 5,* 11–15.

Rolider, A., & Van Houten, R. (1985). Movement suppression time out for undesirable behavior in psychotic and severely developmentally delayed children. *Journal of Applied Behavior Analysis, 18,* 175–288.

Sanford, D., & Nettelbeck, T. (1982). Medication and reinforcement within a token programme for disturbed mentally retarded residents. *Applied Research in Mental Retardation, 3,* 21–36.

Schroeder, S., Mulick, J., & Schroeder, C. (1979). Management of severe behavior problems of the retarded. In N. Ellis (Ed.), *Handbook of mental deficiency* (2nd ed.). New York: Erlbaum.

Schroeder, S. R., Rojahn, J., & Oldenquist, A. (1991). Treatment of destructive behaviors among people with mental retardation and developmental disabilities: Overview of the problem. In *Consensus development conference on treatment of destructive behaviors in persons with developmental disabilities* (Report No. 91-2410). Washington, DC: National Institutes of Health.

White, G. D., Nielsen, G., & Johnson, S. M. (1972). Timeout duration and the suppression of deviant behavior in children. *Journal of Applied Behavior Analysis, 5,* 111–120.

Chapter 11

Rumination

Cynthia R. Ellis, Teresa S. Parr,
Nirbhay N. Singh, and Hollis A. Wechsler

INTRODUCTION

Rumination is the deliberate regurgitation or bringing up of previously ingested food into the mouth (Singh, 1981). In the DSM-III-R (American Psychiatric Association, 1987), it is defined as the repeated regurgitation of food (without nausea) for one month following a period of normality, and to be classified as rumination disorder, the behavior cannot be due to gastrointestinal or other nonpsychiatric medical condition. Further, it may not occur exclusively during the course of anorexia nervosa or bulimia nervosa. Although the DSM-III-R includes weight loss or a failure to make expected weight gain as part of the diagnostic criteria, the DSM-IV draft criteria (American Psychiatric Association, 1993) do not require that there be weight loss or a failure to reach desired weight gain, or that there be an absence of nausea for rumination disorder to be diagnosed. Complications resulting from this disorder include chronically raw chapped lips, severe weight loss, failure to grow, dehydration, aspiration, gastric disorders, tooth decay and erosion, anemia, lowered resistance to disease, severe malnutrition, and death. Further, ruminators are often socially isolated because peers and caregivers view them as being unpleasant to interact with.

PREVALENCE

Rumination is typically reported in infants and individuals with mental retardation (Mayes, 1992). Prevalence studies of individuals with mental retardation have reported that between 6% (Singh, 1981) and 10% (Ball, Hendricksen, & Clayton, 1974) of individuals in residential care engage in rumination. Although rumination may appear as early as 3 weeks of age (Hollowell & Gardner, 1965), the average age of onset in individuals with mental retardation appears to be about 6, with a 3:1 ratio of boys to girls. Further, rumination is more common in individuals with severe and profound mental retardation than in those with mild and moderate retardation (Singh & Dawson, 1980).

DIFFERENTIAL DIAGNOSIS

Before treatments can be considered, an accurate diagnosis must be made. This can be difficult, because certain medical conditions, such as pyloric stenosis, duodenal ulcer, and food allergies, may mimic some of the diagnostic criteria for rumination. Thus, differential diagnosis is essential for proper therapy. Rumination is often preceded by a period of vomiting that is without organic cause. It is important to distinguish this vomiting from involuntary vomiting. The former is often mistaken for habitual vomiting or organic dysfunction, because involuntary vomiting is very common in young children. One way to distinguish between the two is that vomiting due to organic factors disappears once the problem receives proper medical attention.

Several factors should alert the clinician to the possibility of rumination disorder. The client may be emaciated and may have vomitus constantly on his or her chin, neck, and upper shirt but is not seen vomiting. The client may also appear to derive sensory pleasure from mouthing the vomit (Einhorn, 1977). Starin and Fuqua (1987) have suggested that the following steps be undertaken to rule out possible medical or physiological disorders: a careful medical history; a psychiatric assessment; a physical examination; hematological tests; a drug screening; hormone level tests; serum and urine tests; immunological tests; radiological tests of the abdomen and head; upper gastrointestinal tract endoscopy; gastric emptying tests; esophageal, anorectal, and gastrointestinal manometry; a formal psychiatric assessment; and laparotomy and biopsy of the small bowel. Finally, it should be noted that a functional analysis methodology that reliably predicts the learning-based motivation of rumination has yet to be developed.

ETIOLOGY

Our understanding of the etiology of rumination is incomplete, at best. Speculations on possible etiologies range from various medical factors (e.g., gastroesophageal reflux, hiatal hernia, side effects of medication, neuromuscular disorders, and intestinal obstruction) to environmental and psychological factors (e.g., disturbed parent-child relationships). As noted by Singh (1981), most of these theories of etiology have not been empirically verified. However, there is some support for a learning-based theory on the maintenance of rumination in many individuals with mental retardation. Indeed, the majority of the treatment literature is based on the assumption that the behavior is a result of faulty learning and can be treated by manipulating the antecedent and consequent variables that maintain rumination.

TREATMENT

Antecedent Strategies

Strategies involving the manipulation of antecedent conditions are frequently used in the management of rumination and are often the treatment of choice because they are socially acceptable, safe, and nonaversive. Antecedent conditions are stimuli occurring just before a behavior that, when modified or changed, influence the occurrence of the behavior. A large number of antecedent conditions precede or facilitate the occurrence of rumination, including variables in the physical environment (e.g., caretaker attention and interaction, the room temperature, swaddling, and the level of extraneous stimuli), procedural and feeding techniques (e.g., positioning, the choice of foods and feeding utensils, and the methods used to place the food in the individual's mouth), or an individual's internal state. The selection of antecedent strategies as interventions for rumination should be based on an analysis of the conditions that maintain the behavior.

Special Feeding Techniques

The special feeling technique reported by Ball et al. (1974; see Box 11-1) is an example of an antecedent treatment strategy involving a modification in feeding procedures. In contrast to the standard institutional feeding procedures, which involved no active participation by the individual, the special feeding technique required the individual's active participation in the feeding process. Food was no longer passively placed in his mouth; oral movements were required to express liquid from a nipple or to remove food from a spoon. Various means were used to encourage this oral activity, including increasing the length of time the nipple or spoon was in the mouth and moving the nipple or spoon around in the mouth to increase taste and tactile sensations. This procedure was successful in reducing the frequency of his rumination and was easily implemented by his usual caretakers in his natural setting and with minimal training.

Food Satiation

Food satiation is another example of the use of an antecedent strategy in the treatment of rumination. For many individuals with rumination, eating food is a pleasurable experience, and thus, the repeated ingestion of regurgitated food serves as a positive reinforcer for the continued occurrence of the behavior. Food satiation interventions involve manipulation of the quantity of food an individual eats and are based on the assumption that the consumption of

<table>
<tr><td>

Box 11-1

</td><td>

CASE EXAMPLE OF THE USE OF A SPECIAL FEEDING TECHNIQUE

The client was an 11-year-old boy with profound mental retardation and severe visual and motor disabilities. He was on a diet of pureed foods and milk that was fed to him by his caretakers. He was typically fed by staff while lying on his back with little or no active participation in the process or interaction with the staff. The milk was squirted directly from a bottle into his mouth, and the pureed food was placed in his mouth with a spoon. During these feedings, he exhibited unpredictable episodes of vomiting that did not appear to be preceded by coughing, gagging, or choking.

In an attempt to manage his vomiting, a special feeding procedure was implemented. During the special feeding periods, the attendant emphasized the boy's active participation in the feeding process. For example, the bottle was placed in his mouth until he engaged in active biting of the nipple, expressing the milk into his mouth. At times, the nipple was moved around in his mouth to stimulate oral activity. As in the standard feeding procedure, he was fed the pureed food with a spoon. However, in the special feeding procedure, the spoon was placed in his mouth and kept there until the food was removed by biting movements of the boy's teeth. When the oral movements decreased, the spoon was tapped on his teeth to encourage further biting.

The efficacy of the special feeding procedure in reducing his vomiting was compared to his baseline rate of vomiting when fed by the standard feeding procedures. Standard and special feeding were alternated over 25 sessions in which the boy was fed both milk and applesauce. The duration of each feeding session was standardized across the two feeding procedures. The number of episodes of vomiting was recorded for each feeding session. The special feeding procedure proved to be far superior to the standard treatment.

</td></tr>
</table>

excessive amounts of food will cause the food to be less appealing. This decrease in the reinforcement value of the food subsequently results in a decrease in the occurrence of rumination. In the case example in Box 11-2, Rast, Johnston, and Drum (1984) allowed individuals to eat until they indicated that they were full. The authors demonstrated that the occurrence of rumination rapidly decreased following meals in which the subjects were satiated. An advantage of the food satiation procedure is that it can be incorporated into an individual's mealtime routine because no special techniques or changes in the type of food served are required. Consideration should be given to overall dietary management, however, because the increased consumption of certain foods may also result in excessive weight gain.

Response-Contingent Strategies

Response-contingent strategies differ from antecedent strategies in that they involve the use of a consequence following the occurrence (or nonoccurrence)

Box 11-2

CASE EXAMPLE OF THE USE OF FOOD SATIATION

The clients were three adults with profound mental retardation and long histories of rumination. Medical evaluations showed that they were significantly underweight, and that there were no structural physiological conditions known to cause their rumination. Rumination was defined as the presence of food in the mouth that came directly from and went back to the stomach and the esophagus. The amount of time the ingested food was present in the mouth (regurgitation to reswallowing) was recorded as the duration. Each ruminative response and its corresponding duration was recorded for each client during the 60 minutes immediately following breakfast and lunch. The quantity of food presented at each meal varied throughout the treatment period, and meals that were not included in the data collection were matched in quantity and food type to lunch in that phase. Each meal began with a consistent volume of liquid (4 ounces of fruit juice for breakfast and 8 ounces of milk for lunch) and was followed by a standard institutional meal. The food served at each meal was weighed. Only the starch component of the meal (e.g., potatoes, rice, and grits) was increased or decreased during the study. Completion of the meal was indicated by consumption of all the food or a signal by the client that he or she was done.

After the collection of initial baseline data, the quantity of food served to the first two clients was gradually increased over several phases. The meal sizes were then reduced to the baseline quantities for a final period of data collection. The results demonstrated a decrease in the frequency and duration of rumination with each increase in the quantity of food included in the meals. A reversal phase showed a return to baseline levels of rumination. Following the initial baseline phase, the third subject began the treatment phase with a large quantity of food, which was sequentially decreased to the initial baseline amount. As with the other two clients, the frequency and duration of rumination increased as the quantity of food per meal decreased.

of a behavior rather than the modification of a condition that only precedes the behavior. In many cases, rumination is preceded or initiated by one or more physiological or behavioral events, such as abdominal tension, gagging, and tongue thrusting. In addition to focusing on the act of rumination itself, a response-contingent treatment intervention may target any one of these physiological or behavioral events, and thus effectively interrupt the cycle and decrease rumination.

Differential Reinforcement

Although reinforcement is a behavioral technique that is typically used to increase the frequency of a behavior, these procedures can be used in the suppression of a problem behavior by reinforcing (i.e., increasing) the nonoccurrence of the behavior. In general, reinforcement used in this manner is called

<table>
<tr></tr>
</table>

Box 11-3

CASE EXAMPLE OF THE USE OF DIFFERENTIAL REINFORCEMENT OF OTHER BEHAVIOR

The client was a nonambulatory 6-year-old boy with profound mental retardation and blindness who had been institutionalized for five years. He had a four-year history of high rates of self-stimulatory behaviors, primarily sucking, chewing, and biting his fingers and hands. These hand-mouthing behaviors resulted in ruminative vomiting 15 to 20 times per day. As a consequence of his ruminative vomiting, he had become severely malnourished and underweight. Previous treatments, including wearing gloves, verbal reprimands, restraint, extinction, the placement of bitter substances on his hands, and verbal praise for nonmouthing, had all proved ineffective.

It was noted by staff that the only activity the boy engaged in more frequently than his self-stimulatory behavior was rubbing his face, arms, and back against an activated washing machine. As the vibration from the washing machine appeared to be something that he liked, vibration was chosen as a positive reinforcer for him. The vibratory stimulation was administered by a small commercial vibrator that was sewn into the back of a vest worn by the boy. The goal of the treatment was to increase the boy's weight while decreasing his ruminative vomiting and hand-mouthing behaviors. A treatment protocol was designed that reinforced the boy for the absence of hand-mouthing behavior. The reinforcers included initial verbal praise for nonmouthing behavior followed by a 30-second period of vibratory stimulation.

The efficacy of the treatment program was investigated within an ABAB design. The child was observed for two nonconsecutive 30-minute sessions each day for five days per week. Data were collected on the number of episodes of vomiting exhibited during each 30-minute observation period, as well as on the number of hand-mouthing behaviors. The rates of vomiting and hand-mouthing responses during the four-day baseline phase were 30 and 82 per day, respectively. During the initial six-day contingent vibratory treatment phase, the rate of rumination decreased by 47% to 16 per day, and the rate of hand mouthing decreased to 27.5 responses per day. The rates of both behaviors increased during the reversal phase and then decreased substantially in the second treatment phase. The vibratory stimulation was gradually faded following the second treatment phase. The boy's weight increased from 23 to 40 pounds in the year following the treatment.

differential reinforcement, and it may take several forms. In the treatment of rumination, differential reinforcement of other behavior (DRO) increases the nonoccurrence of rumination by reinforcing any behavior other than the target behavior. The differential reinforcement of incompatible behavior (DRI) and the differential reinforcement of alternative behavior (DRA) consist of reinforcing an incompatible or alternative behavior, respectively. The use of a DRO procedure in the treatment of rumination (Barmann, 1980) is described in Box 11-3. In this case, sensory stimulation (i.e., vibratory sensation) was identified as a positive and enjoyable stimulus for the child. Throughout the

> **Box 11-4**
>
> ### CASE EXAMPLE OF THE USE OF CONTINGENT SHOCK
>
> The client was a 21-year-old woman with severe mental retardation and a 19-year history of institutionalization. Over the three-month period before treatment, she had vomited after every meal and had lost 13 pounds. Her weakened physical condition precluded her participation in ward programs and activities, and she was vulnerable to other serious medical complications.
>
> Preliminary observations indicated that vomiting generally occurred during the hour following each meal. Thus, the treatment was implemented during this time on three consecutive days. Following the completion of a meal, the client was given a glass of milk or juice to facilitate the onset of vomiting. She was dressed in briefs to allow observation of the target behavior: the stomach tension that preceded vomiting. A towel placed around her neck in a biblike fashion was changed and weighed every 8 minutes throughout the treatment period to quantify the amount of material regurgitated during the time interval. With each occurrence of stomach tension, a momentary shock (less than 1 second in duration) was administered to the woman's thigh with an electric prod. The number of stomach tensions and the amount of vomited material were reduced to near-zero levels within one day of initiating the shock treatment.
>
> A wardwide program was instituted after the three-day treatment phase. The woman returned to her usual ward activities following each meal and was observed for vomiting by the unit staff. If vomitus was observed, she was confined to a chair for a 1-hour observation period. Any stomach tensions occurring during this time were punished in exactly the same manner as during the initial treatment. Data for 25 days indicated that 64 of 75 meals were vomitfree, and that she had gained 10.5 pounds. The wardwide treatment program continued for five months, and at a ten-month follow-up, vomiting was being maintained at near-zero levels.

treatment period, he was reinforced with a vibratory sensation whenever he did not engage in hand mouthing, a behavioral precursor to rumination for this child. The subsequent increase in behaviors other than hand mouthing resulted in a decrease in his rumination.

Punishment

Punishment strategies can take several forms, including the presentation of an aversive stimulus, the removal of a positive stimulus, or the requirement that the individual engage in an effort-based (i.e., aversive) activity following the occurrence of rumination or one of its precursors. The result is a reduction in the frequency of rumination. Because of its aversive nature and the legal and ethical implications of its use, punishment is rarely used as a first-line treatment. Punishment procedures, however, often lead to a more rapid reduction in rumination than other procedures and may be indicated either when other treatments have proved ineffective or when the rumination has become life-threatening.

Electric Shock

Although the use of contingent electric shock has declined considerably in recent years, it remains an effective punishment procedure for the treatment of rumination, particularly when rumination has proved intractable to other, less aversive treatments. As presented by Kohlenberg (1970) and described in Box 11-4, the administration of an electric shock should be contingent on a well-defined, discrete ruminative behavior, preferably one early in the response cycle. The 1- to 2-second shock is usually delivered whenever rumination or one of its precursors, such as stomach tension, occurs. Although contingent electric shock often results in a rapid reduction in rumination to zero or near-zero rates (usually within one to five days of treatment), the behavior may return to pretreatment levels in the absence of a maintenance program.

Noxious Taste

Singh (1979) described the use of an aversive oral punishment in the management of rumination (Box 11-5). Lemon juice and Tabasco pepper sauce were selected as aversive gustatory (i.e., taste) contingencies for tongue thrusting, a precursor to rumination, and a small amount of either the lemon juice or the pepper sauce was squirted into the individual's mouth for each incident of the preruminative behavior. The results clearly demonstrated that pepper sauce was the more effective of the two substances and that complete suppression of rumination could be obtained with its use.

Effort-Based Consequences

In effort-based interventions, the individual is required to engage actively in aversive physical activity following the occurrence of rumination or its precursor. An advantage of this strategy is that there are a number of simple and familiar effort-based activities that may be incorporated into a treatment protocol, thus eliminating the need for extensive staff training. There may also be beneficial side effects of the treatment, including improvement in the individual's physical condition and maintenance of the physical environment. The use of a contingent exercise procedure (Daniel, 1982) in the treatment of rumination is presented in Box 11-6. In this case, walking was selected as the consequence for rumination because it was aversive to the child and the treatment resulted in near-zero rates of rumination.

Box 11-5

CASE EXAMPLE OF THE USE OF AVERSIVE GUSTATORY STIMULATION

The clients were two institutionalized children with profound mental retardation and a history of rumination that had failed to respond to treatments including thickened feeding, minimal intake of liquid, medication, and positive attention. Two treatment programs were designed to test the efficacy of lemon juice and pepper sauce in the treatment of rumination. The client in the first study was a 4-year-old boy with severe to profound mental retardation who ruminated for approximately 60 minutes following each meal. The appearance and reconsumption of vomitus was preceded by vigorous thrusting of his tongue backward and forward. Therefore, ruminative tongue movements were chosen as the target behavior for the treatment program. An ABAC design, using alternating treatments with lemon juice and pepper sauce (baseline, Treatment I: lemon juice, reversal, Treatment II: pepper sauce), was used to determine the different treatment effects of the two substances on rumination. Throughout the study, the subject was given regular institutional food, and although the contingencies were in effect for 60 minutes following each meal, data were collected only after the midday meal.

During a ten-day baseline period, no consequences were provided for rumination or tongue movements. The boy ruminated at a mean rate of 48.8 responses per 60-minute session. The first treatment condition consisted of 5 to 10 cc of lemon juice being squirted into the boy's mouth on the occurrence of ruminative tongue movements, and his mean ruminative responses decreased to 39 per session during this phase. Baseline conditions were reinstated during a reversal of the treatment contingencies, and ruminative responses increased to 51.5 per session. Diluted pepper sauce was administered in the same manner as the lemon juice during the second treatment phase, and rumination decreased to a mean of 3.5 responses per session. This treatment phase was terminated when the boy did not ruminate for five consecutive days. Posttreatment observations for four weeks following the conclusion of treatment showed no instances of rumination. Follow-up at 12 months also revealed no evidence of rumination.

In the second treatment program, a 6-year-old boy with profound mental retardation received a treatment using only diluted pepper sauce in an ABAB design (baseline, Treatment I: pepper sauce, reversal, Treatment II: pepper sauce). With the exception of the elimination of the lemon juice contingency, the procedures were identical to those in the first treatment program. During the first baseline period, the boy had a mean of 62.4 incidents of tongue movements or ruminations per session. The first pepper-sauce treatment period resulted in a decrease to a mean of 14.2 responses per session. During the reversal phase, his rumination increased to 49.2 per session and then decreased during the second treatment phase to a mean of 3.34 responses per session. The second treatment phase was terminated when there was no rumination for five consecutive days. At 4-week and 12-month follow-ups, there was a complete absence of rumination.

Box 11-6

CASE EXAMPLE OF THE USE OF CONTINGENT EXERCISE

Burt was a nonverbal 10-year-old boy with profound mental retardation who had a six-year history of chronic rumination. Although he engaged in rumination for most of each day, this behavior was most frequent after his noon meal. It was observed that the only significant part of the day during which Burt was not ruminating was while he was walking, an activity that was not spontaneous and seemed to require concentration and effort. Therefore, walking was selected as the contingency for rumination.

The number of episodes of rumination per minute were recorded daily for a 10-minute period following his noon meal. A rumination response was defined as the visual or auditory perception of a distinctive gagging reflex that typically preceded Burt's vomiting. Baseline data were collected for five days, during which time Burt received no treatment. A treatment procedure was subsequently instituted that required Burt to walk around a 5-foot square each time the gagging response occurred. Verbal and physical prompts were used as needed to encourage Burt to walk around the square. In addition, on the first day of treatment, he was also reinforced with a piece of cracker on a 30-second schedule for engaging in walking rather than ruminative vomiting.

At baseline, Burt exhibited rumination on an average of twice per minute. Following the introduction of the walking contingency, there was an almost immediate cessation of the ruminative behavior. This near-zero rate of rumination continued throughout the entire eight-day phase of contingent exercise treatment and was maintained over four subsequent monthly observation periods. Furthermore, near-zero rates of rumination were reported at a one-year follow-up.

Oral Hygiene

Singh, Manning, and Angell (1982) described an oral hygiene procedure in the management of rumination (see Box 11-7). The oral hygiene treatment involved the use of a verbal reprimand, a 2-minute period of enforced toothbrushing with an antiseptic-soaked toothbrush, and wiping of the individual's mouth. Physical prompts were used if the individual resisted the procedure. The treatment resulted in a dramatic reduction in rumination that was maintained over a six-month period. Improved oral hygiene is an obvious beneficial side effect of this treatment.

Overcorrection

Overcorrection consists of two components: restitution (i.e., correction of the environmental effects of an inappropriate act) and positive practice (i.e., the requirement that the individual repeatedly practice an appropriate alternative behavior). Overcorrection has an advantage over other response-contingent interventions in that there is a logical connection between the target behavior and the consequence. However, the behaviors involved in restitution and positive practice may be somewhat complicated and time-consuming and thus

Box 11-7

CASE EXAMPLE OF THE USE OF AN ORAL HYGIENE PROCEDURE

The clients were a pair of 17-year-old monozygotic male twins, Paul and David. Both boys had profound mental retardation of unknown etiology and a ten-year history of rumination, particularly in the hour following each meal. Numerous procedures, including satiation, thickening food, and the use of drugs, had demonstrated only limited success in the management of their rumination.

The effects and side effects of an oral hygiene procedure on rumination were evaluated by the use of a multiple-baseline, across-subjects, and across-situations (meals) design. Rumination was defined as any upward movement of the throat accompanied by the cheeks puffing as they filled with vomitus, or as the chewing or drooling of previously ingested food. Daily observation sessions were one hour in duration and scheduled immediately following meals. Following a baseline period during which no programmed contingencies were in effect, treatment was introduced for Paul in succession after lunch, breakfast, and dinner. After an additional period of baseline data collection, treatment was introduced for David in a similar fashion. The treatment procedure consisted of a verbal reprimand ("No") and the requirement that the boys clean their teeth with a Listerine-soaked toothbrush for 2 minutes following each instance of rumination. In addition, the boys had to wipe their lips with a Listerine-soaked washcloth after cleaning their teeth. Physical prompts were used when the twins resisted treatment. During the subsequent six-month maintenance period, the same procedures were used by the staff throughout the day whenever ruminative vomiting occurred.

Both boys had a high rate of rumination and low rates of appropriate and stereotyped behavior throughout the baseline periods. When the oral hygiene procedures were in effect, both boys demonstrated a dramatic decrease in rumination, along with an increase in their rates of stereotyped behaviors. Paul's already low rate of socially appropriate behavior decreased by about 40% during the oral hygiene treatment phase. However, David showed an increase in his appropriate behavior during the oral hygiene treatment to four times its baseline rate. Data collected at the six-month follow-up showed that the rumination rates of both boys had continued to decrease with the maintenance procedures. David's rates of appropriate behavior remained unchanged, and Paul showed an increase in his rates of appropriate behavior.

may require extensive staff supervision and interaction. The use of an overcorrection procedure in the treatment of rumination has been described by Duker and Seys (1977) and is presented in Box 11-8. An obvious benefit of overcorrection is that, in contrast to other punishment procedures, it focuses on appropriate behaviors and teaches the individual a desirable alternative response.

Combined Treatments

A combination of two or more treatment strategies is occasionally used in the management of rumination. Treatment packages incorporating several differ-

> ### Box 11-8
>
> ### CASE EXAMPLE OF THE USE OF AN OVERCORRECTION PROCEDURE
>
> Carol was a 19-year-old woman with profound mental retardation of unknown etiology and a 14-year history of institutionalization. She engaged in extensive vomiting, primarily after meals. Previous attempts to manage her vomiting using time-out, extinction combined with DRO, and aversive gustatory stimulation had all been unsuccessful.
>
> Restitutional overcorrection procedures were initiated for 8 hours per day in an attempt to decrease her vomiting. With each episode of vomiting, verbal disapproval and physical guidance were used to show Carol the results of her vomiting (e.g., a dirty bib and vomit on the floor). She was then required to complete a 20-minute routine consisting of washing her face with cold water, cleaning the floor at and around the vomitus, and washing a section of the wall, windowsill, and floor. Following this, she was required to change from her soiled clothes into clean clothes. Throughout the overcorrection procedure, she was instructed in a neutral manner, and an effort was made not to look at her. Positive reinforcement was given for nonvomiting behaviors.
>
> A function relationship between the use of the overcorrection procedure and the frequency of vomiting was demonstrated over a 4.5-month period in a repeated reversal design. Carol's vomiting decreased to near-zero levels during each treatment period.

ent components are used in an attempt to maximize the likelihood of treatment success, especially in cases where large or rapid changes in rumination are sought. Box 11-9 presents an example of a combined treatment package incorporating two response-contingent strategies: differential reinforcement and extinction (Mulick, Schroeder, & Rojahn, 1980). Although the treatment as a whole was successful in decreasing rumination, this study was also able to determine the efficacy of each of the individual treatment components.

Murray, Keele, and McCarver (1976) reported the successful use of a combination of antecedent and response-contingent strategies on rumination (see Box 11-10). A disadvantage in this case, as in many combined treatment packages, is that it was not possible to determine which component was responsible for the behavior change. In some cases, all of the components may not be necessary.

CONCLUSION

Rumination can be a very serious behavior problem with potentially life-threatening complications. Although a number of treatment approaches have been used in the management of rumination, behavioral techniques have proved to be the most successful. However, no one behavioral treatment has

<table>
<tr><td>

**Box
11-9**

</td><td>

CASE EXAMPLE OF A COMBINED TREATMENT PROGRAM USING RESPONSE-CONTINGENT STRATEGIES

</td></tr>
</table>

The client was a 15-year-old boy with Down syndrome and profound mental retardation who was referred for the treatment of coprophagy and chronic rumination. Although the consequences of his rumination were not considered life-threatening, he did suffer from raw, chapped areas around his mouth and experienced exclusion from certain activities because of the unpleasant odor and appearance resulting from his rumination. A prior attempt to use food satiation to decrease his rumination had proved unsuccessful. Although his coprophagy was quickly brought under control by the use of tight-fitting pants and an overcorrection procedure, his rumination continued and was particularly frequent following meals.

A combined treatment for his rumination was developed consisting of four different behavioral therapies:

1. *Differential reinforcement of other behaviors (DRO).* The subject was told, "Okay, no vomiting." If he did not vomit for 30 seconds, he received a reinforcer.
2. *Differential reinforcement of incompatible behaviors (DRI).* The subject was told, "OK, no vomiting, but do this. Play!" He was then given a toy. If he did not vomit and maintained play behavior for 30 seconds, he was reinforced.
3. *Extinction and differential reinforcement of other behaviors (EXT-ALTR).* The experimenter said, "OK, let's play." The subject was reinforced for each 30 seconds of continuous play. Vomiting and rumination were ignored.
4. *Extinction alone (EXT)*, during which no behaviors were reinforced or punished. Reinforcement consisted entirely of social praise and pats or touches on the head, arms, or back.

Treatment was provided in a daily one-hour session immediately following the boy's lunch. The sessions were divided into four 15-minute components, and a different behavioral technique was used during each component. The order of presentation of the behavioral techniques was systematically varied across the sessions. Data were collected on vomiting and ruminating. A 12-session baseline phase preceded the 12-session treatment phase. This was followed by a 5-session reversal phase that employed baseline conditions. An analysis of the efficacy of the individual treatment procedures showed that DRI was the most effective procedure in decreasing the frequency of both vomiting and rumination, and that EXT was the least effective. Although the DRO and EXT-ALTR treatments had approximately the same effects on rumination, EXT-ALTR produced a lower frequency of vomiting than the DRO procedure.

emerged as the treatment of choice. The decision regarding which treatment to use should be made on a case-by-case basis, and the risk the behavior poses for the individual should be taken into account. Other considerations include the degree of expertise required to competently execute the desired behavior program and the ability to generalize the treatment to the individual's natural setting. The ethical and legal issues surrounding the use of aversive treatments also need to be factored into a treatment decision.

> ## Box 11-10
>
> ### CASE EXAMPLE OF A COMBINED TREATMENT PROGRAM USING ANTECEDENT AND RESPONSE-CONTINGENT STRATEGIES
>
> Charles was an emaciated and malnourished 6-month-old boy who was hospitalized after he began to vomit following every meal. After each feeding, he appeared to deliberately induce vomiting by repeatedly protruding his tongue and making chewing motions with his jaw. He would continue this activity until his stomach was empty. A complete medical evaluation failed to discover an etiology for his repeated vomiting.
>
> After baseline data were recorded, a combined treatment program designed to intervene during the first phase of ruminative behavior, tongue rolling, was implemented by the nurses and aides on the ward with each feeding. His food was thickened with cereal to make the initiation of rumination more difficult (stimulus control). The boy was held affectionately when he was being fed but was returned to his crib on initiation of tongue rolling (punishment via the withdrawal of reinforcement). Two drops of Tabasco sauce were then placed on his tongue for each episode of tongue rolling (punishment). Although he was not held or touched while he was demonstrating ruminative behavior (extinction), once the behavior ceased, he was picked up again (reinforcement of incompatible behavior). Throughout the baseline and treatment phases, measurements of the number of punishments, the frequency and approximate volume of vomitus, and weight gain were recorded.
>
> Ruminating was brought under control within a few days. Although five or six punishments had to be administered after each feeding on the first day, by the second day only one or two punishments were necessary. By the tenth day, no rumination was observed, Charles's weight had significantly increased, and he had become more alert and interactive with his environment. On follow-up at 10 months of age, his weight had doubled, and there had been no vomiting since his discharge from the hospital.

REFERENCES

American Psychiatric Association. (1987). *Diagnostic and statistical manual of mental disorders* (3rd ed., rev.). Washington, DC: Author.

American Psychiatric Association. (1993). *DSM-IV draft criteria.* Washington, DC: American Psychiatric Press.

Ball, T. S., Hendricksen, H., & Clayton, J. (1974). A special feeding technique for chronic regurgitation. *American Journal of Mental Deficiency, 4,* 486–493.

Barmann, B. C. (1980). Use of contingent vibration in the treatment of self-stimulatory hand-mouthing and ruminative vomiting behavior. *Journal of Behavior Therapy and Experimental Psychiatry, 11,* 307–311.

Daniel, W. H. (1982). Management of chronic rumination with a contingent exercise procedure employing topographically dissimilar behavior. *Journal of Behavior Therapy and Experimental Psychiatry, 13,* 149–152.

Duker, P. C., & Seys, D. M. (1977). Elimination of vomiting in a retarded female using restitutional overcorrection. *Behavior Therapy, 8,* 255–257.

Einhorn, A. H. (1977). Rumination syndrome. In A. M. Rudolph (Ed.), *Pediatrics.* New York: Appleton.

Hollowell, J. G., & Gardner, L. I. (1965). Rumination and growth failure in male fraternal twin: Association with disturbed family environment. *Pediatrics, 36,* 565–571.

Kohlenberg, R. J. (1970). The punishment of persistent vomiting: A case study. *Journal of Applied Behavior Analysis, 3,* 241–245.

Mayes, S. D. (1992). Rumination disorder: Diagnosis, complications, mediating variables, and treatment. In B. B. Lahey & A. E. Kazdin (Eds.), *Advances in clinical child psychology* (Vol. 14). New York: Plenum Press.

Mulick, J. A., Schroeder, S. R., & Rojahn, J. (1980). Chronic ruminative vomiting: A comparison of four treatment procedures. *Journal of Autism and Developmental Disorders, 10,* 203–213.

Murray, M. E., Keele, D. K., & McCarver, J. W. (1976). Behavioral treatment of ruminations: A case study. *Clinical Pediatrics, 15,* 591–596.

Rast, J., Johnston, J. M., & Drum, C. (1984). A parametric analysis of the relationship between food quantity and rumination. *Journal of the Experimental Analysis of Behavior, 41,* 125–134.

Singh, N. N. (1979). Aversive control of rumination in the mentally retarded. *Journal of Practical Approaches to Developmental Handicaps, 3,* 2–6.

Singh, N. N. (1981). Rumination. In N. R. Ellis (Ed.), *International review of research in mental retardation* (Vol. 10, pp. 139–182). New York: Academic Press.

Singh, N. N., & Dawson, M. J. (1980). *The prevalence of rumination in institutionalized mentally retarded children.* Auckland, New Zealand: Mangere Hospital and Training School.

Singh, N. N., Manning, P. J., & Angell, M. J. (1982). Effects of an oral hygiene punishment procedure on chronic rumination and collateral behaviors in monozygous twins. *Journal of Applied Behavior Analysis, 15,* 309–314.

Starin, S. P., & Fuqua, R. W. (1987). Rumination and vomiting in the developmentally disabled: A critical review of the behavioral, medical, and psychiatric treatment research. *Research in Developmental Disabilities, 8,* 575–605.

Chapter 12

Pica

Cynthia R. Ellis, Nirbhay N. Singh,
W. David Crews, Jr., Sharon H. Bonaventura,
Jessica M. Gehin, and Robert W. Ricketts

INTRODUCTION

Pica is an eating disorder characterized by the persistent eating of nonnutritive substances (American Psychiatric Association, 1994). Although it is frequently seen in children, pica is more often observed in individuals with developmental disabilities (Popper, 1988) and, in fact, pica is the most common eating disorder in individuals with mental retardation (Danford, 1983). Pica is a serious behavior problem because it can result in serious medical, psychological, and social sequelae. For example, medical complications ranging from constipation to poisoning and, in severe cases, even death have been reported (Abu-Hamden, Sondheimer, & Mahajan, 1985).

In this chapter, we review a number of treatments for pica that have been demonstrated to be effective in some individuals with developmental disabilities. Case examples are provided as illustrations of the use of the specific treatment strategies in either clinical or natural environments.

PREVALENCE

There have been relatively few published studies reporting the prevalence of pica in individuals with developmental disabilities, and the only available data are from institutionalized samples of individuals with mental retardation. Further, the prevalence data vary depending on the definition of pica, the characteristics of the population sampled, and the methods used for data collection. In one survey of 991 institutionalized adolescents and adults with mental retardation, Danford and Huber (1982) made a distinction between food pica (the compulsive and excessive consumption of food and food-related substances) and nonfood pica (the ingestion of nonfood items). Although only 5.4% of the subjects engaged in food pica, 16.7% engaged in nonfood pica. McAlpine and Singh (1986) broadened the definition of pica to include the mouthing or ingestion of inedible substances and found that 9.2% of 607 children and adults with mental retardation living in a state residential facility engaged in pica. Lofts, Schroeder, and Maier (1990) reviewed the medical records, treatment plans, and behavioral programs of 806 institutionalized individuals with mental retardation for reference to the ingestion of nonfood items and reported a 15.8% prevalence rate of pica. Increasing levels of pica were associated with increasing severity of mental retardation in all of the studies. In addition, pica was less frequent with increasing age, the greatest occurrence being reported in 10- to 20-year-olds (Danford & Huber, 1982; McAlpine & Singh, 1986).

MANAGEMENT APPROACHES

The management of pica in individuals with developmental disabilities represents a complex clinical problem that requires an individualized approach. Most of the treatment studies of pica have been based on the traditional view that pica is a learned behavior, and therefore, the intervention strategies have been behavioral in nature. Indeed, the literature indicates that a variety of behavioral procedures have been used to reduce the frequency of pica, at least over the short term, in many but not all individuals with developmental disabilities (Singh, 1983).

There have been a few studies that have used nutritional and pharmacological treatments for pica. These have been based on theories indicating that some cases of pica may result from underlying biochemical abnormalities. The association between pica and certain nutrient deficiencies, particularly of iron and zinc, is well recognized in some individuals with developmental disabilities, and a significant reduction in pica has been reported when these individuals have been treated for their specific nutrient deficiencies (Danford, Smith, & Huber, 1982; Lofts et al., 1990). Further, the hypothesized link between diminished dopaminergic neurotransmission and the expression of pica suggests a basis on which pharmacological treatment strategies specifically targeting the dopamine system can be developed (Singh, Ellis, Crews, & Singh, 1994). Although there are no published pharmacological treatment studies of pica, drugs that enhance dopaminergic functioning, such as methylphenidate and bromocriptine, may indeed provide treatment alternatives for individuals with pica that is refractory to behavioral interventions.

While a number of treatments have been described that use a variety of medical, nutritional, or behavioral interventions, it is clear that there is no single treatment of choice, and it is unlikely that any one treatment strategy will effectively address the entire spectrum of pica behaviors. Because there are no clear clinical guidelines, the selection of an appropriate treatment for a particular form of pica is a complex process. The nutritional and dietary approaches that have been used have demonstrated success in a limited number of cases, but in general, behavioral methods have been used most often and have resulted in the greatest reductions in pica. As described in Chapter 8 on self-injurious behavior, a comprehensive behavioral assessment and analysis is a prerequisite to the successful matching of the most appropriate (i.e., least restrictive and most effective) treatment to a specific behavioral problem. Although this assessment may take several forms, a functional analysis of the maladaptive behavior—in this case, pica—frequently yields the best results. This information can then be taken into consideration on an individual basis in the selection of a behavioral treatment.

Box 12-1

CASE EXAMPLE OF THE USE OF FUNCTIONAL ANALYSIS

Jim was a 19-year-old nonverbal man with profound mental retardation and cerebral palsy. He had a long history of pica, which was noted to be his predominant behavior during periods of minimal staff supervision. To keep him from ingesting inedible items, Jim wore a helmet with a face shield. Although the helmet offered him a degree of protection (he was still able to wedge small pieces of cloth and other materials between his face and face shield and into his mouth), its use restricted his vision and limited his social interaction.

A functional analysis procedure was designed to examine the relationship between the level of staff interaction and the occurrence of pica. Further, because of the restrictive nature of the current treatment (i.e., the helmet), conditions were incorporated into the functional analysis to determine the minimum level of protective equipment required to control his pica. Baseline observations were made in his natural classroom environment, with Jim wearing his helmet and sitting at a table alone or with a peer. He was presented with a familiar vocational task, and his teacher interacted with him on a variable interval (VI) 8-minute schedule. If he placed inedible objects in his mouth, the object was removed, and he was given a mild verbal reprimand.

The effects of three noncontingent social interaction conditions (frequent, limited, and no interaction) were then assessed daily during 15-minute sessions. During the frequent social interaction condition, the experimenter sat at the table with Jim and provided him with nearly continuous eye contact and verbal interaction on a VI 15-second schedule. The limited social interaction condition consisted of the experimenter's circulating around the room and talking to Jim for 15 to 30 seconds every 3 minutes. During the no-interaction condition, the experimenter sat at another table without looking at or speaking to Jim. Jim wore his protective helmet during all three conditions.

Three helmet conditions were also analyzed experimentally. The first consisted of Jim wearing his usual helmet, with the face shield in place. The face shield was removed in the second condition, and Jim did not wear a helmet in the third. The occurrence of pica was recorded in 15-minute sessions during all three helmet conditions. Social interactions during the three helmet conditions were identical to those in the limited social interaction condition.

The results showed functional relationships between pica and both the level of social interaction and the use of the helmet. Pica decreased with increased social interaction and with decreasing helmet restriction. The analysis-derived treatment plan consisted of limited social interaction in the absence of the protective helmet. The efficacy of this treatment was then tested in Jim's typical dayroom environment in a BAB reversal design. The experimenter provided him with eye contact for 5–10 seconds on a 1-minute schedule and verbal interaction on a 3-minute schedule. He did not wear his helmet during this treatment condition. If he engaged in pica, the item was removed from his mouth without reprimands or eye contact. The subsequent return-to-baseline condition was identical to the treatment condition except that Jim wore his helmet. Jim's pica was significantly reduced during the treatment condition, increased with the withdrawal of treatment, and again decreased with the reintroduction of the treatment.

Functional Analysis

Although the use of functional analysis procedures have been extensively described for other maladaptive behaviors, such as self-injury, there have been relatively few case reports of their use with pica. However, a consideration of the effects of various environmental variables on the expression of pica is an important component in its overall management. For example, Mace and Knight (1986) described the use of a functional analysis methodology to determine the relationship between antecedent and concurrent environmental variables and pica and, subsequently, to derive an appropriate treatment plan (see Box 12-1). In this example, the analyses revealed functional relationships between specific environmental variables and the occurrence of pica, which were then used to derive the most appropriate treatment strategy. In addition to examining the role of antecedent and concurrent stimuli in the expression of pica, functional analyses can also be used to determine the consequences that may be important in maintaining the behavior.

TREATMENT

Antecedent Strategies

Antecedent strategies involve the manipulation of conditions or stimuli that occur just before a behavior and are assumed to set the stage for the occurrence of that particular behavior. If an antecedent condition for a particular behavior can be identified, then manipulation of that condition should result in a change in the occurrence of the behavior. Examples of antecedent conditions include stimuli from the physical environment, interactions with others, and an individual's internal state. The presence of an antecedent condition increases the likelihood that an individual will engage in a specific behavior. Modifying antecedent conditions is a socially acceptable form of treatment because it is nonintrusive, nonaversive, safe, and generally effective. For these reasons, antecedent strategies are often used as the initial form of treatment.

Environmental Stimulation

Madden, Russo, and Cataldo (1980b) demonstrated the efficacy of one antecedent strategy by showing that changes in environmental conditions have a positive impact on the occurrence of pica. As shown in Box 12-2, increasing the stimulation in the environment resulted in decreased pica. It is important to note that the children treated in the enriched and group play settings demonstrated an actual loss of interest in their mouthing behavior rather

> **Box 12-2**
>
> ## CASE EXAMPLE OF THE USE OF ENVIRONMENTAL STIMULATION
>
> Suzie was a 23-month-old girl who had been hospitalized for asymptomatic lead intoxication as a result of her pica. It was presumed that maternal and social deprivation had played an important role in the development and maintenance of her pica, and it was not known if attempts to treat her pica had been undertaken in the past. A treatment program using three environments—group play, impoverished individual play, and enriched individual play—was implemented to determine the effects of environmental influences on the maintenance of her pica.
>
> The treatments consisted of placing Suzie in each of the three settings and observing her for the mouthing of inedible substances, her involvement and noninvolvement in activities, and her interaction with peers and adults. The group environment consisted of a varying number of activities and toys, as well as the presence of several other children and adults. The impoverished individual play environment consisted of a minimal number of activities with no toys or other children present. The enriched individual play environment included numerous activities and toys and an adult. Suzie was placed in each environment six to ten times over a two- to three-week period and was observed for mouthing behaviors during 20-minute sessions.
>
> Mouthing behaviors were low or nonexistent in both the group play and enriched individual play environments. However, mouthing continued to occur at significant rates in the impoverished play environment. Therefore, the enrichment of an impoverished play environment with toys and interaction with other peers and adults led to a reduction in pica.

than an increased difficulty in mouthing objects in those two environmental conditions.

Discrimination Training

Rather than modifying the environment in which pica occurs, discrimination training attempts to directly modify the occurrence of the behavior by changing the individual's response to the antecedent stimulus. This procedure is based on the assumption that pica is less likely if the individual is able to discriminate between those items that are edible and those that are not. In Box 12-3, we present an example of the use of this procedure based on a study by Finney, Russo, and Cataldo (1982). An advantage of this technique is that it is simple to implement. For example, this procedure can be used by parents at home with their children. This technique has been shown to be effective alone, as well as in combination with other behavioral procedures.

Alternate Sensory Activities

Favell, McGimsey, and Schell (1982) addressed the treatment of pica by investigating the role of sensory reinforcement. This approach is based on the idea that socially appropriate alternate activities can be used to set the occasion for

> ## *Box 12-3*
>
> ### CASE EXAMPLE OF THE USE OF DISCRIMINATION TRAINING
>
> Sam was a 3-year, 9-month-old boy with low-average intelligence. He exhibited life-threatening pica that had resulted in at least one prior hospitalization for lead poisoning. Sam had received no previous treatment for pica. Discrimination training was initiated in an effort to directly modify his behavior and decrease his pica.
>
> Before the training, Sam was assessed to confirm that he could discriminate between edible and nonedible items. Discrimination training was then initiated by randomly presenting five edible items and five nonedible items over 20 trials (2 trials per item). Following the presentation of each item, the clinician asked, "What is this?" and "Should you put this in your mouth?" Sam was reinforced with verbal praise and food for each correct answer. The effectiveness of the discrimination training was assessed by the recording of the occurrence of pica behaviors during a subsequent 10-minute observation session. Sam's pica significantly decreased following discrimination training as compared to his pretreatment levels of pica although he continued to display moderate levels of pica at the end of the treatment.

less harmful sensory activities than pica (see Box 12-4). In these case examples, pica was reduced when an alternative sensory activity, whose stimulation was similar to the stimulation provided by the pica, was facilitated. For example, it was neither the sensation of holding objects in their hands nor the sense of fullness following the ingestion of food that reduced pica; the "chewing" sensation associated with the alternate activities was consistently shown to be associated with the reduction of pica. This finding is significant because it eliminates hunger as the motivation for pica and also specifies what type of objects should be used by staff in planning sensory-reinforcement treatment protocols. The use of adult toys and materials may result in increased pica because they do not provide the opportunity for and sensation of chewing to those individuals who desire that form of sensory stimulation. When using sensory reinforcement, it is important to remember that, once pica has been reduced to a satisfactory level, other procedures (e.g., fading) will be required to allow the individual to safely use age-appropriate materials.

Response-Contingent Strategies

Response-contingent strategies can also be used in the management of an undesirable behavior, such as pica. In contrast to antecedent strategies, which modify a condition or stimulus that precedes the occurrence of pica, response-contingent strategies involve the use of consequences that follow the occurrence of the behavior.

Box 12-4

CASE EXAMPLES OF THE USE OF ALTERNATE SENSORY ACTIVITIES

Elsie and Rita were two women, aged 19 and 13, respectively, who had been diagnosed with profound mental retardation. They had been institutionalized for at least eight years and had significantly impaired motor skills that confined them to wheelchairs and restricted their fine-motor abilities. Both women had a long-standing history of chewing on and ingesting their clothing and bed linen. They were at risk for choking and intestinal blockage due to this behavior. Ron, aged 16, had also been diagnosed with profound mental retardation and had been institutionalized for five years. Although he was ambulatory with assistance, he moved around primarily by scooting along the floor in a seated position, during which time he frequently ingested small objects such as paper, pieces of toys from floors, and pieces of bulletin boards and table surfaces.

The treatment consisted of four alternating conditions (no toys, toys, popcorn, and toys and popcorn) presented randomly across 30-minute sessions held daily for each individual in his or her residential dayroom. Another condition, popcorn contingent on toy holding, was then presented for seven to eight consecutive sessions at the end of the study. The three behaviors recorded during the sessions were pica (placing an inedible item into the mouth), chewing on toys, and holding toys in the hands. During the no-toys condition, the clinician removed the available toys and provided no interaction, while in the toys-available condition, two to five designated toys (large rubber balls, squeaky toys, and rings) were placed within reach of the individual, but no prompts or interaction was provided. During the popcorn condition, the clinician placed a bowl of popcorn within the subject's reach in an attempt to provide an alternate form of oral reinforcement and sense of fullness. No prompting or interaction was provided. The toys-and-popcorn condition involved the presentation of a bowl of popcorn and toys to the individual. This condition provided an opportunity for both chewing (popcorn) and toy holding and, at the same time, served as a control for the later use of popcorn to reinforce toy holding. During the condition of popcorn contingent on toy holding, the clinician reinforced the individual with popcorn for a continuous period of holding a toy without chewing on it.

The levels of pica were significantly reduced in all three individuals when they were provided with easy access to toys and/or popcorn. Similar reductions in pica were observed with both toy chewing (involving manual activity) and popcorn chewing (involving little manual activity). Therefore, it appeared that the oral stimulation involved in chewing toys or popcorn rather than the manual (hand) activity was the key factor in reducing pica. Although chewing popcorn reduced pica, it was not a successful reinforcer for toy holding alone (manual activity with no oral involvement). Thus, when the subjects were provided an appropriate alternative opportunity for "chewing," pica was substantially reduced in all three. This finding was confirmed when an attempt was made to substitute the "chewable toys" with age-appropriate, nonchewable toys. This switch resulted in a higher frequency of pica in all three individuals.

Box 12-5

CASE EXAMPLE OF THE USE OF DIFFERENTIAL REINFORCEMENT OF INCOMPATIBLE BEHAVIORS

David was a 38-year-old white male with profound mental retardation who displayed pica for cigarettes. Although the underlying reason for his behavior was unclear, it seemed possible that his pica for cigarettes may have been related to a nicotine addiction. In an attempt to decrease his pica, a treatment program consisting of differential reinforcement of incompatible behaviors (DRI) was instituted.

David's treatment consisted of first prompting him to chew gum as the behavior incompatible with pica. He was also instructed to avoid pica behaviors. For every 5 seconds of gum chewing and abstinence from pica, David was reinforced with one teaspoon of coffee and verbal praise. If the gum was not visibly being chewed, however, David was not reinforced. If the gum was swallowed, he was given another piece and reminded to chew the gum. The intervals between reinforcement were gradually increased in an effort to produce significant periods of independent gum chewing. During treatment sessions, frequent breaks were also given to provide a rest period.

As the DRI training progressed, the latency of David's pica within sessions increased. Further, with the continued use of DRI, his pica decreased to near-zero levels across sessions. The strategy was then generalized to several familiar staff. Initially, David exhibited some variability in his pica as new staff were introduced, but as training progressed, so did the time between pica occurrences and the number of sessions in which there was an absence of pica.

Differential Reinforcement Procedures

Differential reinforcement is a response-contingent reinforcement strategy that has been used with pica. Although reinforcement contingent on the occurrence of a behavior is typically used to increase that behavior, reinforcement can also be used to decrease or eliminate a problem behavior, such as pica, by making reinforcement contingent on the nonoccurrence of the target behavior (i.e., through reinforcement of other behaviors). Differential reinforcement techniques used in the management of pica range from general to very specific. For example, differential reinforcement of other behaviors (DRO) involves the reinforcement of *any* behavior other than pica. When effective, DRO increases the frequency of the "other" behaviors that are reinforced while decreasing pica, which receives no reinforcement. Differential reinforcement techniques that are more specific include differential reinforcement of alternative (DRA) or incompatible (DRI) behaviors. DRA and DRI have the advantage of replacing pica with either more appropriate alternative responses (DRA) or physically incompatible, yet functionally equivalent, behaviors (DRI).

The effects of DRI on pica are shown in Box 12-5 (Donnelly & Olczak, 1990). This approach focuses less on the specific behavior of pica and more on

Box 12-6

CASE EXAMPLE OF THE USE OF VISUAL SCREENING

Debbie was a 24-year-old woman who had a right hemiplegia and profound mental retardation and who had been institutionalized for 13 years. She had a long history of ingesting cigarette butts, buttons, and leaves. Data regarding the effect of a visual screening procedure (blindfold) on Debbie's pica were collected across three settings during baseline, treatment, and maintenance phases. Changes in collateral behaviors were also recorded.

Debbie's pica was defined as the bringing of a nonnutritive substance to her lips or placing the substance in her mouth. Following the collection of baseline data, the blindfold contingency was instituted daily in 15-minute sessions across three settings (dayroom, TV/sunroom, and outside the residential unit). With each occurrence of pica, a clinician physically guided Debbie to remove the pica object from her mouth. A blindfold was then placed over her eyes for 1 minute. Removal of the blindfold was contingent on 1 minute of nondisruptive behavior. An eight-week maintenance period followed the treatment phase with the blindfold contingency in effect 8 hours each day. The blindfold contingency proved effective in rapidly and significantly reducing Debbie's pica to near-zero levels in all settings. Although not targeted by the treatment procedure, positive changes in collateral behaviors, including stereotypy and aggression, were also observed.

increasing behaviors that physically interfere with pica, thus decreasing the undesirable behavior. In this case, the use of an acceptable alternative behavior (i.e., gum chewing reinforced with coffee) demonstrates the effectiveness of matching oral sensory modalities with the target behavior of pica. Differential reinforcement techniques have the advantage that they require less intensive staff intervention than many other behavioral treatments, they typically replace pica with socially appropriate alternative behaviors, and they do not elicit many of the ethical concerns raised by punishment procedures.

A number of punishment procedures have been used in the management of pica, including the contingent withdrawal of a positive reinforcer and the contingent presentation of an aversive stimulus (Singh, 1983). In contrast to other treatments, punishment procedures have generally been less socially acceptable and have been used primarily as a last resort to reduce pica (Rojahn, McGonigle, Curcio, & Dixon, 1987). However, such response-contingent strategies may be highly beneficial in the treatment of pica that has proved unresponsive to other, less aversive procedures or is deemed life-threatening.

Screening Procedures

The contingent presentation of an aversive stimulus can involve any sensory modality. Screening procedures in which an individual's eyes are briefly

Box 12-7

CASE EXAMPLE OF THE USE OF AN AVERSIVE TASTE

John was a 16-year-old boy with profound mental retardation who displayed chronic, life-threatening pica. An array of medications, dietary regimes, and behavioral treatments had failed to manage his pica. Consequently, the oral delivery of lemon juice was initiated in an attempt to decrease his pica.

The initial training sessions, lasting 1 to 3 hours, were conducted by a trained clinician. During these sessions, the delivery of lemon juice was contingent on pica. Specifically, one squirt of concentrated (100%) lemon juice was administered, via a plastic squirt bottle, directly into John's mouth on the occurrence of pica. The clinician also said loudly, "No," with the administration of the lemon juice. Initially, John displayed a negative reaction to the lemon juice, including grimacing, lip smacking, jumping, loud vocalizations, and self-slapping. However, these reactions extinguished over the course of the treatment. Once pica was suppressed during the training sessions, the treatment was undertaken by facility staff and generalized to all waking hours. John's pica decreased to near-zero levels by the tenth session. Further, with continued use of the lemon juice by facility staff, John's near-zero rate of pica was maintained through three- and six-month follow-ups.

covered (i.e., vision restricted) contingent on the occurrence of a target behavior have been used to treat a number of maladaptive behaviors, including pica. For example, Singh and Winton (1984) used a blindfold procedure to systematically examine the effects of this form of visual screening, across three settings, on the pica of a woman with profound mental retardation. In addition to a monitoring of her pica, observations of collateral behaviors were recorded to determine if the screening procedure affected their occurrence (see Box 12-6). This case study illustrates the usefulness of visual screening in the treatment of pica. The blindfold screening procedure was widely accepted by the clinicians involved in the treatment, and following a brief period of resistance, the client complied with the blindfold procedure. In this case, pica decreased, and collateral social behaviors increased, even though there were large variations in the rate of these behaviors across settings.

Aversive Tastes

Paisey and Whitney (1989) described the efficacy of lemon juice as an aversive oral (i.e., gustatory, or taste) contingency in the treatment of pica (see Box 12-7). In this case example, the contingent use of lemon juice as an aversive substance proved highly effective in reducing pica. The treatment required minimal staff training and was successfully generalized across facility staff. Although the client's initial negative reaction to the delivery of lemon juice (grimacing, lip smacking, jumping, loud vocalizations, and self-slapping)

Box 12-8

CASE EXAMPLE OF THE USE OF AN AVERSIVE ODOR AND WATER MIST

Liza was a 16-year-old girl with severe mental retardation, mild cerebral palsy, autism, and a seizure disorder. In addition to self-injury, stereotypy, and aggression, Liza exhibited pica and had ingested items such as tacks, staples, crayons, string, and cigarette butts. Medication and a number of behavioral techniques had proved unsuccessful in managing her pica, and she became aggressive when staff attempted to intervene. Based on the intractable nature of Liza's pica, a treatment program consisting of response-contingent aromatic ammonia and water mist was instituted. A three-phase treatment protocol was designed in such a way that the efficacy of the individual components could be determined.

The first phase of the treatment protocol followed the collection of baseline data and included daily sessions consisting of three 7.5-minute alternating treatment conditions (aromatic ammonia, water mist, and no treatment). The aromatic ammonia treatment condition consisted of crushing an ammonia capsule directly under Liza's nose and holding it there for 3 seconds after observing pica attempts. The second condition, water mist, involved the spraying of water mist at room temperature in her face from a distance of approximately 15 cm when pica occurred. The third treatment condition consisted of no response to instances of pica. The experimenter began each condition by showing Liza photos of an ammonia capsule, a water bottle, or a white surface while explaining to her how and when they would be used. The second phase of the treatment protocol involved dropping the aromatic ammonia contingency and comparing the water mist and no-treatment conditions. In the third phase, the water mist was the only contingency used. The water mist treatment was then transferred from an inpatient to a residential setting, and a number of staff were trained to implement the procedure.

Although an initial brief increase was seen in Liza's pica as a result of the treatment with aromatic ammonia, both the aromatic ammonia and the water mist contingencies rapidly and significantly reduced Liza's pica. However, the water mist treatment was found to suppress Liza's pica more consistently and maintained near-zero rates of the behavior over a three-month follow-up period.

extinguished over the course of the intervention, tolerance and habituation did not develop, and the intervention strategy remained effective. In addition, no long-term negative side effects were associated with this treatment. However, because of the acidity of the lemon juice, prophylactic dental care should accompany this form of treatment to prevent demineralization of the teeth. In this case, the client was given daily fluoride treatments throughout all intervention phases (Paisey & Whitney, 1989).

Aversive Odor and Water Mist

The use of contingent aromatic ammonia (aversive smell sensation) and water mist (aversive physical sensation) procedures on pica (Rojahn et al., 1987) are

Box 12-9

CASE EXAMPLES OF THE USE OF BRIEF PHYSICAL RESTRAINT

John and Tim were two adolescents with profound mental retardation, aged 19 and 12, respectively, who engaged in high rates of pica. In an effort to reduce their pica, a treatment program of brief response-contingent physical restraint was initiated.

Contingent on the occurrence of pica, John's and Tim's treatment consisted of instructing them to remove inedible items from their mouths and, as required, physically guiding their hands away from their faces. John's arms were then restrained at his sides for either 10 seconds or 30 seconds, with no verbal interaction. Tim's arms were similarly restrained for either 10 seconds or 3 seconds. For both John and Tim, the duration of physical restraint was alternated across two different settings (dayroom and sunroom) to determine which restraint interval was most effective. Once the most efficacious restraint interval was determined, it was used exclusively in a number of settings.

In general, all durations of physical restraint resulted in significant decreases in pica. However, 10 seconds of physical restraint, compared to 3 seconds and 30 seconds, was found to suppress pica more rapidly and completely in both individuals and to result in very low levels of the behavior.

described in Box 12-8. The initial increase in pica seen with the use of aromatic ammonia, but not with the water mist, may indicate that the introduction of ammonia was briefly reinforcing, possibly as a novel sensation, before becoming aversive. This possibility supports the notion that the expected outcome of an aversive stimulus may be misleading and that its effects on behavior may quickly change. Treatment with aromatic ammonia has been shown to maintain a reduction to low rates of pica and may be generalized to an individual's natural environment and across therapists.

Brief Physical Restraint

Brief physical restraint is another aversive response-contingent treatment that has been demonstrated to be successful in the treatment of pica. For example, Bucher, Reykdal, and Ablin (1976) used a verbal reprimand and 30 seconds of physical restraint following instances of pica. Although they demonstrated some treatment success, the differential impact of the physical restraint and the verbal reprimand could not be established. In a subsequent study, Winton and Singh (1983) demonstrated the effectiveness of brief response-contingent physical restraint on pica (see Box 12-9). In addition to the demonstrated efficacy of brief physical restraint, other advantages of the procedure include its simplicity, its requirement of minimal staff training time, and the lack of a need for special equipment. Its disadvantages include the need for a therapist on a one-to-one basis during treatment and the difficulties that may be

> ## Box 12-10
>
> ### CASE EXAMPLE OF THE USE OF AN OVERCORRECTION PROCEDURE
>
> Carla and Nora were two women, aged 39 and 34 years, respectively, who had profound mental retardation and resided in an institution. Both had a long history of pica and exhibited high rates of the behavior that had proved intractable to previous behavioral and pharmacological therapies. A treatment protocol consisting of three overcorrection procedures (tidying, oral hygiene, and personal hygiene) was used. Data were collected daily over ten days in three different settings (dayroom, sunroom, and dining room), and one of the three overcorrection procedures was randomly assigned to each setting on a daily basis. Treatment with tidying consisted of having Carla and Nora spit out or throw away the inedible object, pick up the trash can from the floor, put the inedible object in the trash can, and empty the trash can. This sequence of activities occurred for 5 minutes, and physical guidance was used when necessary. With oral hygiene, the women spit out or threw away the object and then brushed their mouths, teeth, and gums for 5 minutes with a soft toothbrush previously soaked in an oral antiseptic. The personal hygiene procedure consisted of spitting out or throwing away the object, then washing their hands and scrubbing their fingernails for 5 minutes.
>
> The data showed that all three overcorrection procedures reduced pica. However, oral hygiene was the most effective in suppressing pica in both women. Oral hygiene could be successfully and easily implemented by several therapists without an increase in pica and had several beneficial side effects, including improvement in the appearance of the subjects' teeth and gums, control of their breath odor, and a reduction in tooth decay.

encountered in restraining a large individual. When implementing a restraint procedure, as well as any response-contingent strategy, the clinician must weigh the potential benefits and advantages of a given strategy against the possible disadvantages for the individual, on a case-by-case basis.

Overcorrection

Various overcorrection procedures have been shown to be successful in the treatment of some intractable cases of pica. Overcorrection procedures require the individual to engage in a single activity or a series of activities following the occurrence of pica that either correct the environmental or physical consequences of the pica or rehearse an appropriate alternative response. Typically, these procedures comprise multiple components and/or specific reinforcement schedules. The intensity of the required staff supervision depends on the complexity of the overcorrection procedure. The prototypical overcorrection procedure for pica, which consists of prompting the individual to spit out the object, oral hygiene training, personal hygiene training, tidying the floor, and emptying the trash can, has been used and modified by several

Box 12-11

CASE EXAMPLE OF THE USE OF A COMBINED TREATMENT PROGRAM

Tina was a 2-year-old girl of average intelligence who was hospitalized for the treatment of lead poisoning secondary to pica. The underlying reasons for her pica and whether there had been attempts at previous treatment were unknown. A combination treatment program consisting of discrimination training, differential reinforcement for other behaviors (DRO), and overcorrection was initiated in an effort to decrease Tina's pica.

The discrimination training consisted of randomly presenting Tina with inedible objects and foods and asking her, "Is this something you should put in your mouth?" For correct responses, she was reinforced with food and verbal praise. Alternatively, the clinician corrected Tina's incorrect responses by stating, "No," and telling her that inedible objects would make her sick. In addition, for incorrect responses, the clinician withdrew attention for 30 seconds. Although Tina's pica transiently decreased after she successfully achieved the mastery criterion of 100% correct responses over 20 trials, it did not remain at these low levels. Thus, a DRO procedure was implemented. She was reinforced with food and 1 minute of interaction with the clinician for each minute she refrained from pica. As this treatment also failed to reduce her pica to near-zero levels, an overcorrection procedure was added to the DRO. With each occurrence of pica, Tina's teeth were brushed with a toothbrush that had been dipped in an oral antiseptic while the DRO procedures were continued. This combined treatment approach resulted in Tina's pica decreasing to near-zero rates and remaining at that level.

investigators in the successful treatment of some cases of pica. Singh and Winton (1985) systematically evaluated the effects of three components of an overcorrection procedure on pica (see Box 12-10). Although all three components of the overcorrection procedure effectively reduced pica, oral hygiene was the most effective component. The component analysis in the Singh and Winton study is important because it isolated a single, simple, yet effective treatment from a more complex treatment package. The use of a single procedure (e.g., oral hygiene) is advantageous because of its ease of implementation and thus its potential for greater consistency in use. In this example, the oral hygiene intervention was effectively and easily implemented by several therapists. In addition, it required less staff time than the prototypical overcorrection procedure.

Sequential Behavioral Treatments

It is not uncommon for pica to be treated with a combination of behavioral strategies. Box 12-11 illustrates how Madden, Russo, and Cataldo (1980a) used a sequence of behavioral treatments, consisting of least restrictive to progressively more restrictive procedures, to produce an individualized and effective means of treating pica. In this case example, three different behavioral techniques were sequentially implemented, but because of the combined nature of the overall treatment strategy, it was not possible to determine the contribution of any single procedure. The successful use of a combination of procedures requires that each case be assessed individually because the selection of appropriate treatments may vary across individuals, based on factors such as cognitive and language abilities.

CONCLUSION

Pica is a very serious behavior problem for many individuals with developmental disabilities, particularly those with severe and profound mental retardation. Although a number of treatments have been demonstrated to be effective in the management of pica, at least in the short run, it is clear that there is no single treatment of choice. While pharmacological and nutritional therapies may hold a promise for success in the management of pica, the current effective treatment strategies are behavioral. The selection of an appropriate treatment strategy is typically based on a number of factors, including the hypothesized motivation of the behavior, the risk the behavior poses for the individual, and the technical sophistication of the treatment staff. Further, to be truly successful in the management of pica, the treatment should be generalizable across settings and therapists and should include long-term maintenance procedures.

REFERENCES

Abu-Hamdan, D. K., Sondheimer, J. H., & Mahajan, S. K. (1985). Cautopyreiophagia: Cause of life-threatening hyperkalemia in a patient undergoing hemodialysis. *American Journal of Medicine, 79,* 517–519.

American Psychiatric Association. (1994). *Diagnostic and statistical manual of mental disorders* (4th ed., rev.). Washington, DC: Author.

Bucher, B., Reykdal, B., & Albin, J. (1976). Brief restraint to control pica in retarded children. *Journal of Behavioral Therapy and Experimental Psychiatry, 7,* 137.

Danford, D. E. (1983). Pica and zinc. *Progress in Clinical Biological Research, 129,* 185–195.

Danford, D. E., & Huber, A. M. (1982). Pica among mentally retarded adults. *American Journal of Mental Deficiency, 87,* 141–146.

Danford, D. E., Smith, J. C., & Huber, A. M. (1982). Pica and mineral status in the mentally retarded. *American Journal of Clinical Nutrition, 35,* 958–967.

Donnelly, D. R., & Olczak, P. V. (1990). The effect of differential reinforcement of incompatible behavior (DRI) on pica for cigarettes in persons with intellectual disability. *Behavior Modification, 14,* 81–96.

Favell, J. E., McGimsey, J. F., & Schell, R. M. (1982). Treatment of self-injury by providing alternate sensory activities. *Analysis and Intervention in Developmental Disabilities, 2,* 83–104.

Finney, J. W., Russo, D. C., & Cataldo, M. F. (1982). Reduction of pica in young children with lead poisoning. *Journal of Pediatric Psychology, 7,* 197–207.

Lofts, R. H., Schroeder, S. R., & Maier, R. H. (1990). Effects of serum zinc supplementation on pica behavior of persons with mental retardation. *American Journal on Mental Retardation, 95,* 103–109.

Mace, F. C., & Knight, D. (1986). Functional analysis and treatment of severe pica. *Journal of Applied Behavior Analysis, 19,* 411–416.

Madden, N. A., Russo, D. C., & Cataldo, M. F. (1980a). Behavioral treatment of pica in children with lead poisoning. *Child Behavior Therapy, 2,* 67–81.

Madden, N. A., Russo, D. C., & Cataldo, M. F. (1980b). Environmental influences on mouthing in children with lead intoxication. *Journal of Pediatric Psychology, 5,* 207–216.

McAlpine, C., & Singh, N. N. (1986). Pica in institutionalized mentally retarded persons. *Journal of Mental Deficiency Research, 30,* 171–179.

Paisey, T. J. H., & Whitney, R. B. (1989). A long-term case study of analysis, response suppression, and treatment maintenance involving life-threatening pica. *Behavioral Residential Treatment, 4,* 191–211.

Popper, C. W. (1988). Disorders usually first evident in infancy, childhood, or adolescence. In J. A. Talbott, R. E. Hales, & S. C. Yudofsky (Eds.), *American Psychiatric Press textbook of psychiatry* (pp. 649–736). Washington, DC: American Psychiatric Press.

Rojahn, J., McGonigle, J. J., Curcio, C., & Dixon, M. J. (1987). Suppression of pica by water mist and aromatic ammonia. *Behavior Modification, 11,* 65–74.

Singh, N. N. (1983). Behavioral treatment of pica in mentally retarded persons. *Psychiatric Aspects of Mental Retardation Review, 2,* 33–36.

Singh, N. N., Ellis, C. R., Crews, W. D., & Singh, Y. N. (1994). Does diminished dopaminergic transmission increase pica? *Journal of Child and Adolescent Psychopharmacology, 4,* 93–99.

Singh, N. N., & Winton, A. S. W. (1984). Effects of a screening procedure on pica and collateral behaviors. *Journal of Behavioral Therapy and Experimental Psychiatry, 15,* 59–65.

Singh, N. N., & Winton, A. S. W. (1985). Controlling pica by components of an overcorrection procedure. *American Journal of Mental Deficiency, 90,* 40–45.

Winton, A. S. W., & Singh, N. N. (1983). Suppression of pica using brief-duration physical restraint. *Journal of Mental Deficiency Research, 27,* 93–103.

Name Index

Abidin, R. R., 30, 46
Abu-Hamdan, D. K., 254, 268
Achenbach, T. M., 29, 46
Ackerman, A. B., 62, 86
Agran, M., 223, 234
Albin, J., 265, 268
Albin, R. W., 35, 38, 47, 89, 97, 118, 127–129, 147
Alexander, D., 62, 86
Alwell, M., 100, 116, 124, 147
Aman, M. G., 8, 18, 24, 29, 46, 48, 150, 151, 157, 160, 163, 164, 166, 168–171, 173–175
Anderson, S. R., 125, 145
Angell, M. J., 247, 252
Asmus, J., 43, 45, 47
Asnes, R., 104, 115
Ault, M. J., 88, 94, 105–107, 120
Ault, M. H., 128, 145, 181, 197
Axelrod, S., 3, 18, 29, 46, 103
Azrin, N. H., 210, 216, 227, 235

Bachman, J. E., 101, 112
Baer, D. M., 71, 86, 110, 112, 119, 123
Baer, R. A., 101, 112
Bailey, D. B., 88, 89, 94–96, 101, 105, 107, 112, 117, 120, 145
Bailey, J. S., 3, 19, 100, 117
Ball, T. S., 238, 240, 251
Bannerman, D. J., 104, 112
Barlow, D. H., 130, 145

Barmann, B. C., 243, 251
Barrera, F. J., 48, 227, 234
Bashir, A., 132, 148
Bauman, K. E., 42, 43, 47, 123, 147, 180, 181, 183, 185, 198
Baumgart, D., 133, 147
Beach, D. R., 29, 47
Beale, I. L., 167, 176
Bechtel, D. R., 232, 235
Beck, S., 222, 234
Becker, B. J., 100, 115
Belfiore, P., 110, 117
Bell, L. K., 104, 116
Bellack, A. S., 137, 145
Bellamy, G. T., 88, 120
Bennett, D., 110, 113
Benson, B., 223, 224, 234
Benson, H. A., 104, 115
Berberich, J. P., 70, 86
Berg, W., 97, 99, 107, 108, 119, 123, 125, 148, 186, 190, 197
Berkowitz, S. F., 132, 148
Berler, E. S., 231, 235
Bernal, M. E., 102, 118
Bernstein, C., 2, 18
Best, A. M., 48, 155, 175
Bijou, S. W., 128, 145, 181, 197
Billingsley, F. F., 90, 97, 98, 112, 115
Bird, F., 124, 145

Subject Index

TO THE OWNER OF THIS BOOK:

I hope that you have found *Prevention and Treatment of Severe Behavior Problems* useful. So that this book can be improved in a future edition, would you take the time to complete this sheet and return it? Thank you.

School and address: _____

Department: _____

Instructor's name: _____

1. What I like most about this book is: _____

_____

_____

2. What I like least about this book is: _____

_____

_____

3. My general reaction to this book is: _____

_____

4. The name of the course in which I used this book is: _____

_____

5. Were all of the chapters of the book assigned for you to read? ____

  If not, which ones weren't? _____

6. In the space below, or on a separate sheet of paper, please write specific suggestions for improving this book and anything else you'd care to share about your experience in using the book.

_____

_____

_____

_____

_____

Optional:

Your name: _____ Date: _____

May Brooks/Cole quote you, either in promotion for *Prevention and Treatment of Severe Behavior Problems* or in future publishing ventures?

Yes: _____ No: _____

Sincerely,

Nirbhay N. Singh

FOLD HERE

FOLD HERE